REDEFINING THE POLITICAL

ALEX J. MOFFETT-BATEAU

REDEFINING
THE POLITICAL

Black Feminism and the Politics of Everyday Life

TEMPLE UNIVERSITY PRESS

Philadelphia • *Rome* • *Tokyo*

TEMPLE UNIVERSITY PRESS
Philadelphia, Pennsylvania 19122
tupress.temple.edu

Library of Congress Cataloging-in-Publication Data

Names: Moffett-Bateau, Alex J., 1985– author.
Title: Redefining the political : Black feminism and the politics of
    everyday life / Alex J. Moffett-Bateau.
Description: Philadelphia : Temple University Press, 2024. | Includes
    bibliographical references and index. | Summary: "Identifies
    socio-political concepts and frameworks that can be used to recognize
    and understand the styles of political engagement, political rebellion,
    and political identity creation used by poor Black women living in the
    United States"— Provided by publisher.
Identifiers: LCCN 2024006730 (print) | LCCN 2024006731 (ebook) | ISBN
    9781439921173 (cloth) | ISBN 9781439921180 (paperback) | ISBN
    9781439921197 (pdf)
Subjects: LCSH: Womanism—United States. | African American
    women—Political activity—Illinois—Chicago—Case studies. | Poor
    African Americans—Political activity—Illinois—Chicago—Case studies.
Classification: LCC HQ1197 .M644 2024 (print) | LCC HQ1197 (ebook) | DDC
    305.48/896073—dc23/eng/20240402
LC record available at https://lccn.loc.gov/2024006730
LC ebook record available at https://lccn.loc.gov/2024006731

9 8 7 6 5 4 3 2 1

Contents

Part I Recognizing Extrasystemic Politics via Black Feminist Political Theory

Part II Recognizing Extrasystemic Politics outside Academia and without Polling

List of Table and Figures

Preface

I started this project thirteen years, three institutions, dozens of hospitalizations, and seven surgeries ago. Back then, I was a very young and very sheltered middle-class Black girl from the West Side of Detroit. But while I had never been inside a public housing development prior to the beginning of this work, I knew that no matter who they were, every Black adult needed and deserved to be greeted how they wanted to be greeted, as mister, miss, doc, Baba, auntie, or a chosen name. In the early days of my research, I knew nothing about the Chicago Housing Authority (CHA) or the developments they built and managed. It was only through transparency about my lack of experience, a lot of humility, and a community of Black women who took a young researcher under their wing that this project was able to come to completion.

When I first spoke with Bernadette Williams, the president of the Local Advisory Council (LAC) of the Altgeld Gardens and Phillip Murray Homes development on the far south side of Chicago, she was reluctant to communicate with me. Her first question was, "What makes you any different? Why should I talk to you?" I told her that my intention was to study the lives of Black women in public housing to make a substantive difference in their lives (as cliché as that likely seems now in 2024, I was young!). Unenthusiastically, Ms. Bernadette scheduled a meeting with me for a couple of days later. When I arrived at her office, the genuine surprise on her face was palpable. Since I'd introduced myself over the phone as a doctoral candidate from the University of Chicago, she'd automatically assumed that I was white and much older. Almost immediately, she said that she "didn't expect [me] to look like" I did. In fact, she was convinced that I looked just like one of her younger cousins and corroborated this with the other women in the office. At the time, I was a very young looking twenty-six-year-old with soft fuzzy black hair and big round glasses. I was still skinny enough to squeeze through the iron gate on my mother's back door in Detroit, Michigan.

The conversation that followed with Ms. Bernadette was familial in tone. She told me repeatedly that she was proud of me for getting a Ph.D. from the University of Chicago (this was a theme repeated throughout my time at Altgeld). Open about her challenges and victories, Ms. Bernadette was also generous in sharing the dates and times of Altgeld LAC meetings, CHA Board meetings, and Tenant Services meetings. This initial meeting with her was critical because it served as my opening to a community with deep-rooted suspicions of researchers. Because of her negative interactions with academics in the past, Ms. Bernadette was clear that she expected me to keep in regular contact with her, as well as to show her my final dissertation. I agreed to these terms readily, but over the course of my time at Altgeld, it proved challenging to keep in touch with Ms. Bernadette, largely because she was difficult to find. I would call the office, as well as visit the office repeatedly and miss her. The challenge for Ms. Bernadette as the LAC president was that the position was a full-time job that paid her a mere $200 a month. In the end, it was Ms. Bernadette's initial enthusiasm about my project and her willingness to introduce me at meetings, as well as to individual residents, that allowed my project to take root.

Toward the end of April 2011, I was able to schedule an initial meeting with Cheryl Johnson. My meeting with Ms. Cheryl was similar to my meeting with Ms. Bernadette, familial in tone. Ms. Cheryl was similarly open about the challenges she faced as an activist in the Altgeld Gardens development. Ms. Cheryl is the daughter of Hazel Johnson, the founder of People for Community Recovery (PCR). A well-known Chicago environmental activist, Ms. Hazel was responsible for introducing a young Barack Obama to a number of other residents within the development and was infamous for hosting him at her kitchen table. After Ms. Hazel's death, Ms. Cheryl followed in her mother's footsteps, staying within public housing in large part to continue her mother's work. When I met Ms. Cheryl, she was organizing activist actions within the development, providing training workshops, hosting "toxic doughnut" environmental racism tours of Altgeld Gardens, and facilitating activities for local youth. My meeting with

Ms. Cheryl turned out to be another critical moment in the development of this research. She provided information about my project to a number of women who live in Altgeld and also informed me of meetings and protests hosted by PCR.

A consistent theme throughout my interviews within Altgeld Gardens was the surprise and relief many respondents seemed to experience when I showed up at their door. Because of our screening conversations over the phone, almost all of them expected me to be a much older white woman. In 2011 and 2012 I appeared to be much younger than I actually was, so many respondents assumed that I was an undergraduate in college when they initially met me. Many also expressed relief over our shared racial identity. Throughout the study, I heard many times that I looked just like a respondent's sister, cousin, or daughter. One other theme that appeared in many of my interviews was a sense of pride from respondents when they discovered I was working on my Ph.D. Woman after woman congratulated me for being in school and encouraged me to finish the degree and "do something with my life." Perhaps this was an expression of Michael Dawson's concept of linked fate (*Behind the Mule*, 1994). Many women seemed to closely identify with my perceived achievement and had an urgent desire to express a personal sense of pride. It meant a lot to me.

The intersection of my race, age, and gender provided a certain level of access, trust, and comfort throughout my interviews. But while a shared racial and gender identity created a certain level of vulnerability in many instances, it also created an assumption of a shared lived experience on the part of some respondents. There was so much I did not know and could not hope to understand about their lived experience as Black women living below the poverty line. Many respondents told me poverty was the identity that had the most power over their lives. Race and gender were a very distant second and third factor for a number of the women I interviewed. However, my lack of shared experience provided rich opportunities for me to listen in silence as I recorded the narratives they told me about their political lives, aspirations, and dreams. Ultimately, the data I collected is rigorous, rich, and theoretically meaningful. It centers a political community rich with its own political legacy and history.

In *Two Cheers for Anarchism: Six Easy Pieces on Autonomy, Dignity, and Meaningful Work and Play*, James C. Scott (2014) argued that "the largest class in world history" is "the peasant class." In simpler terms, the majority of the people who ever have and likely will ever walk this earth are the working class, the working poor, and those living below the poverty line. A famous proverb says that "history is written by the victors," and while that may be true, it rings hollow on the realization that the vast majority of the people—soldiers, cooks, domestic workers, factory workers—who move civilization forward are never recorded in the history books, even when they happen to be on the winning side.

In humanity's long history, there are very few records about the people who only had power over themselves and their local communities. We know precious little about those who came before us. Even as researchers, most of us study the wealthy, the elite, the exceptional, the special, and the especially gifted of humanity. Of course, this feeling is only exacerbated via the realities of being a person of African descent, anywhere in the global diaspora. Most Black people of African descent who are also descendants of enslaved people have precious little written about them in the Western historical record of the last one thousand years. But we know even less about the Black poor and the Black working class as they have existed throughout history. We know precious little about the internal politics and social community structures of enslaved people throughout the Americas. This must change.

The growth in published work centering the lived social and political experiences of poor Black people throughout the Americas is only the first step. We must build on the work of the scholars who came before us and continue to develop research that values documenting, archiving, and critically engaging with the politics of poor Black people as legitimate and knowledgeable political actors. Through the centering of the sociopolitical communities of the Black poor and the Black working class, not only will the rigor and general applicability of our research increase but so will the quality and relevance of our politics. After all, Black liberation is an all-or-nothing deal. As Fannie Lou Hamer instructed us, "No one is free until everybody is free." *Redefining the Political* is not a history book or even a traditional ethnography. Instead, I use these pages to argue that the sociopolitical strategies, knowledge, and community networks of poor Black people are worth studying as critical political thinkers working within a very different political environment.

Acknowledgments

As cliché as it may sound, every book truly comes together via the collective effort of a community. It is only through the support of the many contributors to this project that *Redefining the Political* has come into the world. First and foremost, I would like to thank all of the Altgeld community members and subject experts I spoke with throughout the Altgeld Gardens and Phillip Murray Homes development, and Chicago Public Housing more broadly. I especially must thank Cheryl Johnson of People for Community Recovery (PCR) and Bernadette Williams of the Altgeld Gardens LAC. Your guidance helped me at a critical moment. Thank you to Natalie Y. Moore for your openness and kindness to a very young and very naive graduate student thirteen years ago. I am grateful for the support of Janet Dykstra, Kate Babbit, and Andi Cumbo. Your care and generosity throughout the birth and development of this book project helped me reach the finish line. Thank you to all of the funders who contributed to the research, development, writing, and editing of this project.

A special thank you to the University of Chicago Social Sciences Division, the Carter G. Woodson Institute at the University of Virginia, and the Collaborative for Equity through Research on Women and Girls of Color at the University of Connecticut, Storres. Thank you to my John Jay College and CUNY colleagues here in New York City. I am especially grateful to my friends and family who kept me going when I lost track of my path. I deeply appreciate my mentors and my dissertation committee; thank you to my dissertation cochairs Cathy J. Cohen and Omar McRoberts, as well as Michael C. Dawson and Bernard Harcourt. Thank you to the University of Michigan faculty who encouraged me every step of the way. In particular I would like to express my gratitude to my undergraduate thesis advisers, Tiya Miles and Vincent Hutchings. I am especially thankful for my patient and rigorous editor Aaron M. Javsicas, the three peer reviewers for this manuscript, and all of the staff and board members at Temple University Press for their support of this project. *Redefining Political* has been a long time coming; I am very grateful to be crossing the finish line.

List of Abbreviations

BFDC Black Feminist Definitional Criterion
CAC Central Advisory Council
CHA Chicago Housing Authority
CPS Chicago Public Schools
EJO Environmental Justice Organization
LAC Local Advisory Council
PPS Political Possible-Self
REP Race, Ethnicity, and Politics
SES Socioeconomic Status
TPT The Plan for Transformation
TSC Tenant Services Committee

Redefining the Political

I

Recognizing Extrasystemic Politics via Black Feminist Political Theory

1

Introduction

What Do the Words "Politics" and the "Political" Mean?

*P*olitics and the *political* are ideas shaping almost every area of our lives.* Traditional definitions of *politics* and the *political* were originally limited to interactions between the public and government institutions, bureaucracies, politicians, policymaking, and electoral politics more generally.[1] However, this missed the presence of *politics* and the *political* throughout daily Black life.[2] Because of that dissonance, for decades Black scholars, writers, artists, and others have published work pushing the boundaries of traditional understandings of *politics* and the *political* (ideas, concepts, definitions, theories, frameworks, etc.).[3] Across academic disciplines and mainstream book publishing are books about Black people with the word "*politics*" or "*political*" in the titles.[4] Books about the politics of Black spirituality, the political work of hip-hop music, the politics of survival, and the politics of rioting.[5] However, when *politics* and the *political* are discussed among the public, the media, politicians and bureaucrats, the academy and mainstream writers, does everyone mean the same thing?[†] What do the words *politics* and *political* mean? In the literal sense?

---

* *Ideas* can also be understood as *concepts*. I will use both words interchangeably throughout the book.

† I *italicize* a word when I am using it a theoretical/conceptual framework (instead of using the word's standard definitional meaning—e.g., *politics, the state,* or *citizenship*).

I am interested in examining the words, concepts, definitions, and theories used to understand the politics of poor Black people living in the United States.* Specifically, I continue the work of Black feminist and Black politics scholars in further developing understandings of *politics* and the *political* capable of recognizing the political power of marginalized Black women.[6] With that in mind, I am concerned with a central question: What concepts and theories are capable of recognizing and documenting the political engagement and political identity development of marginalized Black women living in poverty within the United States? I argue that, to fully understand how marginalized Black women living below the poverty line gain sociopolitical power, studies must extend and sometimes reimagine existing theories on the politics of Black marginalized communities.

There is no such thing as *politics* or the *political* without power.[7] I argue that "politics" and "political" are the words used to describe the distribution of power and resources among people, nations, geographies, and groups.[8] *Politics* is a concept used to understand who and which communities have power.[9] Yet for Black women living below the poverty line, especially Black women who are the beneficiaries of U.S. government policies (e.g. welfare, Aid to Families with Dependent Children, public housing, etc.), amassing any amount of social, political, or cultural power is a difficult task.[10] However, this is not the same as saying they have no access to sociopolitical power whatsoever.[11] Originally, traditional definitions of *politics* and the *political* were often too narrow to accurately recognize and document the political identities and political engagement of poor Black people living within the United States.† As a result, more writing and research will con-

---

* Throughout this book I will use the words "ideas" and "concepts" interchangeably. If you understand what an *idea* is, you understand what a *concept* is. "Theory" is a word academics use to describe the *process* of *defining* and *understanding* ideas, structures, and processes. When I mention *political power*, in this sentence, I mean *sociopolitical power*, better understood as *power-over* the social, political, and cultural spheres of influence (Cudd, *Analyzing Oppression*).

† When I refer to an individual as a marginalized Black person, marginalized Black woman, or something similar, I am referring to someone with multiple sites of high-stigma intersectional identity. In this case, I describe Black communities living below the poverty line as marginalized Black communities.

This is what political scientist Cathy J. Cohen calls *"secondary marginalization"* or *"advanced marginalization"* (Cohen, *Boundaries of Blackness*).

Cathy J. Cohen defines secondary marginalization as the oppression and exclusion experienced by people with multiple sites of marginalization. Specifically, when marginalized identity groups stigmatize more marginal group members. In other words, secondary marginalization is usually referring to the oppressive experiences of people with multiple sites of high-stigma identity. In this manuscript, I describe Black communities living below the poverty line as marginalized Black communities. Secondarily marginalized populations, like Black women

tinued to be needed in order to further the work of documenting and understanding a sociopolitical community with firm sociopolitical genealogies dating back to the enslavement period.[12]

In *Redefining the Political*, I used past scholarship and original ethnographic data to make two contributions. First, I developed the *Black feminist definitional criterion* (BFDC), a rubric students, scholars, activists, and policymakers can use to identify traditional and nontraditional politics and political engagement as they occur in everyday life.* The *Black feminist definitional criterion* for *extrasystemic politics* understands everyday habits, speech, and patterns as being a part of the broader makeup of individual political identity. Second, I created an alternative framework used to recognize and document political identity, *the political possible-self* (PPS). The PPS is made up of two concepts: (1) belonging to a sociopolitical community and (2) political imagination. I discuss several respondent case studies throughout the book to demonstrate why studying individual political imagination and belonging to local sociopolitical community is central to the study of politics. Ultimately, *Redefining the Political* argues that belonging and political imagination are two key factors in accurately recognizing and documenting the politics of Black marginalized communities.

To begin, I collected original ethnographic data and thirty-one in-depth interviews over the course of a year in Chicago, in collaboration with Black women who were residents (past and present) of Altgeld Gardens, a Chicago public housing development.† I documented how belonging and political imagination were used to create moments of collective sociopolitical power among their community in a public housing development on the far south side of Chicago. Through this research I found Black women living below the poverty line in the United States who developed a subversive extrasystemic politics.[13] However, I do not use this research to make a causal

---

living in Chicago public housing, are consistently targeted via government, bureaucratic, and residential violence because of the stigma attached to their intersecting sites of marginalization.

    * *Redefining the Political* focuses on the expansion of public understandings of *politics* and the *political*. I do this by focusing the research in this book on *extrasystemic* approaches to the political.

    Throughout the book, the terms "quotidian politics" and "nontraditional politics" will be used interchangeably, in service of developing a conceptual framework of *extrasystemic politics*. In short, *extrasystemic politics* is political power developed outside of mainstream public spheres. For a detailed definition of extrasystemic politics, please see pages 24–26.

    † I collected qualitative data at the Altgeld Gardens and Phillip Murray Homes development in Chicago Housing Authority public housing. It is one large development of approximately 1,900 apartments. I will refer to it throughout the book as Altgeld, Altgeld Gardens, Altgeld Gardens and Phillip Murray Homes, and similar names.

argument. I cannot and would not claim that the cases examined in this book are applicable to all Black women or to all Black communities within the United States more generally. However, the cases do provide important insight into the sociopolitical lives of marginalized Black communities within the United States.[14] I hope the insights garnered here will be useful to other marginalized communities struggling for language to describe their unique sociopolitical contexts, communities, and power. I use *Redefining the Political* to create tools aimed at recognizing and documenting the politics and political identities of Black women living below the poverty line.

The Origins of a Political Language Problem

Race, ethnicity, and politics scholars have noted that existing theories and concepts designed to explain or describe the political engagement of people living in the United States (e.g., words like "politics," "alienation," "efficacy," "cynicism," "trust," and "freedom") do not completely or accurately capture the politics of Black people living in poverty nationwide.[15] Mainstream large-N surveys and polls (organized around more traditional definitions of *politics* and the *political*) can miss the political engagement of Black women living in poverty.[16] As Amy Lerman and Vesla Weaver argue, "existing models of American Politics provide little theorizing to make legible the perceptions and experiences voiced by marginalized Black communities across the United States."[17] Black feminist political scientists Zenzele Isoke and Evelyn Simien argued that traditional definitions of politics and the political frequently miss the politics of marginalized Black women. Likely because those frameworks were originally designed to study the political engagement of middle-class white Americans living in the United States.[18] Out of necessity, race, ethnicity, and politics and Black feminist scholars expanded their conceptual and theoretical frameworks of *politics* and the *political* with an eye toward understanding the under-studied and the nontraditional political engagement of marginalized Black communities.[19]

Scholars like Gary King, Ronald Schmidt, and Jane Junn have argued that key concepts and terminology used within mainstream U.S. politics research (e.g., *efficacy, cynicism,* and *alienation*) were developed within a specific social, political, cultural, and spatial context, a white American context.[20] Evelyn Simien, Nikol Alexander-Floyd, and Julia Jordan-Zachery noted that the mainstream U.S. public sphere has imposed political language [originating from white patriarchal, heteronormative Western thought], onto electoral politics, the study of government more broadly understood, and the arts and sciences.[21] Subsequently, Western political language and theory are mapped onto every community whose culture is examined within the academy.[22] This includes the politics of Black communities living below the poverty line. In *Redefining the Political*, I argue that dominant mainstream approaches to the study of *politics* and the *political* are insufficient when used as a singular paradigm through which scholars seek to understand the sociopolitical worlds of marginalized Black women.

Why Focus on Black Women Living in Poverty in the United States?

During the in-depth interviews in their homes, respondents frequently discussed extrasystemic political engagement throughout their sociopolitical community. Some of the nontraditional (extrasystemic) political engagement described to me included, but was not limited to, protesting oppressive institutions within their communities, filling in the gaps left behind by public housing authority policies of benign neglect, subverting the formal rules and structures of public meetings to be heard by Chicago Housing Authority (CHA) executives, organizing art shows and community meals, volunteering at local public schools, and holding meetings to increase the political confidence of public housing tenants by educating them on navigating government bureaucracies.[23]

While the crossroads between race and gender has had a significant influence on the development of politics within Black communities, the intersection of race, gender, and class can also predetermine who can access particular forms of politics.[24]

> Today, systemic racism, sexism, and classism make it difficult, challenging, and nearly impossible for Black mothers—especially low- and zero-income Black mothers—to survive. Yet they do; yet we do. Poor Black women have often been erased from public and academic discussions of politics. Even when Black women are lauded for "saving America" through voting or framed as an influential voting bloc in Brazil, the discussion addresses Black women in general and places little focus on poor Black women.[25]

As a result of frequently being locked out of more mainstream Black politics, historically the Black working class and Black poor also engaged in extrasystemic political engagement (e.g., rioting, creating meal programs, providing low-cost childcare, gossiping, storytelling, rumor spreading, creating music, being loud on the bus, participating in rent strikes, or simply refusing to show up to an underpaid backbreaking job).[26] Given the U.S. government's history of intrusion on and exploitation of Black women, documenting the political genealogies of Black women who have pushed back against government power is critically important.[27]

Black women constituted the majority of the tenants who showed up for tenants' meetings, protests, and CHA Board meetings while I was in the field from 2011 through 2012. Similarly, scholars frequently find that adult Black women make up a large proportion of on-the-ground grassroots labor throughout Black political work across the United States.[28] Additionally, consistent with my own findings, feminist historians have noted that marginalized Black women found creative and nontraditional means to subvert oppressive power structures generation after generation.[29] Because of their habitually ignored political past, present, and future, it is critical that scholars of politics continue to develop tools and frameworks capable of accurately recognizing and documenting the politics and political worldview of Black women living below the poverty line.[30]

Staggering levels of poverty plague Black communities throughout the United States. According to the U.S. Census Bureau, in 2020 "the Black population had the highest poverty rate (19.5%)," despite accounting for approximately 12.4 percent of the total U.S. population.[31] According to the National Partnership for Women and Families, in 2022 nearly 80 percent of "Black mothers [were] key breadwinners for their families . . . and nearly 30% of family households headed by Black women in the United States, live[d] below the poverty level."[32] Similarly, in 2011 Black women made up most of the "heads of household" within CHA public housing. Black women made up the majority of the residents serviced by the CHA (84 percent) and also a significant portion of Chicago's urban poor. In 2004, 39.5 percent of those serviced by welfare offices in Illinois were Black Americans—a reality that worsened after the Great Recession of 2008. U.S. social entitlements policy for people living in poverty has become critical for their survival, particularly in the COVID-19-endemic era.[33] Unfortunately, people who receive federal and local financial subsidies are closely surveilled by government bureaucracy.[34] They are required to regularly check in with their caseworkers (who can also randomly and without warning stop by for inspections of their home, children, or workplace).[35] Food insecurity, domestic violence, residential violence, exposure to state and law enforcement violence, joblessness, economic insecurity, and housing insecurity all function to make Black women living in poverty exceptionally vulnerable to the state.[36]

Their unique vulnerability is a result of living in the United States, where anti-Blackness has been built into social entitlements and public housing policy for the poor.[37] However, their lack of protection from oppressive power(s) has made marginalized Black women uniquely informed about the nature of government power, how it functions, and how to fight back. Black feminist Mariame Kaba, whose political work focuses on Black liberation via abolition, made it plain when she said, "It is those closest to the problem who often have the answers." Simply put, I focused my study on the community best positioned to accurately understand the nature of power, politics, and the political: in this case, Black women living below the poverty line.

An Overview of Chapter 1

Below I lay out the relevant principles of the radical Black feminist political theories which altogether represent the jumping-off point for *Redefining the Political*.[38] I then discuss the origins of the project and my introduction to the Altgeld Gardens and Phillip Murray Homes CHA public housing development on the far south side of Chicago. I spend the second part of this introductory chapter laying a path through the frameworks of the key concepts and theories developed in this book. Finally, I end with a brief overview of each chapter to come.

The Black Feminist Principles Organizing This Book

By allowing marginalized Black communities to speak for themselves, scholars, storytellers, and knowledge workers can provide an accurate description of Black sociopolitical life within communities living below the poverty line.[39]

> Black feminism . . . is a framework used in academic writing to offer a more complete analysis of racialized, classed, and gendered structures that shape Black women's daily experiences. It is also a practical tool of self-empowerment that can be used by individuals and activists. Black feminists are aware of and struggle against the multiple oppressions Black women face and acknowledge how these oppressions are symbolized in stereotypes meant to dominate and oppress Black women.[40]

This project builds on the work of scholars of quotidian politics, Black politics, Black feminist social scientists, and radical Black feminists who created theories and concepts designed to contribute to the study of marginalized Black populations and their politics.[41] The concepts I propose and define in this book (e.g., *sociopolitical tools, sociopolitical community*, and *extrasystemic politics*) act as the hinges and screws of the mechanisms within both theoretical frameworks (the BFDC and the PPS). Ultimately, fully appreciating the politics of marginalized Black communities will in many ways require the union of the old and the new: language, theoretical frameworks, and conceptual tools.* While I introduce theoretical frameworks and concepts within the pages of this book, beyond this project much has already been accomplished, and there is still much work to be done. Simply put, documenting the lived experiences of marginalized Black women is central not only to the work of this project but to the study of politics more broadly.[42]

Terrion L. Williamson argued that for political or intellectual work to be Black feminist, it must first prioritize the voices of Black women and femmes and seek to root itself within the "politics of the everyday."[43] Meaning, being a Black feminist requires the presence of Black women, girls, and femmes within the everyday of your life.

> I define black feminist practice as a radical commitment to the significance of black female life and the humanity of all black peoples,

---

* Scholars of race, ethnicity, and politics have continued to point out characteristics unique to the political engagement and political identity formation of various marginalized groups (e.g., Afro-Cuban immigrants, Black trans women, Deferred Action for Childhood Arrivals [DACA] students seeking citizenship, etc.). When it comes to Black women in the United States, survey data often misses them altogether (Alexander-Floyd, "Why Political Scientists" Jordan-Zachery, "Beyond the Side Eye"; Jordan-Zachery, "'I Ain't Your Darn Help'"; D. Harris, *Black Feminist Politics*; Simien, *Black Feminist Voices in Politics*; Junn et al., "What Revolution?"; Junn, "Participation in Liberal Democracy"; Richie, *Arrested Justice*). We know they are being missed because of the onslaught of qualitative data (and some quantitative data) that shows how concerned marginalized populations are with whether power and politics affect their everyday lives (Weaver, Prowse, and Piston, "Too Much Knowledge"; Prowse, Weaver, and Meares, "State from Below"; Michener, "Medicaid and the Policy Feedback Foundations"; Cohen, *Democracy Remixed*; Dawson, *Black Visions*; Simien, *Black Feminist Voices in Politics*; Alexander-Floyd, "Why Political Scientists"; Jordan-Zachery, "'I Ain't Your Darn Help'"; Prestage, "In Quest of African American Political Woman"; N. Brown and Young, "Ratchet Politics").

In an effort to contribute to the ongoing knowledge production around the politics of marginalized Black women and of Black women more generally, this book builds upon Evelyn Simien's work in *Black Feminist Voices in Politics*. Most centrally, the ethnography and the in-depth interview questions were informed "by an appreciation of the lived experience and the political objectives of both African American women and men" (Simien, *Black Feminist Voices in Politics*). In practice this meant the study was centrally concerned with centering the words and experiences of the Black women involved, all of whom were incredibly generous with their time, experience, and stories.

regardless of whether the practitioner identifies with feminism as a formalized ideological commitment or holds some views that might ultimately be deemed antithetical to feminism itself. . . . Thus, what it means to take up "practice" here is to turn our attention to the "politics of the everyday."[44]

As a result of the Black feminist foundations of Williamson's and Zenzele Isoke's projects, they prioritized the collection of Black women's sociopolitical stories and used those narratives to construct the theory of resistance politics and the politics of the everyday they described in their work.[45] It is their example and the example of the Black feminist writers and scholars who preceded them that illuminate this book.

What does it mean to have a radical Black feminist theoretical framework as the foundation of *Redefining the Political*? Political scientist Duchess Harris argues that Black feminism has three key components: "an understanding of intersectionality, a focus on community-centered politics, and an emphasis on the particular experiences of black women."[46] I have taken those three components and created a set of subtle variations, which operate as the three radical Black feminist organizing principles of *Redefining the Political*'s methodology, theory, and analysis:[47] (1) the creation of a theoretical framework that will allow political practitioners to center Black women's voices and allow respondents to speak for themselves, (2) a focus on community-centered politics, and (3) a politics wherein marginalized Black women constitute the vanguard center.[48]

Because I chose to use radical Black feminist political theory and Black feminist methodology, when organizing the research design for this project, I focused on one community of Black women for twelve months.[49] As Black feminist political scientist Gladys L. Mitchell-Walthour notes, Black feminist methods prioritize "[relying] primarily on the narratives of participants."[50] I interviewed thirty-one Black women who were currently living or used to live in the Altgeld Gardens and Phillip Murray Homes, a public housing development on the South Side of Chicago. Across the street from Altgeld Gardens are several abandoned steel mills. As a result, residents frequently complained about the chemicals emitted from the old mills and the illness they caused within the community. There have been lawsuits and generations of tenant activism attempting to fight back against the environmental racism foundational to Altgeld Gardens' very existence.[51]

When I began this research, historic public housing developments (and their tenant sociopolitical communities) were being demolished across the city of Chicago via the Plan for Transformation housing policy.[52] Given Altgeld's long political history and its absence from the demolition list, it made sense to focus my research there.[53] The Altgeld Gardens and Phillip Murray Homes public housing development is owned and managed by the CHA. Altgeld accommodates a little more than 1,900 row houses throughout the development (or what respondents called walk-up apartments, versus the high-rise apartments Chicago public housing was well known for).[54] In addition to conducting the in-depth interviews, I also observed how their community and neighborhood context informed resident extrasystemic politics and the development of political identity.

I center poor Black women in this study because they constitute the vanguard center within radical Black feminist political theory, what Deborah King calls "the hallmark of Black feminist thought."[55] Literally, the "vanguard center" are the military troops who are front and center, leading the way into battle. In simpler terms, when Black feminists mention "the vanguard center," they mean the people and the communities who live on the margins.[56] Black feminist social scientists argue Black women living below the poverty line often have the most lived experience and knowledge fighting and confronting oppression.[57] So it follows that the people with the most experience should be members of the leadership within any movements for liberation. In the words of Benita Roth, "the liberation of Black women—who were oppressed by the multiplicative systems of gender, race and class domination—would lead to the liberation of all."[58] Generations of radical Black feminists have argued that, to achieve a fully robust sociopolitical freedom, we must first free the people with the most intersecting sites of oppression (intersectionality).[59] Scholar Benita Roth articulates this idea:

> Black feminists constructed an ideology of liberation from racial, sexual, and class oppression, what I call at various points in this chapter a "vanguard center" approach to politics. Since Black women were at the intersection of oppressive structures, they reasoned that their liberation would mean the liberation of all people (Roth 1999a; Roth 1999b). This legacy of intersectional feminist theory—of analyzing and organizing against interlocking oppressions—would come to have a profound impact on feminist theory as a whole.[60]

As Roth noted in the preceding vignette, Black feminist writers and Black feminist social scientists argue that when you liberate the most oppressed, you will liberate everyone.

At the vanguard center, marginalized Black people lead while being central to Black feminist organizing, as well as Black feminist political theory. Their breadth of experience, navigating multiple high-stigma sites of marginalization and liberating themselves whenever possible, means their lived sociopolitical experience is invaluable.[61] Notably, Black women living below the poverty line in the United States have significant political experience, which needs to be reckoned with and taken seriously, intellectually, politically, and creatively.[62]

Central to a radical Black feminist political theory is the idea that Black feminist intellectual and political work prioritizes the building and maintenance of intentional community with a shared set of political values.[63] In order to purposefully build Black feminist sociopolitical community, you must allow Black and brown people, of all backgrounds, to speak for themselves and to *actively choose their own politics*.[64] As Zora Neale Hurston modeled in her work, I argue that any radical Black feminist intellectual or political project must allow the Black people within it to speak for themselves, to choose for themselves, and to articulate their own politics for themselves, using whatever language, dialects, slangs, or creoles they desire.[65] With that in mind, one of the goals of this project is to build a theoretical framework which will (1) allow scholars to consistently recognize and accurately document the sociopolitical tools of marginalized Black communities and (2) provide a scaffolding that will guide political practitioners through centering the voices of respondents in their work.

The prioritization of Black women's own words and style is the reason in-depth interviewing was a central component of *Redefining the Political*'s methodology.[66] It is also why, throughout the book, I avoided breaking respondent transcripts into small pieces. My goal was to allow each respondent enough room and to give the reader enough context for our conversation, to ensure each woman's point of view was clear. To many an editor's dismay, I repeatedly refused to list or add up respondent answers so they could be aggregated and displayed via various charts. Each respondent, each Black woman in this study, is an individual person with a distinct set of experiences and point of view. It was critical to me, as a Black feminist political theorist writing within a radical tradition, that their personhood remain clear throughout the book.[67]

The Combahee River Collective were a formation of radical Black feminists who pushed for the sociopolitical liberation of all people. In their 1977 "Combahee River Collective Statement" Combahee noted, "even our Black women's style of talking/testifying in Black language about what we have experienced has a resonance that is both cultural and political."[68] In their statement, Combahee described a unique socio-political-cultural style of communication used within Black women's public and private communities, meaningfully specific to how we move through the world and how we understand power.[69] This is not to say only Black folks can study Black folks or only Black women can study Black women. But it is to say a Black feminist theoretical framework demands that political practitioners allow marginalized groups, especially groups we are not a part of, to speak to, identify, describe, and participate in their own unique style of sociopolitical communication. A BFDC of politics and the political must be indifferent to whether political elites and scholars want to recognize the work as political.

Marginalized Black communities throughout the United States (and throughout the world) have developed *extrasystemic politics*, which as Lester Spence points out frequently go unrecognized within the mainstream public sphere, as well as the mainstream Black counterpublic:[70]

> Focusing solely on inter-racial inequality causes us to erase the inequality that exists within black communities . . . and this causes us to gloss over the fact that neoliberal ideas and policies are not simply produced and reproduced by whites to withhold resources from blacks. Black institutions and ideas have themselves been transformed. Black elected officials and civil rights leaders reproduce these ideas, participating in a remobilization project of sorts, one that consistently posits that the reason black people aren't as successful as their white counterparts is because of a lack of hustle, is because they don't quite have the work ethic necessary to succeed in the modern moment. A remobilization project that consistently posits that the greatest danger black people face is one posed by other black people, black people who are not only not productive but are in fact counter-productive. This remobilization project posits that there are two types of black people—black people who have the potential to be successful if they take advantage of their human capital, and black people who have no such potential.[71]

My hope is that the idea making within these pages will assist in pushing back against political gatekeeping, which can prevent marginalized Black communities who live and move outside of the social circles of the Black wealthy and Black middle class from accessing sociopolitical and financial support from their communities, as well as from foundations, organizations, and governments.[72] By creating a BFDC for politics and the political, I hope to fully recognize and document the unique sociopolitical capacity, contributions, and political worldviews of marginalized Black communities.

Perhaps with an understanding of the sociopolitical power cultivated within marginalized Black communities, more people will be able to identify, connect with, and ultimately advocate for fights for liberation. I believe that, with a clearer understanding of the power each community can bring to the forefront, it is possible for marginalized Black populations to find comradery in their fights for freedom.[73] In that way, Black feminism within the social sciences can be used in service of its original mission, to help Black sociopolitical communities create a firm foundation for the building of sociopolitical power, self-sufficiency, and interdependence.[74]

Origins of the Project

In April 2011 I conducted a two-month pilot study in the Altgeld Gardens and Phillip Murray Homes, a public housing development on the far south side of Chicago, to assess if my proposed research was viable. The project went on to become a yearlong ethnography. Ultimately, my research at Altgeld Gardens became much larger than my dissertation could hold. Thirteen years later, I have finally finished creating a container (the book you are holding in your hands) capable of holding *some*, if not all, of the stories I listened to and learned from the women of Altgeld Gardens.

To build relationships with tenants living in Altgeld Gardens, I began by reaching out to residents who were local activists throughout the development. I contacted researchers and journalists from around Chicago who had previously published writing about the Altgeld Gardens development.[75] Journalists recommended I contact two women: Khadijah James, the Local Advisory Council (LAC) president of Altgeld Gardens, and Maxine "Max" Shaw, the president of a local community organization, Environmental Justice Organization (EJO).

Sociopolitical Education as the Key to Political Imagination

It was Ms. Shaw who introduced me to Regine Hunter. Both Regine and Ms. Shaw grew up in Altgeld Gardens. When I interviewed Regine in 2011, she had been living in Altgeld Gardens for forty-one years. When she was eight years old, she moved there with her mom and dad during the Great Migration.*[76] Because of their close community ties, Regine received a sociopolitical education from her community throughout the development.

---

* Journalist Isabelle Wilkerson defines the Great Migration as "the outpouring of 6 million African Americans from the Jim Crow South to the cities of the north and west from the time of World War I until the 1970s." She goes on to say that the Great Migration "stands out be-

A: What kind of activities do you participate in? Are you involved in any groups, volunteer work, or organizations?

R: No, most of the things I get involved with is like sometimes with Max Shaw, in her organization, you know. You know, they have meetings or things like that or flyers or things to get the word out to people and stuff like that. So I get involved with her like that. I try to do as much as I can. It's hard right now because of my illnesses that I have, that I have a few things wrong with me. So that kind of slowed me down. That slows me down some, but I still be trying to push myself, you know. And like I said, with the LAC, I was trying to stay involved with that. But I'm trying to get back into that. I'm just trying to take care of myself right now, because I always was involved in the community in some kind of way.

A: How did you get involved? Why?

R: From growing up out here and working out here, and then we get flyers on different things and asking did people want to volunteer, and then I would volunteer, you know, because it's my neighborhood, to try to keep it together. Try to make it safe and try to have something for these children to do. So I try to still put my finger out there, get on the phone, do as much as I can do. And then spread the word so the kids have something to do so they don't just be bored so they get into trouble being bored. It's nothing for them to do, so we try to, I try to put the word out there, send them up there, take them over there, you know. Yeah.

A: Do you find that more women or more men participate in the kind of activities you participate in? Why? Do you think more women are participating in these kinds of activities in society more generally?

R: Well, they middle age, like me. You might have some that are under my age group, you know. And that's who participates. We still, as older ones, the oldest ones is more or less out here. We try to help the younger ones to help get something done out here,

---

cause this was the first time in [U.S.] history that [U.S.] citizens had to flee the land of their birth just to be recognized as the citizens that they had always been. No other group of [U.S. citizens] have had to act like immigrants to be recognized as citizens. So, this Great Migration was not a move. It was a seeking of political asylum within the borders of one's own country. They were defecting a [system of oppression] known as Jim Crow. It was an artificial hierarchy in which everything that you could and could not do was based upon what you looked like" (Zomorodi 2021).

so these kids can have something to do. So you'll have people come, we going to do this, or you going to get involved . . . it's for the kids, so I try to get involved because it's the kids, you know.

A: So you feel like you're able to recruit a lot of different people to come and participate?

R: Yeah. 'Cuz it was somebody always recruiting us when we was kids. We always had an adult over us, and that's how we grew up, with taking us to different developments, playing softball, and stuff like that. We always had someone over us, so we try to put it back in our community, you know.

A: Do you vote or participate in any political activities?

R: I vote. But I haven't been participating. Like I say, with my illnesses I can't really get around as much as I used to.

A: Why? Do you think this [voting] makes a difference?

R: You have a right to vote, you know. Equal opportunity, you know. I mean schooling, it's a whole lot. Respect, everything, you know. This is America, so I feel like freedom. We have a right to vote. Everybody do.

A: Do you have those skills and knowledge to participate [in politics]?

R: No. No. They would kill me! [*Laughs.*] No. No, it's a whole lot. I wouldn't even want to go that route.

A: But what about the political work you do on the development? You don't see that as political?

R: It is, but it's not as deep. See, it's not as deep. Now, I can understand, I can relate to that more better than being down there in them offices with them people. They use them big words that I don't understand, and I'd be sitting up there dumbfounded, like wait a minute, what did he say, 'cuz all that I don't understand.

A: How do you define politics? When I say the word "politics," what do you think of?

R: Far as with the government and stuff, the world, what's going on, like presidents and what's going on in the world. That's politics, dealing with them . . . government.

This conversation with Regine followed a consistent pattern I heard repeatedly across multiple interviews. Black women who were (objectively speaking) active in their communities volunteered, registered people to vote, and even served as poll workers. Yet when I asked the women I interviewed,

"Do you consider yourself capable of participating in politics?" many of them said no. Regine said, "No. No. They would kill me! [*Laughs.*] No. No, it's a whole lot. I wouldn't even want to go that route." I remember this interview with acute clarity because I was so surprised by her answer.

Regine Hunter was a woman who ran for block captain (an elected position), who spoke up and pushed back against city elected politicians regularly, who even led a protest outside the local grocery as part of a collaboration with another local activist group, Occupy the Hood.*[77] But the follow-up question I asked almost every respondent became critically important; "When I say the word 'politics,' what do you think I mean?" Once I analyzed all the data, I concluded that the word "politics" was consistently generating a different set of meanings among people living in Altgeld and throughout the city (as compared to the formalized definitions of "politics" and the "political" academics learn within the university context).[78] Early on, my research began to corroborate the findings of scholars who have uncovered cultural incomparability between more traditional political science survey questions and nonwhite, non-U.S.-born, and non-middle-class populations.[79]

As I mentioned at the beginning of this chapter, Black feminist social scientists, race and politics scholars, and political methodologists have found that this political language standard originates from white, patriarchal, heteronormative, and Western thought.[80] Political language developed within the U.S. academy and the broader U.S. culture has established political meaning and political power from its sheer pervasiveness throughout the public sphere. However, despite that power, words like "citizenship," "cynicism," and "efficacy" often fail to fully reflect the everyday sociopolitical lives of many marginalized Black communities living in the United States.[81] Some of this language confusion is a function of cultural incomparability.†[82] Quite simply, diverse cultures understand, describe, and relate to their sociopolitical identities from diverse points of view, and as a result, the language marginalized communities use to describe their politics and political worldview can be different and distinct.[83]

---

* Occupy the Hood Chicago was a spin-off organization that developed after multiple failed attempts at getting Occupy Wall Street Chicago (and the national formation) to become serious about integrating the needs and demands of Black people more generally and poor Black people specifically. When I started visiting Altgeld Gardens, Occupy the Hood Chicago and Environmental Justice Organization would occasionally collaborate.

† The distinctive political engagement practices and the unique political identity characteristics of populations like poor Black women are often missed in large-*N* surveys because of cultural incomparability. Put another way, the politics of Black women living in poverty frequently register as nonexistent within political survey data because of differing cultural interpretations of the survey questions.

A Structural Lack of Access to Civics Education and the Structural Vulnerability of Poor Black Women

Quite a bit of the political language confusion however, is due to a structural lack of access to civics education within the United States.*[84] As Ray Acheson makes clear in *Abolishing State Violence*, people who are educated within the United States are frequently taught a limited sociopolitical toolkit.[85] In 2023, many students in U.S. public schools lacked a comprehensive civics education.[86] As of 2023, the state of Massachusetts is the only state requiring every student to complete a full year of civics instruction.[87] Access to civics education in the United States is inequitably distributed along the intersections of race, class, and ethnicity.[88] Students with access to civics classes are often limited to discussions of voting, protesting, letter writing, and making financial donations as legitimate and effective means of influencing politics.[89] Overall, as Acheson notes, the socialization around what counts as a "legitimate" political behavior is strong within the United States:

> We are told and taught that this is the way the world is and there is no way to change it. Tweak it, maybe, but change it—not a chance. There's an age-old saying that it's easier to imagine the end of the world than the end of capitalism—well, that is also true for most when it comes to prisons, police, borders, nuclear bombs, or war. . . . This framing of the inevitability of it all, the disorientations, and the deceptions necessary to lull us into acceptance of the oppression of the majority. . . . From offshore detention . . . to erasing indigeneity and Native realities from U.S. history and current life. . . . What we can't see, we won't object to; what we don't know, we can't fight. "Certain images do not appear in the media," explains philosopher Judith Butler, "certain names of the dead are not utterable, certain losses are not avowed as losses, and violence is derealized and diffused"[90]

In the United States, political education has a narrow scope and is accessible to a limited few.[91] As one example, Acheson notes that other countries in the Western world, such as New Zealand, Australia, or even Canada,

---

*According to the New York State Education Department, through civic education, students learn how to identify and address problems in their community or school community. Students also learn how to demonstrate respect for the rights of others, respectfully disagree with other viewpoints, and provide evidence for a counterargument (Office of Standards and Instruction, "Civic Readiness Initiative").

provide some relatively superficial instruction within their public schools about the destruction of Indigenous North American peoples at the hands of European colonialists.[92] But in the United States, the bloody and brutal genocide of Indigenous populations has been structurally excluded from the history books taught in U.S. public schools, as well as from the discipline of political science.[93] Students at public institutions are frequently denied the opportunity to learn about Black American history makers, slave revolts, the many attempts by Black enslaved people in the United States to escape bondage, Indigenous genocide, or Indigenous fights for sovereignty.[94]

In short, people who live in the United States are rarely taught the tools to analyze what they are told about politics, power, culture, and sociopolitical change.[95] This is even truer for those who are Black, poor, and living in a community with low access to resources.[96] Marginalized Black communities are not taught the sociopolitical tools to imagine alternative political possibilities. As Lester Spence points out, housing segregation ensures that "Blacks are concentrated in poor neighborhoods, cities, and educational systems"; it makes sense that they might reject politics and the political altogether.[97] In doing so, they give-up on imagining an alternative world of their own making. Without political imagination, individuals and communities are unlikely to develop an active, let alone visible, political life.

> "Reformism limits the horizon of political possibility to what is seen as achievable within the limits of existing institutional structures," writes Dylan Rodríguez, whether in relation to electoral politics, racial capitalism, heteronormativity, the nation-state, or whatever. Not only does it limit our imaginations, reformism "defers, avoids, and even criminalizes peoples' efforts to catalyze fundamental change to an existing order." It makes it *more* difficult to achieve the real transformations we need in our societies—both because the act of reform legitimizes the overall system, but also because it takes away energy, resources, and people power from more meaningful changes.[98]

When framed in such a clear and precise way, the many limitations placed on the capacity of CHA residents to develop and enact radical sociopolitical changes become abjectly clear. Spence argues the neoliberal turn created an environment where Black urban neighborhoods are increasingly stripped of their right to public aid and where meaningful aid is being replaced with more lectures about "personal responsibility."[99] Ruthie Wilson Gilmore further contextualizes neoliberalism by arguing that organized abandonment is replacing the basic services promised by the social safety net in the United States.[100] The public schools serving Altgeld Gardens are regularly under probation by the Chicago Public Schools for poor performance.[101] In 2010–2011 Altgeld had a 200 percent higher violence rate than the rest of the city.[102] To add insult to injury, as journalist Debra Williams reported, Altgeld Gardens is "flanked on three sides by sanitary and hazardous waste landfills, manufacturing plants and shuttered steel mills, the area is now distinguished by poor air quality, with both adults and children suffering from above-average rates of respiratory ailments."[103] When the system itself has never met the obligations it committed to in the development of public housing and welfare policy, how can residents take morality and respectability politics lecturing seriously?

As a singular example, Altgeld Gardens is a testament to just how much marginalized Black women living below the poverty line are expected to take on.[104] They were faced with unconscionable environmental racism, which left many children, adults, and elders with significant health issues, many respiratory in nature.[105] There was limited public transportation, and Altgeld tenants without a car were completely reliant on one bus that came in and out of the development.[106] They lived in a food desert, with little access to fresh groceries, let alone regular household goods. Altgeld Gardens public schools were in a constant state of neglect, and there were rarely any opportunities to earn a living wage.[107] It is no wonder these conditions, when taken altogether, seemingly result in marginalized Black communities who believe that the work of their local sociopolitical communities lacks political power or political meaning.

However, because of high tenant vulnerability to the bureaucratic policy changes via law enforcement and housing bureaucrats, it was urgent for residents at Altgeld Gardens to develop a sociopolitical curriculum for one another, as well as fast and effective neighborhood communication networks.[108] Incredibly, these conditions did not crush the sociopolitical spirit of every woman I interviewed. Instead, many developed unique sociopolitical tools and cocreated their own formulations of political identity to address their particular needs. Ironically, because they bore multiple intersecting sites of high-stigma marginalization, it seemed as though Black CHA residents were in many ways more politically adept than their wealthy white counterparts at navigating government bureaucracies.[109]

If the organizing work in your community is routinely glossed over as having no meaningful political power (by your community, by the academy, by philanthropic funders, or by the state), you will either stop doing it or continue but consider yourself apolitical.[110] The latter was something

I saw repeatedly among respondents. Women would be involved in parent-teacher associations, church councils, flyer campaigns for local politicians, and other community-based work, but when I asked them if they considered themselves capable of participating in politics, some would consistently say no. Respondents would regularly use their standing in the community to advocate for themselves and others in front of various CHA and city power brokers. Yet they did not see themselves as political practitioners because their education on what counts as politics was too narrow. Civics education in the United States, alongside ongoing reinforcement via media, the academy, and other political power brokers (better known as *the mainstream public sphere*), routinely teaches U.S. citizens that the only legitimate forms of political engagement are voting and occasionally peaceful nonviolent protest.[111] As a result, some respondents believed that their community engagement and knowledge did not merit what they perceived as the formal designation of "political."

The nontraditional function of Black sociopolitical tools and the extrasystemic politics of many marginalized groups are in no small part a direct result of oppressive structures and institutions built within the United States to create obstacles for Black communities who want to participate in any public, let alone explicitly political, sphere.[112] Thus, Black people throughout the diaspora, as well as Indigenous and Latinx communities throughout the United States, have had to adopt at least a few extrasystemic sociopolitical tools to access the power needed to shift and change their communities in the way they imagine and desire.[113] As political scientist Michael Hanchard reminds us, Black people globally have at times *had* to use sociocultural, religious, and home-based nontraditional sociopolitical tools (extrasystemic politics) to enter broader political conversations about which communities get what.[114]

Conceptual Frameworks Created via Black Feminist Political Theory

Rather than trying to create one-size-fits-all theoretical frameworks in the name of "objectivity," political practitioners can focus on developing more flexible and sophisticated theoretical frameworks that can be remixed in several ways to ensure maximum cultural and contextual applicability.[115] In *Redefining the Political*, I have developed two such theories, *the political possible-self* (PPS), a holistic framework designed to help political practitioners recognize and place value in the language everyday people use to describe their politics and political identities. The second theoretical framework is the *Black feminist definitional criterion of politics and the political* (BFDC), designed to facilitate the recognition of traditional, extrasystemic, and subversive sociopolitical tools.

It is unlikely that both frameworks will apply to everyone; no political concept or theoretical framework can (or should) capture 100 percent of the total range of human sociopolitical expression.[116] However, the PPS, as well as the BFDC of politics and the political, take politics research an important step closer to a broader understanding of U.S. politics and political engagement. I would like to create an opportunity for political practitioners to systematically ask themselves if their political language choices represent the political language(s) used by the communities they are researching, polling, embedded in, or doing outreach to.

The goal of the BFDC of *politics* and the *political* is to help students of politics recognize the search for liberation in all its many forms. After all, at its core, politics is a subjectively creative enterprise.[117] Most importantly, when political practitioners can recognize the political realities or even possibilities in students, community members, neighbors, children, friends, respondents, researchers, and others, the practitioner can ask questions that encourage people to describe their politics and political empowerment in their own words, from their unique socio-cultural-political point of view.

Political Practitioners

I use the term "political practitioner" to describe anyone engaged in any form of politics or anyone who uses sociopolitical tools. In alignment with Black feminist methodology, the research within *Redefining the Political* is organized around the necessity of allowing respondents to speak for themselves.* Interestingly, many respondents did not self-define as scholars, activists, politicians, or organizers. Even respondents who ran for office occasionally described themselves as nonpolitical. These included respondents who ran for elected office within the Altgeld Gardens development and respondents who ran for citywide elected resident positions on CHA committees charged with serving all the CHA housing developments. Many respondents who volunteered for electoral campaigns (mayor, senator, or alderman) did not consider themselves "political," and they did not identify as electoral organizers. Even respondents who participated in the Oc-

---

* The word *respondent* is how academic researchers describe anyone we interview. Occasionally researchers will also use the word "sample," or "subjects," to describe everyone who is participating in their research.

cupy movement, ran their own nonprofits, or ran Altgeld cleanup campaigns did not consistently consider themselves "political." More directly, some respondents did not culturally identify with my word choice. They reported "white people" immediately coming to mind when I asked them what they thought of when I said the word "politics." On a more complicated level, many respondents associated "politics," "political work," "activism," and similar language with dishonesty, lying, and a disdain for poor Black people.

However, Altgeld Gardens residents and CHA street-level bureaucrats were engaged in politics and political work. But they also had differing ideas about how to categorize, recognize, or describe their work to people outside of their community. As a result, I ultimately settled on "political practitioner" as a catch-all term for a variety of people doing various kinds of socio-political-cultural work.* If a person engages in politics or political work, as understood via the BFDC of politics and the political, then I refer to them as a political practitioner. I also use the term "political practitioners" for anyone engaged in the work of developing political ideology (e.g., political theorists). Political practitioners include, but are not limited to, political scholars, pollsters, data scientists, activists, organizers, nonprofit organizations, executive directors, foundations, program officers, institutional review board directors, get-out-the-vote campaigners, political educators, protestors, rioters, journalists, writers, artists, and anyone else engaged in sociopolitical work of any kind.

Extrasystemic Politics

"Extrasystemic politics" describes methods of political engagement that function outside of traditional government institutions, bureaucracies, and electoral or even protest politics in the United States.[118] In other words, "extrasystemic politics" describes sociopolitical power developed outside of mainstream public spheres. The phrase is literal; in simpler language it can be broken down to "extra," "in addition to," or "outside of" systems, or "the system." In this case, it is a form of politics operating outside of the system for "correct" or "traditional," "respectable" politics, as defined by U.S.-based systems of power.[119]

At the beginning of this chapter, I initially used the phrase "nontraditional politics" to get at this idea for accessibilities sake. Via the work of scholars who developed conceptualizations of *quotidian politics* and *non-*

---

* After asking respondents for a year how I should categorize people who fell into my Black feminist definition of politics and the political, most respondents had no idea, or disagreed with one another, and ultimately just wanted me to deal with it.

traditional politics, I developed the conceptual framework for *extrasystemic politics*.[120] The concept of extrasystemic politics refers to sociopolitical tools used outside of what are considered formal government institutions, organizations, elections, lobbyists, or politicians.*[121] In short, it can be any politics or sociopolitical tools that function outside of traditional political structures. Extrasystemic politics can also include activities like riots, quilting, breakfast programs for people without housing, or a potluck in the home of a community member.[122] Philosopher Sally Scholz contends that if oppressed people are to engage in sociopolitical resistance, someone must teach them how.[123] Black women who live in poverty in the United States regularly engage in sociopolitical resistance by educating one another about extrasystemic politics.[124]

Political theorists interested in quotidian politics have done important work recognizing the extrasystemic politics of marginalized Black communities living in poverty. As political scientist Michael Hanchard noted, his "explication of quotidian politics serves as a corrective to political and cultural analysis that reduces all politics to the state or macroeconomic factors."[125] In other words, politics is about more than direct engagement with government and government institutions. Hanchard's quotidian definition of the political is central to the extrasystemic definition of politics I propose. In short, Hanchard argued that politics is "the art of the possible, for opportunities and the lack of opportunities in a given situation or dynamic."[126] Simply, politics is about the push to change what is into something else. It is also important to note what Hanchard distinguished as nonpolitical. In short, "non-political acts are behaviors that are not generative of political community."[127] This is why drive-by shootings and gunplay within neighborhoods are not political. While they may be moments of rebellion or deviance in the strictest sense, in reality, this particular sort of violence causes a "breakdown of political community not its affirmation or creation."[128]

James C. Scott, Michael Hanchard, and Robin D. G. Kelley (1994) emphasized that struggles over identity, dignity and fun, also constitute formations of political communities that not only matter but also have influence and power within broader political conversations.[129] Ultimately, I am not dismissive of traditional formulations of politics, but I am aiming toward the continuation of the work of the aforementioned scholars in the expansion of what we understand as politics. It is critical that we consider politics,

---

* In simple terms, street-level bureaucrats are white-collar workers who work with the local, city, county, state, or federal government. They are the nonelected bureaucrats who work in government and interact directly with the public. Scholar Michael Lipsky developed this term in 1980 (Lipsky, *Street-Level Bureaucracy*, xi–xx).

at least in part, as the negotiation of power in what is currently understood as public and private space. Michele Berger argued that the political work of Black women to "create and re-create a sense of community" resulted in "labor [that] overlaps and often resists easy public or private distinctions."[130] Black feminist scholars have asserted, time and time again, that a comprehensive definition of politics must push back on the desire of sociopolitical elites to draw firm lines separating the public and private spheres. Instead, they have argued that much of Black women's political work at the very least begins in their homes or in other spaces often designated as private (e.g., hair salons, churches, or drug treatment centers).

Extrasystemic politics are a politics defined by what is culturally considered deviant, subversive, or quotidian.[131] Other sociopolitical tools of extrasystemic politics include but are not limited to protesting oppressive institutions (or organizations) within communities, organizing art shows and community meals, organizing neighborhood cleanups, planting thorny roses around a walk-up public housing building, and holding educational meetings to increase the political confidence of public housing tenants by providing instruction on how to efficiently navigate institutional bureaucracies.[132] Extrasystemic politics can also manifest within traditional politics when political practitioners approach activities like voting or attending a city council meeting in subversive ways.[133] Ultimately, to engage in an extrasystemic political strategy, you need sociopolitical tools to bring that strategy into existence.

Sociopolitical Tools

I use the term "sociopolitical tools," rather than "political engagement," because the concept of sociopolitical tools has more breadth and flexibility. "Sociopolitical tools" can include traditional political engagement behaviors like voting, but significantly, it can also include political behaviors, political dynamics, political ideologies, or political strategies that historically have been excluded by traditional definitions of "politics" and "the political."[134] In short, *sociopolitical tools* can include any method or strategy meant to subvert or push back against power structures, institutions, bureaucrats, or representatives, acting as an oppressive force in the life of an individual or the lives of a sociopolitical community.[135] For example, imagine that a political group decided they wanted to cocreate political power via a grassroots, extrasystemic, arts-based campaign. Various activist-artists could use poetry, painting, or writing as their sociopolitical tool of choice.

As I will explain later in the chapter, the capacity for political imagination is needed within all political practitioners, including scholars of politics. Without it, the study of politics can become too tightly wound up around ultranarrow definitions of power: who is powerful, what makes up politics, and what are "legitimate" forms of political engagement or political strategies. The concept of sociopolitical tools uses language to break the political practitioner out of tried-and-true ideas about what constitutes "real" political engagement. The concept of sociopolitical tools encourages the consideration of a potentially vast number of behaviors that could count as tools in our extrasystemic kits. When I spoke with the respondents who participated in this research project, most, if not all, of them learned their sociopolitical tools from other Black women. From their neighbors, their mothers, friends, or play aunties, the social networks within the Altgeld local sociopolitical communities were incredibly effective at informal information dissemination.

Sociopolitical Community

I was regularly blown away by the effectiveness and efficiency of the neighborhood communication networks within the Altgeld sociopolitical community. However, residents did not feel that it was anything special. In some ways, the inability of respondents to see their work as political reflects their inability to see their relational work as meaningful, let alone powerful. As I will flesh out more thoroughly later in the book, in the simplest sense, power is the ability to compel others to act.* In the same vein, the more power held by members within a sociopolitical community, the greater the community's capacity to compel other groups to act.[136] Black women who could not recognize power within their daily lives were less likely to recognize themselves as members within a greater sociopolitical community. While a full understanding of the politics of recognition is critically important for Black communities in the United States who want to successfully fight against systems of power, it is important to remember that recognition is only one step on a broader staircase of the politics within those communities.[137] The sociopolitical community is the container marginalized Black communities in the United States use to develop extrasys-

---

* In *The Power of Feminist Theory: Domination, Resistance and Solidarity*, Amy Allen argues that power is simply the ability or the capacity of a set of actors to act. While Allen thinks about three different types of power and the way they show up within important concepts like solidarity, resistance, and domination, ultimately she gets to a core idea of power that considers how we create or act on capacity building in our day-to-day lives.

temic power and subversive sociopolitical tools.[138] Notably, some sociopolitical tools are only passed down via Black oral traditions within local Black sociopolitical communities.[139]

The framework of sociopolitical community builds upon a diverse set of scholarship that interrogates political community as a sociopolitical concept.[140] Sociopolitical tools are birthed in the home and developed within the spatial context of residential neighborhoods.[141] A person's interpersonal relationships in their home and neighborhood spatial qualities like basic building maintenance (e.g., heat, access to water and electricity, and clean public throughways), state violence, physical health, poverty, domestic abuse, environmental racism, residential violence, and access to public space all play a role in whether an individual learns and develops a firm and clear politics.[142] This matters not only because the materiality of residential spaces (e.g., the CHA's neglect of the public housing infrastructure and the surrounding ecological space) gives birth to a specific set of sociopolitical tools among residents but also because residential spaces circumscribe the behavioral boundaries of members within the sociopolitical community.[143]

My data showed that the logics of politics are deeply tied to the relational bonds within sociopolitical communities, as other feminist and Black feminist scholars have shown before.[144] A sense of belonging is critical to understanding an individual's political identity.[145] To what extent does the individual feel they belong to their neighborhood? To their city? And to their nation? Because of the stigma and the lack of access tied to being a Black public housing resident, many respondents in the CHA understood their sense of belonging within the space of a couple of neighborhood blocks.[146] As public housing scholars have shown, the activism in public housing is often geographically limited because of residential violence, gang activity, limited time and resources, and state monitoring.[147]

Structures, institutions, spatial context, social norms, and culture collectively create the politics of the people living in a given sociopolitical community.[148] The more restrictions citizens have on their ability or capacity to move from one place to another, the more unique and specific their sociopolitical community (and its sociopolitical tools) will be.[149] Chantal Mouffe was correct when she argued that the concept of the "free individual" (as understood in the contemporary Western world) is only possible within the United States because of the specificity of U.S. sociopolitical history.[150] Similarly, nation-states and the populations who live within them end up developing their own unique understandings of justice, as well as sociopolitical community. Hanchard defines political community, in part, as follows:

The creation of political community necessarily entails more than recognizing a problem or phenomena, such as racism. It encompasses the combination of ideas, peoples, and practices mobilized in response to a set of circumstances that involves other political communities, peoples, and institution.[151]

Building on Hanchard's ideas about political community, I use the concept of "sociopolitical community" to describe a voluntary grouping of people who profess a sense of sociopolitical loyalty to one another. Specifically, sociopolitical communities are made up of people who intentionally, conspicuously, consistently, and publicly attest to their mutual linked-fate.[152] In the cases I analyze within this book, the shared identity that linked the respondents' fates was the residential public housing development they lived in, Altgeld's neighborhood, and the surrounding community, as well as their shared race and class identities. In short, membership within a sociopolitical community requires members to understand their social identity, neighborhood, workplace, or circumstances (for example) as more than a descriptive identifier.[153] A sociopolitical community understands a shared reality as a shared political destiny.[154]

Central to the interventions of Black feminisms within the social sciences is an understanding that politics is rooted in local community.[155] It is through interpersonal relationships, specifically those relationships rooted within larger communities (residential communities, communities made up of political party members, digital communities, etc.), that Black women navigate the social and political impact of marginalization(s) throughout their lives.[156] For some Black women living in poverty within the United States, their sociopolitical isolation created an environment where few places within the public sphere welcome and encourage their social, cultural, or political contributions.[157] As a result, scholars of public housing politics, as well as Black feminist social science scholars, have noted that community building, home building, being in home-adjacent spaces, and belonging are all central to the politics of many Black women within the United States.[158] Black feminist political theory provides a framework through which we can better understand how politics and sociopolitical tools come together in the lives of Black sociopolitical communities within the United States.[159]

Mainstream feminists and Black feminist scholars have argued that residential spaces shape political behavior and identity.[160] Research has also shown that friendship is an important site of political identity formation.[161] Similarly, social networks shape political beliefs and engagement.[162] However, consider the following: if individuals are approved to live in public housing, they can be placed anywhere in Chicago upon submission of their application to the local housing authority. Given trends in Chicago public housing policy over the last twenty years (e.g., mass demolitions of public housing high-rises), many CHA residents are being placed in developments that isolate them from friends, family, and job opportunities.[163] As a result of the CHA's Plan for Transformation, the sociopolitical communities of those receiving public assistance are being tremendously—and forcefully—transformed.[164] A process that continues to this day.

Theoretical Framework: Black Feminist Definitional Criterion of Politics and the Political

The pervasive forces of state and residential violence in the lives of Black women living below the poverty line requires close attention to the means through which marginalized Black populations create political power.* It is critical to consider politics as the negotiation of power within what is frequently divided into public space and private space. Political scientist Michele Berger argues that the political work of Black women to "create and re-create a sense of community" often results in "labor [which] overlaps and often resists easy public or private distinctions."[165] Black feminist scholars like historian Rhonda Y. Williams have asserted that a comprehensive reframing of politics and the political pushes back on the desire of sociopolitical elites to draw firm lines separating public and private spheres:

> Although poor people and black women had to contend with onerous and intrusive regulations as public assistance recipients, numerous low-income black women did receive a political education through their engagement with the welfare system. The federal government's subsidy of low-rent housing implied a right to decent

---

* Patricia Hill Collins argues that violence has become so routinized in the lives of Black women, the public tends to overlook the centrality of violence in their daily lived experience (Collins, "On Violence, Intersectionality and Transversal Politics"). Beth Richie rightly notes, "Because few scholars or activists respond to incidents of police brutality as the gender violence that it sometimes is, the experiences of Black women in public housing where police uses of excessive force seldom appear in estimates of violence against women" (Richie, *Arrested Justice*, 23). Key to the invisibility of the violence visited upon Black women's bodies is a reluctance of knowledge workers to name it as violence (Collins, "On Violence, Intersectionality and Transversal Politics").

living conditions for U.S. citizens. From the beginning, this implied right highlighted poor people's low citizenship status and politicized groups of tenants. For poor women, in particular, subsidized housing created a sense that the previously private sphere of home had become public and political space.[166]

Black feminists have found that much of Black women's political work begins in the home, home-adjacent spaces, or other spaces typically designated as private (like hair salons, churches, or drug treatment centers).[167] Therefore, it is critical that a definitional criterion of politics and the political be broad enough to capture extrasystemic politics and sociopolitical tools, even when they do not fit neatly into categories of "public" versus "private."[168] To create a set of conceptual categories capable of capturing the breadth of politics and the political described here, we must understand politics and the political as expressions of the individuals' and the community's relationship to power. After all, sociopolitical possibilities are only created when power, of one sort or another, directs effort and resources toward doing so.

Iris Marion Young pointed out that power, at its root, is relational. Specifically, she said, "Power consists in a relationship between the exerciser and others through which he or she communicates intentions and meets with their acquiescence."[169] In short, for Young, power is the ability to get others to meet your demands. She said, "Politics must be conceived as a relationship of strangers who do not understand one another in a subjective and immediate sense, relating across time and distance."[170] Young was particularly focused on the aspect of politics that requires one group to have the power to extract their demands from another group. Similarly, Michael Hanchard focused his definition of quotidian politics on *the art of the possible*; he understands politics as the capacity to create "opportunities" or to limit "opportunities, in a situation or a dynamic."[171] I argue that the *political* starts one step before Hanchard's window of opportunity is opened or closed. The work of the political begins when the work to imagine [or limit] the possibilities within the window of opportunity is initiated. The political includes the work to imagine *what is possible* or *what can possibly be limited*. I argue that a BFDC of the political understands the political *as the work of imagining, and then creating (or limiting) possibilities, within or around the substantive reality of the world*.

As I mentioned early on in the chapter, my framing of the political is flexible enough to capture demands for material resources, as well as action. Besides incorporating what is understood as traditional political engagement, the definitional criterion for the political must be capable of capturing what Rhonda Williams names as "activism at the point of consumption—that is, around housing, food, clothing, and daily life in community spaces."[172] But this BFDC of the political must also be able to hold what Berger terms "purposive action":

> One definition of political activity for our purposes is purposive action, which helps to create and define a self or group identity, which then allows for individuals and groups to redress perceived injustices and grievances. This definition helps to open up new spaces between the public and private realms, where many of the activities of the women fall. Thus, the definitions of community work . . . combine with the idea of informal politics.[173]

In attempting to expand how the political is understood more broadly, it is important not to fall into the trap of limiting struggles with power, an inevitable aspect of the political, to distributive politics. Besides purposive action and activism at the point of consumption, a politics of recognition is central to understanding what orients Black women's relationship to the political, particularly in the U.S. context: the demand to be recognized as a full citizen, or even person, within the public and private spheres, who has all the rights every other citizen has.[174] My focus on substantive politics allows for the spectrum of the political to be captured conceptually.

Like Young, I understand the *political* as the effort to achieve compliance from a specified target via negotiation, force, persuasion, education, traditional politics, or extrasystemic behaviors and actions.[175] The political is the work of imagining and ultimately creating (or limiting) possibilities, in the service of a goal—for example, working with nongovernmental organizations to bring global attention to issues of perceived public injustice as part of the work of cognitive liberation.[176] This framing of the political provides a breadth and flexibility allowing political practitioners to capture institutional, bureaucratic, cultural, and community-based politics. Young argues that politics does, can, and should concern all aspect of sociocultural life.

> Politics in this sense concerns all aspects of institutional organization, public action, social practices and habits, and cultural meanings where they are potentially subject to collective evaluation and decision making. When people say a rule or practice or cultural meaning is wrong and should be changed, they are usually making a claim about social justice. This is a wider understanding of the meaning of politics than that common among most philoso-

phers and policymakers, who identify politics as the activities of government or formal interest group organizations.[177]

But amid the enlarging of the conceptual understanding of extrasystemic politics and sociopolitical tools, requires clear boundaries and criteria around what is political and what is nonpolitical are of the utmost importance.

Cathy J. Cohen argues that analytic precision is needed when considering the dividing line between the political and nonpolitical.[178] Without precision, at best I risk creating a set of interesting intellectual ideas for scholars to debate. At worst, I create a messy, repetitive set of criteria lacking the intellectual and sociopolitical weight needed to meaningfully add to a Black feminist conception of the Black sociopolitical world. What I do not want is to end up with a set of terms so convoluted that everything and anything is political.

> While an act of defiance can be misinterpreted as having political intent and a direct challenge to the distribution of power and may result in the actual redistribution of power, I would contend that the initial act was not one of resistance. Thus, understanding the distinction between deviance, defiant acts, and acts of resistance lies in recognizing the perspective or intent of the individual. It is my emphasis on understanding intent as it relates to the agency of marginal individuals where I believe I part ways with Kelley and Scott.[179]

Cohen is right in arguing that there are important differences to be found in the distinctions between "deviance, defiance, and resistance." However, I disagree with her emphasis on intent as the core mechanism through which political practitioners differentiate between behaviors intended to increase individual agency, versus those meant to increase political resistance. Cohen codes "*intent* [as] marking politicized resistance."[180] While I understand why some argue that political intent is required to make acts political, intent is a misnomer.

Scholars do not use intent as a barometer for coding traditional political activities are coded as political or not; there is simply an assumption that activities like voting are political for everyone. We code the intent of our neighbors when they go out to vote as political, instead of presuming that their intent is social (for example, maybe they want to spend time with their neighbors or signal social sophistication to their coworkers). Similarly, individuals can collectively engage in several extrasystemic sociopolitical tools effectively considered political, regardless of what the participants' *intent* might have been. The most obvious example of this is rioting. While the individuals who are participating in a riot might report their behavior to be about expressing anger, many argue that rioting has important sociopolitical implications across the United States.[181]

If I assess rioting using the Black feminist criteria of the political (the work of imagining and then creating [or limiting] possibilities within or around the substantive reality of the world around you), rioting comfortably meets those requirements. Duchess Harris reminds us that "a focus on community-centered politics" is central to Black feminist theoretical frameworks.[182] A BFDC of politics and the political does not allow for a politics centrally concerned with meeting the needs of a singular person. A secondary requirement is critical to the creation of such a criterion: the acts, ideas, or set of behaviors named as "politics" *are rooted in the effort of two or more people attempting to use power to create (or limit) possibilities* via acts or behaviors in service of a sociopolitical goal.

Returning to the example of the riot, there is no such thing as a one-person riot and there is no such thing as a riot without power. Rioters typically target economic centers, because under capitalism, businesses and institutions are where power rests in the United States.[183] Ultimately, the theoretical requirements for a Black feminist framework of politics and the political facilitate enough precision to allow for an effective assessment of which political behaviors legitimately constitute politics and the political, while not depending on an understanding of the state of mind of the people engaged in the behaviors in question. Particularly, given *intent* is not a bar set for assessing whether traditional political behaviors are "political."

I ground my BFDC of "politics" and the "political" in the following requirements: First, the acts, ideas, or set of behaviors named as "politics" are rooted in the effort of two or more people attempting to use power to create (or limit) possibilities via acts or behaviors in service of a sociopolitical goal. Specifically, this is the set of behaviors people engage in together to have possibilities created (or limited) by (or for) their targets. Second, the persons, groups, or tools named as "political" are engaging in work to achieve (or limit) substantive possibilities (via power) within or for their targets.[184] In short, a BFDC of politics and the political understands these concepts as centered on imagining, achieving, creating, or limiting possibilities (be they distributive, purposive, sociocultural, policy related, symbolic, consumption based, or recognition based) and engaging in various forms of relational power dynamics. Using this criterion, "politics" is not about a singular individual, and the "political" requires power. "Politics" requires the effort of multiple people, given that politics is "fundamentally relational" and cannot be accomplished in isolation.

As I've argued throughout this chapter, Black feminist social scientist understandings of politics and the political are centered within the community and on behalf of the community.[185] Another useful example of this point is politically oriented parenting. Activist mothering can be an important form of politics.[186] If activist mothering is done by one person in an isolated silo, it should be understood as *deviance* and not necessarily politics.[187] But, when a group of mothers engages in the work of activist mothering collectively, then their activist mothering becomes the work of politics, and the mothers engaged in that resistance work (as well as the mothering itself) become *political.*

It is important to remember that whether the mothers *intended* to act within a group context is not the central mechanism. It is also not important whether the mothers intended to become political. Instead, I argue, it is shifted behavior, en masse, that matters most. Thus, meeting the principal requirement of the political—*the work of imagining and then creating (or limiting) possibilities within or around the substantive reality of the world around you.* In this example, a group of mothers became *political practitioners* via their resistance work. Activist mothering, accomplished by *a collective of people* with *shared political values,* become an important form of *politics* within their *local sociopolitical community.* Ultimately, these political practitioners transform their parenting (an attempt to raise children mindful of principles of liberation and a just society) into an important sociopolitical tool.

Theoretical Framework: Political Possible-Self

The theoretical frameworks developed in *Redefining the Political* have two primary functions: first, reframing how politics and the political are understood, and second, expanding everyday understandings of political identity via the PPS. The PPS framework helps provide clarity around the politics an individual develops within the context of their sociopolitical community. Consistent with the research of Kevin Fox Gotham and Krista Brumley, I argue that knowledge of a sociopolitical community (and its spatial context) is required to understand how multiple divergent political needs grow within cities, states, and nations.*[188]

The theory of the PPS refers to the extent an individual feels they belong (or do not belong) to their sociopolitical community and the extent

---

* The PPS framework is made up of two components. First, to what extent does the individual respondent feel they belong to a sociopolitical community? Second, how much political imagination does the individual have, and how much do they think they have?

to which they believe change—for themselves or their sociopolitical communities—is possible. Thus, the concept of the PPS is closely linked to individual and group political imagination. The BFDC understands politics as *the acts, ideas, or set of behaviors rooted in the effort of two or more people attempting to use power to create (or limit) possibilities via acts or behaviors in service of a sociopolitical goal.* In short, politics is about developing the political imagination and political power to shift individual or group circumstances. Robin D. G. Kelley clarifies this idea:

> Politics is not separate from lived experience or the imaginary world of what is possible; to the contrary, politics is about these things. Politics compromises the numerous battles to roll back constraints and exercise some power over, or create some space within, the institutions and social relationships that dominate our lives.[189]

Focusing on whether an individual believes change is possible allows us to better understand—and recognize—the political behaviors of a broader subset of the population.

Ultimately, a sociopolitical community is defined by the political imaginations of the people within it. Political theorist Clarissa Rile Hayward notes that Black people in the United States who live below the poverty line have a political imagination like most U.S. residents. It is a political imagination consumed with and in some ways defined by the concepts of homeownership and a sense of belonging to a particular neighborhood, sociopolitical community, or country.[190] The public housing residents I interviewed were particularly concerned with their ability, or inability, to access stability, housing, adequate food, adequate education, and adequate health care.[191] When these necessities are absent from sociopolitical communities, they become politics at the point of consumption.[192]

Public housing, via the stigmas it attaches to residents, the spatial realities, and the lived experience it creates for its residents, can shape the individual PPS of anyone who lives or works there. Identifying the mechanisms through which sociopolitical community and spatial realities could shape the PPS was central to this project. One could imagine that some residents feel so ignored and mistreated by the government or street-level bureaucrats, their PPS does not allow them to imagine the possibility of change, let alone the possibility of interpersonal relationships. However, one could also imagine residents who are highly motivated by the conditions of their lived experience and develop a PPS with a political imagination fueled by a desire for change.[193]

An individual's residential neighborhood is formative in the development of their politics and the sociopolitical tools they find most useful.[194] The concept of the possible-self is based on social psychology literature that examines how individuals envision their future. The possible-self literature argues that how people imagine their future and what they believe themselves capable of ultimately determine what behavior they will engage in, in the present moment.[195] I theorize the PPS as a framework for understanding how the individual imagines their sociopolitical possibilities. This possible-self can influence whether a young person will go to school, whether an ill person will take their medications, and ultimately, as I will argue, whether an individual will develop a sense of politics or any sociopolitical tools.

The PPS can allow for several possibilities in terms of understanding the political identity of an individual. The concept of the PPS is not totalized and allows for agency. There is room for a broad range of sociopolitical reactions to sociopolitical communities and the residential spaces they occupy. This theory does not suggest that residential spaces are the only factor shaping the PPS. However, spatial realities play a large enough part in the development of the PPS to require meaningful examination by empiricists and theorists.[196]

The PPS and Sociopolitical Tools

Now that I have fully explained how politics and the political are understood within the context of *Redefining the Political*, I will further flesh out my framework for understanding political identity. The PPS encapsulates two concepts: (1) a sense of belonging to a sociopolitical community and (2) political imagination. "PPS" is an umbrella term meant to facilitate an understanding of the spectrum of political identity resulting in individual politics. Given the centrality of *political imagination* to the PPS, I will briefly define it. *Political imagination* is the aspect of the PPS that envisions political possibilities. It is the part of the individual capable of imagining success in running for block captain or a sense of purpose when protesting CHA policy. In short, it is the future-oriented aspect of the PPS.

The extent to which an individual feels they *belong* to a particular space, time, people, and place seems to be a significant indicator of their connection to politics. Individuals who feel socially and politically isolated frequently withdraw from their local sociopolitical community and rarely visibly engage politically, civically, or socially.[197] An increasing sense of isolation from a residential space likely creates a set of behaviors often referred to as sociopolitical "alienation."[198] "Physical community" designates the

High Belonging	Community PPS	Liberatory PPS
	Alienated PPS	Visionary PPS
Low Belonging	Low Political Imagination	High Political Imagination

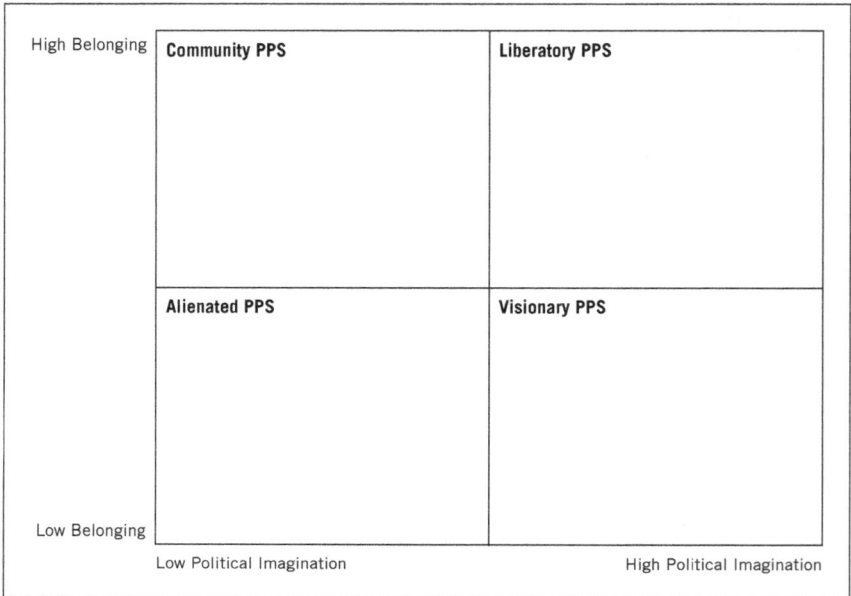

Figure 1.1 Political Possible-Self Matrix

residential spaces where people own, rent, or occupy homes, apartments, rooms, shelters, or outdoor spaces.* The theoretical framework of the PPS helps political practitioners understand the connection between the spatial realities within a given residential neighborhood, the extent an individual feels they belong to a sociopolitical community, and political imagination. Figure 1.1 shows a matrix representation of the PPS and its associated domain areas (alienated, visionary, community, and liberatory). The individual PPS is constantly moving and evolving; it is not static. The PPS matrix helps pinpoint the PPS of any one person or group of people.

Individuals with a high sense of belonging to one or more sociopolitical communities can imagine a future where they can create or limit political possibilities, and they generally have a more liberatory PPS. The liberatory PPS helps to explain how an individual could be described by survey data as simultaneously highly efficacious, highly cynical, and highly politically engaged. People with visible sociopolitical tools can imagine their sociopolitical world changing for the better, while being critical of it.

---

* I focus on "physical" local communities in *Redefining the Political* because I collected data and conducted my theoretical analysis with a focus on the physical space of Altgeld Gardens. However, it is important to mention that I suspect this dynamic could be (and maybe already is) replicated in digital online spaces (e.g., Facebook groups, Discord, or Reddit).

Community PPS

Liberatory PPS

Alienated PPS

Visionary PPS

High Belonging

Low Belonging

Low Political Imagination

High Political Imagination

Legend

Respondent developed interpersonal relationships within their sociopolitical community and increased their sense of belonging.

Respondent accessed political education resources and developed interpersonal relationships within their sociopolitical community. This increased their belonging and political imagination.

Respondent accessed political education resources and developed additional political imagination.

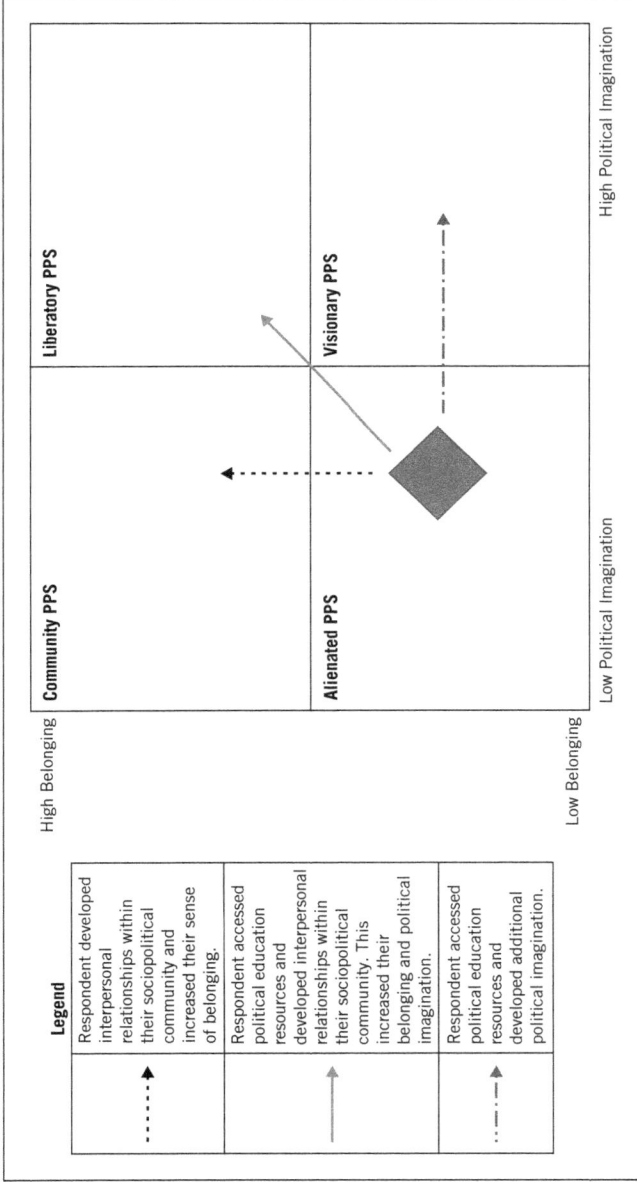

Figure 1.2 PPS Development When Accessing Sociopolitical Education

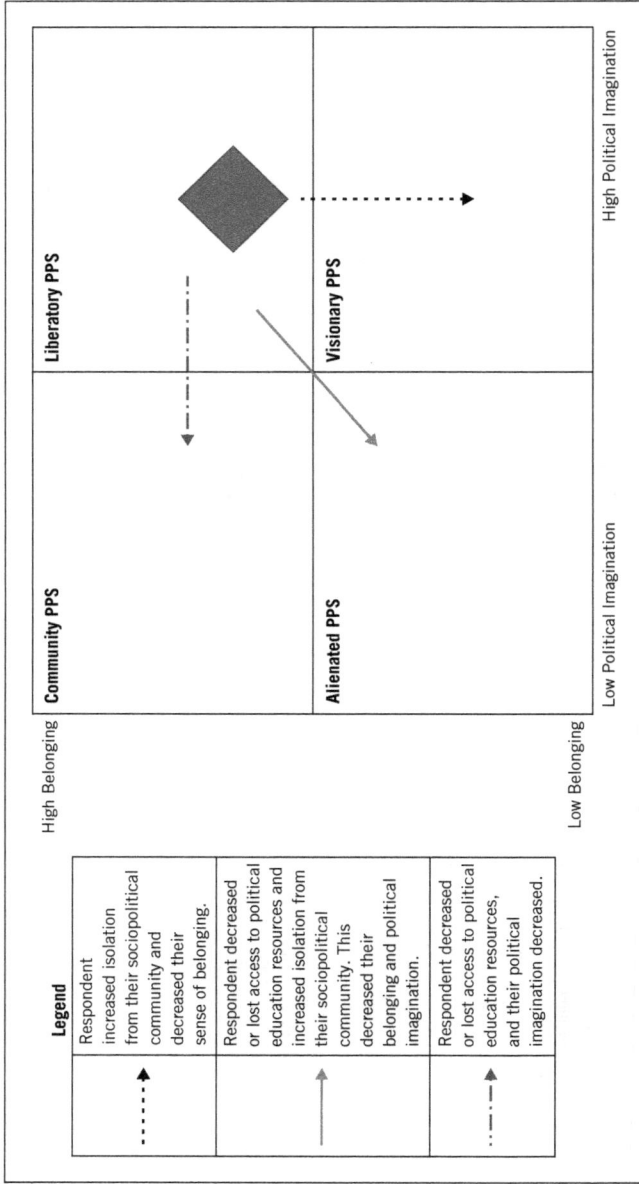

Figure 1.3 PPS Development When Losing Access to Sociopolitical Education

The most meaningful aspect of the PPS framework is its understanding that the politics of any person or community of people can shift and change over time via a process of sociopolitical education.

Changes in the Individual PPS over Time

Individuals (or groups of people) can move around the PPS matrix over the course of their lifetime. Being connected to a sociopolitical community provides individuals with the impetus and motivation to be part of whatever political possibilities they can collaboratively imagine, create, or limit. Respondents with high levels of belonging frequently had neighbors or friends with visible sociopolitical tools. As Figure 1.2 demonstrates, receiving political education from sociopolitical community members allowed an individual (or group of people) to move up, diagonally, or across the PPS matrix.

In contrast, becoming increasingly alienated or isolated from sociopolitical community seemed to result in an individual (or group) gradually losing access to political education and sociopolitical resources from the local sociopolitical community. Losing access to political education and sociopolitical resources could also cause an individual (or group) to move down, diagonally, or across the PPS matrix.

Respondents who did not feel they belonged to any sociopolitical community, and who could not imagine or create any sociopolitical possibilities, generally had nonvisible sociopolitical tools. A person who cannot imagine any sociopolitical possibilities has no reason to be active within their sociopolitical community even if they describe themselves as highly efficacious or politically capable. The disconnect facilitated via sociopolitical isolation adds another level of detachment from the political. In short, those who were disconnected from their local sociopolitical communities tended to be focused solely on escaping those communities. In subsequent chapters, I delve more deeply into the PPS visual matrix and ways individuals can move from domain to domain over the course of their lifetime.

Book Organization

Part I Overview

In *Redefining the Political*, I am concerned with a central question: What political concepts and theories are capable of recognizing and accurately documenting the political engagement and political identity development within marginalized Black communities in the United States?

Chapter 1

I developed the BFDC of *politics* and the *political* to help political practitioners recognize the unique features of sociopolitical life within Black marginalized communities. These criteria can also operate as a rubric or checklist to identify extrasystemic and traditional politics and political engagement. I also developed the PPS as an alternative measure of individual political identity—a theoretical framework informed by Black feminist political theory, as well as the politics and sociopolitical tools of the least of us.[199] In this introductory chapter, I explain why the lived experiences of Black women who live below the poverty line are central not only to the work of this project but to the study of politics more broadly.[200]

Chapter 2

Chapter 2 explains my theoretical and conceptual contribution to the expansion of "commonsense" understandings of political identity, the PPS. I outline the theoretical foundation of the PPS and flesh out the mechanisms supporting it. I go on to show the applications of the PPS via respondent vignettes. Black feminist social scientists and writers have consistently argued that community is a central and defining feature of Black sociopolitical life throughout the United States. A clear understanding of respondents' spatial context and sociopolitical community is foundational to this theoretical framework.

Chapter 3

In this chapter, I flesh out how and why *sociopolitical community*, the *public sphere*, and *spatial context* function as key conceptual mechanisms within the BFDC of *politics* and the *political* and the PPS. I go on to describe the methodological process behind my ethnographic, interview, and observational data. At the end of Chapter 3, I provide a brief history of Black women's organizing within public housing and the impact of neoliberalism on the sociopolitical work of Black marginalized communities more broadly.

Part II: Overview

In Part II, I discuss what the PPS looked like in the context of the Altgeld Gardens' sociopolitical community. I use each of these cases, not as empirical evidence, but as case studies that illustrate the theoretical frameworks developed in this book. Each chapter will focus on a particular axis of the PPS matrix.

Chapter 4

Chapter 4 focuses on the axis of political imagination and on the roles pleasure, intellect, and alienation play in understanding the individual PPS. I argue that political imagination absent interpersonal relationships connecting the individual to their residential sociopolitical community seemed to result in an individual politics disassociated from the public sphere and the local sociopolitical community. Among the women I interviewed at Altgeld Gardens people who landed on the more imaginative end of the PPS spectrum seemed to experience social isolation or alienation. However, the same respondents tended to have higher levels of creativity or intellect, which appeared to fuel a curious and at times even visionary internal political life. This disassociated internal political life seemed to deal almost exclusively in the realm of words, beauty, alienation, and ideas.

Chapter 5

Chapter 5 discusses the belonging axis and explores in depth the centrality of interpersonal relationships to individual sociopolitical development. Throughout my research on the politics of Black marginalized communities, one truth consistently came to the forefront in discussions about political identity: it begins in the local residential community. To be invested in national or even city politics, people need to feel like they belong to a residential neighborhood, or a group of people living in their local community. Without a sense of belonging, some people may haphazardly note that, yes, they feel like an American or a Chicagoan, but it rarely seems to result in visible sociopolitical tools. In Chapter 5, I consider the role of public housing as a Black enclave public sphere, a sociopolitical community where many respondents felt they could belong. My analysis considers Nina Eliasoph's work in *Avoiding Politics: How Americans Produce Apathy in Everyday Life* and builds on it through an assessment of the intersections of marginalized identities and their impact on a sense of belonging to the local sociopolitical community. Specifically, this chapter focuses on the y axis of the PPS matrix, the representation of individual sociopolitical belonging.

Chapter 6

In this chapter, I walk through what this work of Black feminist political theory adds to politics research and its understanding of the sociopolitical lives of Black women living below the poverty line. I also review the eight key findings of *Redefining the Political*. Last, I briefly discuss what this work adds to the study of Black politics and Black feminist political theory and describe the work I am leaving for future scholars to accomplish.

Conclusion

What if we separate understandings of politics from ideas about formal governance altogether? Can communities take part in politics without engaging government or its subsidiaries? Some political scientists have persuasively argued that economic buy-cotts and political consumerism are important sociopolitical tools.[201] Others have considered the role social media plays in the development of political identity and political communication.[202] Anthropologist James C. Scott and historian Robin D. G. Kelley, among others, have documented marginalized communities who engage in rent strikes, gas strikes, the destruction of private and public property, and takeovers of public property. They argue that political practitioners should take these sociopolitical tools seriously.[203]

In a similar vein, political scientist Diane Wong has argued that everyday "shop talk" in neighborhoods like Chinatown in Manhattan is "how women . . . [politically] strategize around gentrification."[204] Scholars like Wong and Zenzele Isoke have pushed political science to think about how politics manifest in everyday life, particularly in urban neighborhoods, on street corners, and in the home.[205] They argue that "the daily face-to-face conversations people have with each other are essential to understanding the development of political thought."[206] Ultimately, the key to capturing the politics, sociopolitical tools, and PPS within residential neighborhoods, cultural institutions, community spaces, and marginalized populations is making space within politics research for frameworks of *politics* and the *political* decentered from government and state institutions.

Like the Black feminist and Black politics scholarship preceding it, *Redefining the Political* is invested in recognizing and accurately documenting the sociopolitical worlds of Black marginalized communities. Using Black feminist political theory, I have developed concepts and theories to help scholars seek out respondents as experts in their sociopolitical context and socio-political-cultural point of view. Using the words and experiences of Black women living below the poverty line in Chicago public housing, I build on the work of Black feminist political theorists and continue the legacy of nontraditional definitions of politics and the political.[207] In interdisciplinary conversations, several studies on nontraditional political engagement center on cultural exchanges (dance, hip-hop, etc.). While arts and culture are a valuable and important component of the Black sociopolitical world, they are not the totality of extrasystemic political activism. I suggest that the interpersonal, at both the individual and community levels, is a fruitful place to find nontraditional political contributions that are expansive, beautiful, meaningful, and powerful.[208]

2

Extrasystemic Politics and the Political Possible-Self

Introduction

During the spring of 2011, I began a yearlong ethnography on the far south side of Chicago, Illinois. For the next year, I observed the lives, politics, and spatial realities of thirty-one Black women who at some point lived in the Altgeld Gardens and Phillip Murray Homes, a CHA public housing development. I knew if I hoped to document the community within Chicago public housing, the only means toward a fuller and more accurate assessment of Black sociopolitical life was a path that understood the political expertise of Black women in the United States who live below the poverty line.[1] As several political scientists and policy feedback scholars have demonstrated, marginalized Black political communities in the United States have tremendous sociopolitical knowledge because of their proximity to street-level bureaucrats and government institutions.[2] To meet key survival needs (food, clothing, and shelter), Black people who live in poverty in the United States engage, push back, and efficiently navigate several government institutions.[3] With this in mind, *Redefining the Political* takes up a central question: What theoretical framework of political identity can capture the sociopolitical lives of Black women living below the poverty line in the United States?

Chapter 2 explains my theoretical and conceptual contribution to the expansion of mainstream understandings of political identity, the PPS. I outline the theoretical foundation of the PPS and flesh out the mechanisms enabling it. Last, I show the applications of the PPS via respondent vignettes.

Political Engagement and Political Identity Frameworks Are Not Enough

Marginalized Black communities living below the poverty line in the United States may not always replicate all the sociopolitical tools used by more privileged groups, they are politically active, engaged, and knowledgeable. The unique nature of their political knowledge and sociopolitical tools matters when considering how politics are developed within communities. While some of the Altgeld residents I interviewed were demonstrably politically engaged in ways the mainstream public sphere would recognize, others were less traditional. Lisa was fifty years old when I interviewed her, and she spent most of her life living in Altgeld Gardens. However, three years before I interviewed her, she had taken CHA's offer of Section 8 housing and left Altgeld with her elderly mother.*

Lisa described her life, her community, and her support network as still being at Altgeld. She went back frequently to feel connected to a community she loves. She even requested we conduct her interview in the home of a friend still living in Altgeld Gardens. This was one of my favorite interviews. Originally it was scheduled to be a typical one-on-one interview, but Lisa did not want to do her interview alone. As a result, I ended up facilitating a lively three-person interview between Lisa and her longtime friends (amd former neighbors). Lisa was a good example of a respondent who did extensive work in service to her community and in service of sociopolitical possibilities. Her sociopolitical tools fell outside the traditional boundaries of what is typically considered political.

A: Do you go to CHA meetings?
L: Yes.
A: What are they like?
L: Phony.
A: Why do you say that?

---

* When the CHA initiated the demolitions of deteriorating buildings in Altgeld Gardens as part of their Plan for Transformation, CHA began offering residents vouchers they could use to leave the development. The Section 8 vouchers allowed residents to apply for market-rate apartments and have a portion of their rent paid by CHA.

L: I mean, you gave your opinions, but most of the time I just go to listen and everything, but I really just was in there.

A: The people that go to those meetings, what are they like?

L: They ask questions, but I have to give people credit out here; they do go to the meetings. Then like when we had that lawsuit with Levy, he beat us out of all our money. Then we had that spill real bad over there; we got beat out all our money then.

A: What spill?

L: Gas. In Block 2, my auntie, her curtain was green; it turned to orange.

R2: It turned orange to green.

A: So they spilled gas out on the highway?

L: It was a chemical thing.

R2: On 115th.

A: OK, so there was a lawsuit because of that too?

L: Mm-hmm.

A: And was that through EJO or something else or . . . ? (For more information on environmental issues at Altgeld Gardens, please see the endnote.)[4]

R2: Sister, what was that leak when we were evacuated and every-body went to Carver? That bad gas?

R3: Oh, yeah, yeah, we had a gas leak!

A: What year was that?

R2: 'Cuz Mama panicked! She come to get her mama. Man, that was so bad . . .

R3: That was like the early eighties.*

A: What kind of activities do you participate in? Are you involved in any groups, volunteer work, or organizations?

L: I used to do volunteer work. I used to do CAPS [Chicago Alter-native Policing Strategy] and all that. I got certificates in all that, arts and crafts . . . that's like the police I was telling you about, CAPS.†

* It is hard to know exactly which chemical spill the respondents were referring to here. Unfortunately, there have been a number of environmental accidents near Altgeld Gardens. However, I believe they might have been referencing "a small explosion inside a stainless steel hose joining a tanker truck to a storage tank on the property of Chicago Specialties Inc., a chemical manufacturer near East 115th Street and South Champlain Avenue" (Ferkenhoff, 1997). The spill caused a cloud of sulfuric acid that resulted in hundreds of people being evacuated from the area.

† "CAPS . . . brings the police, the community, and other City agencies together to iden-tify and solve neighborhood crime problems, rather than simply react to their symptoms after the fact. Problem solving at the neighborhood level is supported by a variety of strategies, in-

A: Oh, OK.

R: Then that's what I told you, when they raided my house one of the police used to come . . . we used to look out for him and stuff.

L: So it was like a neighborhood watch or something like that?

A: Well, back then it was. I was staying out here, but when they raided my house, he just stood there. He didn't even try to search my house. He was like, "I'm so sorry." That happened the day after the Fourth of July, 'cuz my Coleman [grill] sat out. When they did that, he stopped it 'cuz he knew somebody called the police on me. For what, I don't know. Wasn't nothing in my house.

A: So you said you did like arts and crafts . . .

L: Yeah, at the community building, volunteer. I got all kind of certificates. I been a lot of volunteering and stuff.

A: How did you get involved with all the volunteer work?

L: Just being in the community, helping out with the kids. Like they have a little after-school parade, they have barbecue and stuff for the kids, and I go up there and help.

A: Why?

L: I don't know, 'cuz I want to help the community. Like I said, it ain't that bad out here; it's just the gangs. Far as that, this is beautiful.

Lisa's political work centered on serving her community from within the local schools and the Altgeld Gardens community center. The late Dorothy Gautreaux, the tenant organizer who became the lead plaintiff in the 1966 *Gautreaux v. Chicago Housing Authority* lawsuit, also started her sociopolitical work in the local Altgeld schools.*[5]

In Chicago, the civil rights movement first took shape around de facto segregated schools. Dorothy Gautreaux took advantage of this situation to improve the quality of education in the all-Black Carver schools that served the students from Altgeld-Murray. She was in-

---

cluding neighborhood-based beat officers; regular Beat Community Meetings involving police and residents; extensive training for both police and community; more efficient use of City services that impact crime; and new technology to help police and residents target crime hot spots" (Chicago Police Department 2018).

* Helmed by Gautreaux, a group of public housing residents charged that the CHA and Department of Housing and Urban Development (HUD) violated the Fourteenth Amendment by concentrating over ten thousand public housing units in isolated Black neighborhoods. A federal judge agreed three years later, and, in 1976, the Supreme Court did as well.

strumental in establishing a separate administration for the high school, and served as president of its PTA. Her focus expanded as she organized her fellow tenants to go to demonstrations and support boycotts around the city.[6]

There is a long history of U.S.-based Black sociopolitical organizing in and around schools.[7] Those publicly funded institutions are an important site of political work. Beyond the schools, Lisa regularly participated in Tenant Services meetings, LAC meetings, and the CHA Executive Board meetings. If we are using the B.F.D.C. of politics, *the effort of two or more people attempting to use power to imagine and then create (or limit) political possibilities via sociopolitical tools*, then it becomes clear that Lisa's work in her community was political.[8] Her work with CAPS was an effort to create a more peaceful coexistence between residents and the Chicago Police Department. Lisa's work as a volunteer at the community building was an effort to build meaningful relationships within Altgeld, as well as to give the local children a space where they could take part in safe and educational activities.

Black women residents, throughout the history of Altgeld Gardens, have been engaged in meaningful politics.[9]

As the civil rights movement took greater shape and eventually joined forces with Dr. Martin Luther King, Jr. to form the Chicago Freedom Movement, Dorothy [Gautreaux] became the tribune of the CHA tenants within its councils. The image of tenants she projected was not that of abuse but of people with potential to be tapped, she was constantly nurturing that potential, in one housing development after another, holding workshops to help tenants gain the voice she knew was theirs, organizing carloads of neighbors and new-found friends to join the next demonstration. With great pride, she brought Dr. King to Altgeld for a rally.[10]

Beyond the long history of tenant organizing within Chicago Public Housing developments, political labor can be found throughout public housing nationally.[11] While low-income Black people may not be engaged in the same political arenas as other, more privileged groups, they are in fact active, engaged, and sophisticated.[12] This political knowledge and political engagement matters to discussions of how political identity is developed.

While A. Campbell and colleagues and Yvette Alex-Assensoh have argued that poverty depresses political engagement, additionally scholars have argued that when everything else is held constant, poverty does not dampen overall political engagement.[13] In their article, Henry Brady, Sidney Verba, and Kay Lehman Schlozman examine the influence of a variety of sociodemographic factors on the political engagement of a diverse sample of U.S. residents.[14] After testing the impact of class, race, civic knowledge, and political interest on political participation, they found that the major influence on political engagement is the extent to which an individual is interested in politics.

Other scholars note that the home and the neighborhood can become a space where political learning and engagement happen.[15] Chapter Four and Chapter Five recount the process of respondent sociopolitical learning via their neighbors and family members. Ultimately I agree with Terrion L. Williamson, a sense of belonging to a particular geographic place can be key to developing an individual desire to change sociopolitical possibilities for the self or community. Without a sense of belonging and connection, the individual may become apolitical or politically alienated.[16]

Sociopolitical Community as a Key Sociopolitical Tool

Community (both residential and political) plays a significant role in the Black feminist theoretical foundation of this project. The BFDC for politics and the political understands politics as relational. Understanding individual relationships is also foundational to my framework of the PPS, a theory of political identity development. Assessing the extent an individual feels they belong to their local sociopolitical community is critical to fully understanding their PPS. A sense of belonging is central to the development of an individual's sociopolitical tools and also to the BFDC of politics and the political.[17] Sociopolitical tools are birthed in the home and raised in the spatial realities of residential neighborhoods. As I show in subsequent chapters, a person's interpersonal relationships within their home and neighborhood create specific sociopolitical tools illustrated and articulated within the PPS matrix.

The aesthetic infrastructure of the home also helps to shape who the individual becomes politically. Additionally, spatial qualities like basic building maintenance (e.g., heating, hot water, and air-conditioning), state violence, residential violence, and access to public space, all play a role in whether an individual can learn and develop a firm and clear PPS.[18] This matters, not only because the physical space (e.g., the neglect of the public housing infrastructure and the surrounding ecological space by the CHA) is giving birth to a specific set of sociopolitical tools and PPS within its residents, but also because residential spaces circumscribe the ways residents can behave as members within the sociopolitical community, individually, and with one another.

Attention must be paid to the aesthetics, physicality, and spatial realities of sociopolitical development. Political identity is not simply about the political party an individual ascribes to or the boxes they check off on a voting ballot. Instead, political identity encompasses a daily set of behaviors that shift and evolve, depending on the community the individual lives in and the relationship they have to the people within their neighborhood. Neoliberal logic has convinced many that placing residents in more "attractive" housing around wealthier people will solve the problem of systemic inequality and poverty.[19] However, one cornerstone of individual sociopolitical health, well-being, and safety requires a sociopolitical community the individual feels they can belong to.[20] In the absence of a sense of belonging and sociopolitical support, the individual can be thrown into an ever-constant cycle of survival and alienation.[21]

Why Belonging Matters

Within public housing, an individual does not always have complete control over their sense of belonging and the extent of their sociopolitical support networks within their neighborhood. Because public housing residents are living on the dividing line of public and private space, their day-to-day lives can be completely uprooted by federal, state, and local public housing policy. One consequence of the first ten years of the Plan for Transformation ("the Plan") in Chicago public housing was the displacement of residents from all over the city, who were uprooted and replanted in what appeared to be a random fashion. As a result, the policy disconnected entire communities from a sense of belonging cultivated over fifty years.[22] When activists say the Plan destroyed entire voting blocks, they mean that entire communities of people, who felt linked to one another other through shared spatial realities and local sociopolitical community, were separated by state policy.[23] The Plan-fueled resident displacement led to an erosion of community, creating large groups of people no longer invested in their local sociopolitical communities.[24] Groups of people who formerly may have been invested in making sure their neighborhoods continued to have new sociopolitical possibilities, were later consumed with escaping to the next place.[25]

The logics of politics are deeply tied to the relational bonds within communities. As a result, a sense of belonging is a mechanism critical to understanding an individual's political identity.[26] To what extent does the individual feel they belong to their neighborhood? To their city? And to their nation?[27] Because of the stigma and lack of access tied to being a Black public housing resident, many CHA residents frequently understood their sense of belonging as existing within the space of a couple of neighborhood blocks.[28] As scholarly literature and ethnographic studies confirm, the activism in public housing is often geographically limited, not only due to time and resources but because residents feel comfortable, safe, and understood within their local sociopolitical community.[29]

Much of the literature I have examined points to a strong tendency regarding politics: it begins in the local community.[30] In their interviews, various respondents linked their investment to national or city politics, to their sense of belonging to their neighborhood or some other group of people to whom they were in physical proximity (like former neighbors living in the respondents' previous neighborhood). Without that, a respondent may have haphazardly noted that, yes, they feel like an American or pride in their hometown, but such feelings rarely resulted in a visible or active political engagement. Regarding this point, Nina Eliasoph is instructive; in *Avoiding Politics*, she asks, "How do citizens create context for political conversation in everyday life?" She concludes that,

> without a vibrant public sphere, democratic citizenship is impossible: there are no contexts to generate the kinds of selfhood, friendship, power and relations to the wider world that democracy demands. The point is dual; participation in the public sphere helps cultivate a sense of community, so that people care more and think more about the wider world; and second, participation becomes a source of meaning-making power.[31]

My goal is to extend Eliasoph's point by considering how the intersections of race, gender, space, and class affect the cultivation of sociopolitical community. The vulnerability of CHA residents to the neoliberal state can destabilize their ability to establish, form, and act upon a coherent sense of sociopolitical community. Simply put, when a state bureaucracy can move you, evict you, or blackball you from public resources, they can undermine your sociopolitical capacity in a way that cannot be understated.[32] Before the Plan for Transformation, Chicago public housing could serve as a public sphere where sociopolitical communities exchanged ideas and social resources.[33] When the Plan for Transformation dislocated residents, moving them into neighborhoods that were unfamiliar, violent, and unstable, numerous residents' political sense of self became more individualized and isolated from communitarian ethics.[34]

Deepening the PPS Matrix Using
a Black Feminist Perspective

For some Black women living in poverty within the United States, their sociopolitical isolation has created an environment where few places within the public sphere welcome and encourage their political contributions. As a result, many Black feminist scholars have noted that Black women living in poverty use their political imagination to create sociopolitical spaces in venues that are historically understood within political science to be private spaces, or spaces for "civic" (traditionally understood as nonpolitical) engagement. Scholars of public housing politics, as well as Black feminist social science scholars, have noted that community building, home building, being in home spaces, and belonging are all central to the politics of many Black women within the United States. Black feminist political theory provides a framework for understanding how politics and sociopolitical tools come together in the lives of Black sociopolitical communities in the United States. So much so, Beth Richie's Black Feminist Violence Matrix and her larger intellectual project within *Arrested Justice* inspired some of how I articulate and graphically depict the PPS.

As Evelyn Simien argues, "Black feminist consciousness has three core ingredients: an understanding of intersectionality, a focus on community-centered politics, and an emphasis on the particular experiences of Black women."[35] To understand how Black feminist political theory furthers the analysis of this project, an appreciation of intersectionality as a key concept is necessary. Intersectionality provides important analytical leverage towards the study of Black women living below the poverty line and their political lives. Intersectionality as critical social theory is especially helpful in the context of Michelle Berger's framing of *intersectional stigma*.

> a theoretical framework composed of the recognition of and attention to *intersectionality* (or acknowledgement of race, class, and gender subordination as interlocking forms of oppression), and *stigma* (or the ways in which people become socially defined as 'other'). . . . Furthermore, intersectional stigma represents the total synchronistic influence of various forms of oppression, which combine and overlap to form a distinct *positionality*.[36]

As Richie notes, "an evaluation of the interlocking oppressions that Black women face allows for a much more comprehensive understanding" of the violence Black women confront. Intersectionality also illuminates the role their interlocking oppressions play in shaping their individual personhood, their worldviews, and the political engagement strategies they feel safe using day-to-day.[37]

A Black feminist theoretical analysis requires as a key starting point, an acknowledgment of identity, agency and community. Marginalized identities, and the intersecting stigmas they bring with them, are key to accurately understanding how everyday experiences shape how individuals understand power. I agree with the argument that a sense of belonging is a key component of political action.[38] However, I disagree that what brings Black women or Black feminists together is an experience of oppression. Instead, the everyday experiences of shared joy and shared pain facilitate a sense of belonging and linked fate, resulting in a somewhat communal politics.[39] As I discussed in the Introduction, community building, particularly sociopolitical community building supported by political homemaking, is central to many Black feminist understandings of Black women's sociopolitical work.*[40]

Particular to the interventions of Black feminism within the social sciences, as well as Black feminist political theory, is an understanding of interpersonal relationships, specifically those relationships rooted to larger communities (residential communities, sociopolitical communities, digital communities, etc.), that help Black women navigate the sociopolitical impact of intersectional stigma throughout their lives.[41] Another feature of Black feminist political theory is centering Black women's lives and voices. Black feminism throughout the social sciences, as well as Black feminist theory, has consistently argued that it is impossible to research or write about Black women without centering them.[42] By centering Black women, political practitioners stand to grow, not only in their understanding of politics and the political but in their core understanding of sociopolitical tools and extrasystemic politics.[43]

---

* "The Politics of Homemaking" is a theoretical concept developed by Zenzele Isoke, who defines the politics of homemaking as follows:

> Homemaking, as an affective form of resistance, involves more than just being attentive to and providing care to individuals. It also requires building an enduring affective relationship to the physical environment. It is the imaginative political work that transforms the built environment of the city into a home: a place of belonging, a place of remembrance, and a place of resistance. Homemaking, then encompasses black women's efforts to build the will to resist the alienating and dehumanizing practices and ideologies that continue to ghettoize and minoritize black people. (Isoke, "Politics of Homemaking," 119)

The PPS, Political Imagination, and Sociopolitical Tools

The PPS framework understands sociopolitical belonging and political imagination as directly connected to the development of individual and community politics. The PPS encapsulates several key political science concepts without being overly determined by them. For example, the concept of the PPS allows us to think about and measure concepts such as political "efficacy" without being limited to the questions typically used to measure efficacy—for example, "do you feel capable of participating in politics?" Instead, there is room for respondents to define for themselves what it means to be political and, subsequently, to describe whether they are a person capable of participating in politics. The PPS allows respondents to explain how they define their capacity to participate in politics. The idea of a PPS begins with self-definition and self-identification and then considers how communities and environments influence individual perceptions of the self as a political person (or not).

The PPS allows us to understand the connection between belonging and political imagination. In short, the PPS develops from a sense of belonging to a community and one's capacity to imagine new or different political possibilities. Membership in sociopolitical community is defined by a politics seeking to create sociopolitical possibilities. This could be as simple as cleaning up the block outside one's home or as complex as participating in local and national political campaigns.[44] The PPS matrix (see Figure 1.1) helps to illustrates the dynamic nature of politics and sociopolitical tools. The PPS matrix has four domain areas; this matrix can help us understand the political possibilities in people, and maybe even communities.

Individuals with a high sense of connection or belonging to one or more sociopolitical communities, seem to have a more active and visible politics. People with a visionary PPS can imagine new sociopolitical possibilities. Being highly connected to one of their sociopolitical communities provides them with the impetus and motivation to be a part of whatever possibilities they imagine. Individuals with high levels of belonging seem to have more visible interpersonal relationships, and more visible politics. Individuals without a sense of belonging to any sociopolitical community are also frequently alienated from politics and political life. The person who cannot imagine new sociopolitical realities has no reason to be active within the sociopolitical community even if they describe themselves as highly efficacious or capable. The disconnect resulting from the isolation experienced by those who are not connected to any sociopolitical communities adds another level of nonengagement from the political. In short, those who are disconnected from their sociopolitical communities tend to be solely focused on escaping those communities.

The PPS clarifies the roles that belonging and political imagination play in the development of individual-level politics, as well as community-level politics. Political imagination is the process of individuals or groups who go about envisioning a different sociopolitical reality for themselves or their targets. Political imagination often leads to political education, which can later lead to cognitive liberation. In short, the belief that something is possible can lead some to self-educate about their local sociopolitical community, the broader world, power, sociopolitical capital, or alternative solutions and perspectives. Via this process of political education, the individual, or sociopolitical community, is presented with the opportunity to achieve cognitive liberation, to free themselves from the sociopolitical norms and assumptions of everyday life. As I will explain later, political education also allows respondents to move from one PPS domain to another.

The first axis of the PPS matrix represents the continuum of political imagination in the overall development of PPS and the *utilization* of sociopolitical tools. At one end of the spectrum are individuals with low political imagination. An alienated PPS maintains an apathetic and/or ambivalent sense of their capacity to exert influence over state power or any government apparatus, more broadly conceived. Citizens exhibiting low-political imagination are described in Amy Lerman and Vesla Weaver's *Arrested Citizenship*.

> Across our interview sample too, nearly all the individuals with whom we spoke described feeling that political participation was an exercise in futility, and that the voices of people "like them" carried little weight in the public sphere. Most spoke of government as distant and unhelpful, of politicians as untrustworthy and even corrupt.[45]

A number of respondents told me stories about terrifyingly violent encounters. Domestic abuse, bureaucratic abuse, and police brutality were an ever-present part of many respondent realities.[46] Consistently, respondents who experienced physical violence at the hands of the state sat in the low-political-imagination and low-belonging domains of the PPS matrix. Among the Black women I interviewed, respondents who experienced the govern-

TABLE 2.1 POLITICAL POSSIBLE-SELF TEXT MATRIX			
	Low Political Imagination	Neutral Political Imagination	High Political Imagination
High Sense of Belonging	**Community PPS** They engage in sociopolitical tools focused on helping local community thrive and grow. They help local organizations, churches, and institutions support their community. If they use any sociopolitical tools, they are limited to traditional politics. They have many interpersonal ties to their community.	They engage in traditional sociopolitical tools in and around their local community. They are open to hearing and learning about new political, civic, or social ideas. They will consider extrasystemic politics if the ideas come from a person they trust. They have multiple interpersonal relationships tying them to a sociopolitical community.	**Liberatory PPS** They have visible sociopolitical tools and close ties to their local community. They understand extrasystemic politics and traditional politics. They have multiple interpersonal relationships tying them to a sociopolitical community.
Neutral Sense of Belonging	If they use any sociopolitical tools, they are rooted in community-based activities via volunteering, civic activities, or political activities organized and directed by others. They have, at most, a handful of interpersonal relationships within their community.	They engage in a traditional set of sociopolitical tools. They have, at most, a handful of interpersonal relationships within their local community. They understand the power of the government. They may also have a cursory knowledge of extrasystemic politics.	They may use traditional or extrasystemic sociopolitical tools. They have, at most, a handful of interpersonal relationships within their community. Their understanding of extrasystemic politics has led to a vocal politics.
Low Sense of Belonging	**Alienated PPS** They are politically alienated. They have no interpersonal relationships tying them to a community. They do not understand state power. They do not use any visible sociopolitical tools.	They use limited sociopolitical tools. They have few interpersonal relationships tying them to a community. They understand the power of the government. They may have a cursory knowledge of extrasystemic politics.	**Visionary PPS** They use select sociopolitical tools. They have few interpersonal ties to their local community. Their understanding of extrasystemic politics has led to a vocal politics.

ment as a physically violent force in their lives believed that maintaining a politics of invisibility was safest.*

The stories residents and respondents told each other served as warnings, requests for help, and a sociopolitical education on how to navigate the unpredictable spatial realities of their neighborhoods. As Joe Soss and Vesla Weaver note, when state violence happens, "such encounters with

---

* The *politics of invisibility* is a concept developed by Cathy J. Cohen in *Democracy Remixed*. For more, please see Chapter 4 and the subsection titled "The Politics of Invisibility within a Sociopolitical Community," pages 128–133.

police are retold and become elements of collective memory. . . . Stories of police brutality or unfairness are passed through family and friendship networks, the routines of black comedians, rap lyrics and black media."[47] Marginalized populations, Black and brown people in the United States, and people living below the poverty line frequently learn about the state via personal, everyday experiences. When I would attend public CHA meetings, violence was frequently reported by Black women who were living in CHA public housing. Here, I provide some examples from a Central Advisory Council meeting I attended in April 2011:

> One resident was on the CHA waiting list for twenty-four years. She finally received an emergency transfer from CHA because somebody was threatening her. Unfortunately, the resident was still being threatened by the violent resident who managed to find her. At the meeting the resident alleged that the CHA and the police failed to protect her.
>
> Another resident came to the front to speak and complained that residents could not sign others into their apartments. If a guest came to visit and did not have government identification, the guest would not be allowed in the building. This particular tenant felt that the policy was unfair. She believed she should be able to have guests visit her apartment, at her discretion. However, the next resident speaker stated that she was in favor of requiring state identification prior to entry, because of prior violent experiences within her public housing development. The resident recounted a story of an unidentified young man who showed up at her apartment door, threatening to kill her gay son.

CHA residents shared their experiences with violence throughout the community via their social networks, public meetings, social media, and cultural production. Stories about violent encounters were consistent throughout the study. The mainstream public frequently mistakes police brutality as an issue only encountered by Black men. However, for Black women living below the poverty line, this could not be further from the truth.[48] As is illustrated in my field notes, the multiple iterations of violence that respondents experienced were made clear to me after an interview I conducted in November 2011:

> I knocked on Toni's back door and there was no answer, so I started to walk around to the other side but I saw a rustling by the window, and Toni began to open the door.

Toni was a heavy-set woman, she had brown skin with brown spots on her face. Toni's hair was lightly pressed with grey streaks, pulled back into a ponytail. She had a grey t-shirt on, pants and house slippers.

Toni initially estimated she moved to Altgeld around 1976 or 1978. But later she realized her father passed around 1976, so the original move might have been closer to 1968 when she was 10 years old.

Early on, Toni's experience at Altgeld had its difficult moments. Twenty-eight years ago, her brother was shot and killed at Altgeld Gardens.

But overall, she remembered Altgeld being a beautiful, community orientated place that she loved growing up in. However, Toni reported that in the present moment [2011], she experienced Altgeld as being "like a plantation" that she was constantly embattled with.

She was in the midst of fighting a case against East Lake Management Company, because they were trying to evict her.* Toni's son was on parole, he violated parole because "he had reefer in his system." As a result, her son was on house arrest. Toni did not think there was any chance he would be released before the end of his sentence, so she put down her address for the house arrest. He could not go to his girlfriend's home and Toni did not want him bothering her sister-in-law. But Toni said "my little trick didn't work," Her son was released. According to Toni, the house arrest paperwork said she could decline at any time, so she declined right away. However, the prison bureaucracy was slow with the paperwork and CHA residents are forbidden from having individuals on house arrest in their homes.

Ultimately, Toni did not let her son stay with her, and the police came to her home looking for him when he was not there. According to Toni, one of the police officers started swearing at her and yelling epithets and threatening her. As a result, Toni eventually let them in, and when they found out her son was not in her apartment they left.

Toni said that she encouraged her son to turn himself back in. But he kept telling her he just wanted to set aside some money before he went back to jail for his last month. Sometimes he would unexpectedly pop-up at her home for showers, etc.

---

* East Lake Management Company was one of a handful of private management firms CHA hired to manage their developments.

The last time Toni's son came by for a shower, the police showed-up soon afterwards. The police surrounded Toni's home with guns drawn, screaming and beating on the door. The same officer from the previous CPD [Chicago Police Department] visit was yelling and screaming epithets at Toni (bitch, etc.). Toni kept yelling up the stairs asking her son to come down, and he pretended not to be there. Since the officer she previously had a bad experience with was at the front door, she let the officers at the back door in first.

The police officers continued to call Toni a bitch and other racial epithets, her brother, who was with her, told her to ask for a warrant. But Toni did not feel she could ask for paperwork. She was afraid she would get kicked out of her home.

[At this point in the interview, Toni began to cry.]

The police officers tried to put handcuffs on Toni and pushed her on to the couch. The police threatened that she would get kicked out of her home. Toni said the police intimidated her and made her so nervous she couldn't advocate for herself. All of this happened over the summer in June or July of 2011.

A especially aggressive police officer told Toni, "I'm the one who pays your rent." Toni told me she thought he made that statement because he thought she was on section eight, which she was not. Toni went on to say that the police officers' statement did not make any sense because taxpayers pay his salary. She then told me all of the police officers were white.

Toni went on to tell me about a young woman who lived in one of the apartments across the street from Toni's apartment. The young woman called the police due to domestic violence. The police officers called her a bitch and started destroying her belongings, breaking a glass table, some of her windows and a number of other things. Toni heard the young woman screaming from her apartment. Interestingly, the young women actually called 9-11 on the police. Toni thought the strategy must have worked out for her neighbor, because she now has constant surveillance around her home to protect her. Her neighbor was also able to get all of her belongings and windows replaced. Toni wished she had been brave enough to do the same thing. Toni then said, "I have a lot of respect for the police, but a lot of them are prejudiced."

Respondents told stories of police running through the front door of their apartment and out the back door in pursuit of suspects. Some spoke of threats made by Child Protective Services if they did not comply with a variety of orders. Multiple respondents reported being unable to receive an emergency housing transfer order to another public housing development after suffering through violent sexual assaults within the development they currently lived in. These experiences resulted in residents developing a wide range of knowledge about the extent government could be depended on, trusted, or even consulted when they were in need.

Soss and Weaver argue that this knowledge becomes part of a community knowledge network; in Altgeld Gardens, these networks of Black women operated within public housing developments, in welfare offices, and on the street.[49] Ultimately, this knowledge frequently produces a hard-won skepticism of the state, which sometimes results in a low level of political imagination.[50] However, political imagination is not a static quality among citizens. As Harold Baron writes in his tribute to the late Dorothy Gautreaux (a Altgeld Gardens resident), there are many Black women within Altgeld Gardens who refuse to concede their individual and community power.[51] Gautreaux was the lead plaintiff in a historic 1966 federal case against the Chicago Housing Authority for racial discrimination and housing segregation.[52] As a result, women like Dorothy not only occupied the liberatory domain of the PPS but also insisted that other residents join them there.

> Dorothy Gautreaux was of, by, and for the tenants in public housing. Her very being contradicted the perceived wisdom that CHA tenants lived under such heavy control and threat from the political machine that they could not be expected to stand up for themselves. Her view was that tenants both could and ought to direct their own lives. She set out to prove that proposition by example.[53]

Some women I interviewed recounted how they moved from a *community PPS* to a *liberatory PPS* because of the political education they received via the interpersonal relationships they developed in their neighborhoods. Testimonies about Dorothy Gautreaux's life speak frequently about her political education work throughout the Altgeld-Murray development. She created community and built a sense of belonging among residents by "organizing Girl Scouts, Boy Scouts and the PTA."[54] Through her work, Gautreaux built a sense of belonging among her neighbors and helped several move to the liberatory PPS domain as they grew in their sociopolitical education.

Regine Hunter is a example of an Altgeld resident who benefited from the sociopolitical intervention of her neighbors. As I mentioned in Chapter

1, I interviewed Regine in 2011. Regine had been living in Altgeld Gardens for forty-one years, after moving in with her mom and dad during the Great Migration. As was clear in the first series of vignettes from our interview, Regine is a great example of how interpersonal relationships within the neighborhood can move an individual in any direction around the PPS matrix. In Regine's case, it was her neighbors and the women she grew up with in Altgeld Gardens who moved her from a *community PPS* to a closer iteration of a *liberatory PPS*. Because of living in Altgeld Gardens for most of her adult life, Regine was well acquainted with the private management company that controlled most of the resources available to Altgeld residents. She was also a frequent participant in various CHA resident groups, and she held an elected position in the development for three years, as block captain.

A: Do you go to CHA meetings?

R: Oh, yes.

A: What are they like? What do you think of them? What are the people like?

R: Well, the meetings, really, they don't get anything done. I mean, we goes to the meeting; we voice our concerns; they let us talk to different representatives of CHA. OK. They always tell us that they'll get back to us, and they never do.

A: So what specific kind of meetings are these?

R: The commissioner meetings we're going to. And I go to the LAC meeting. Actually, I used to be a block captain, so I was involved with the LAC. So we meet about different things going on in the neighborhood, and really, we don't achieve anything at the meetings. We don't get anything out of those meetings.

A: Why don't you?

R: Well, they tell us that they get our complaints and our concerns, but every time we look up, it's another meeting a month later or two months later we go, and then it's the same old, same old. And then when we do try to talk to the people and they say, "Well, you'll hear from us," we never do. We never do.

A: So what was your experience like being a block captain?

R: Oh, that was fun because I interacted with the neighbors, all these different folks that I didn't know. You know, the kids. And then like I say, we would give them, like, lunches and stuff like the summer and school supplies and things like that with the kids. Like I say, I was more involved with the kids than with the parents, because we had a lot of working parents, and then the few that didn't work, they didn't never come out. So the kids did, so it was fun with the kids.

As I mentioned in chapter one, Regine's PPS developed over time with the support of her local sociopolitical community.* Her initial intuition directed her toward volunteering on the development to support young people and senior residents. But relationships with neighbors like Max Shaw, a nationally known environmental justice and public housing advocate, began to transform Regine's sociopolitical engagement.

Max Shaw is the daughter of Harriet Shaw, a nationally known environmental justice advocate who was the founder of Environmental Justice Organization (EJO). When Harriet passed, Max took on the leadership of EJO and as a result developed a formidable political reputation in her own right. While I discuss EJO and Max Shaw in Chapter 5, what is important to know is that Max and everyone in EJO had an intentional ethic about bringing as many Altgeld residents into their political organizing work as possible. Whenever I came to the development, it was common to hear women reference Max or the EJO meetings when discussing the formation of their politics. Regine often looked to Max and EJO for guidance when it came to understanding the political issues of the day.

A: What kind of skills and knowledge are needed to participate in politics?

R: Politics . . . well, one thing you need some kind of education. You need education. That's number one. And you need to understand English and reading, and you know what I'm saying, in politics. Because I don't understand it all myself. I'm going to tell you that now, I don't, 'cuz it's a whole lot I don't understand 'cuz I'm not all into it, you know what I'm saying? . . . But like I say, I listen to the news every day to try to get an understanding . . . it's so depressing though. It's so depressing.

A: Yeah, you have to be careful about listening to it all the time.

R: Yeah, it don't make you don't want to listen to it, but you still try to get, want to know what's going on out here in this world too, you know. But no, I understand a little. I don't understand a whole lot of it. And I'm being truthful, I don't. And if I don't I ask . . . I ask my mom. I ask either Max Shaw or different people that might know a little more than me.

---

* See pages 15–18.

As Regine continued to grow in her political knowledge, her political capacity, and her political imagination, her interpersonal relationships facilitated the development of a more *liberatory PPS*. For many of the respondents in the study, a site of more radical politics was regarding entitlements policy, specifically how state resources should be shared and disbursed among people living below the poverty line.

A: Are people treated equally in this society?

R: I don't think so.

A: Why is that?

R: I think some people are and some people aren't. Some people get a fair chance. Are you talking about all over or just out here?

A: Everywhere.

R: Well, I'm going to say out here, they have their picks. They choose their picks, who they want. And I don't know, we don't get a fair chance out here when it comes to maintenance and, like, people trying to get applications and with the company called You Can and things of that nature. So I know everybody not getting a fair, equal chance. I already know that from experience out here.

A: So who does get those opportunities?

R: They family members, stuff like that, somebody real close, best friends, and stuff like that. 'Cuz we see with our eyes, you know. . . .

A: Do people in government care about the people who live in Altgeld Gardens?

R: I don't think they care. They should care, but I really don't think they care.

A: Why don't you think they care?

R: Because it's a lot of things we need, like a lot of different programs they could put out here, build different facilities, give monies, you know, to have these kids off the streets. You know, do a clubhouse or something, you know, 'cuz every time . . . you know they have these little gym rooms out here, but now these kids got to be paying a dollar, two dollars to go in the building to play balls and stuff like that.

A: So to go in the park district building, they've got to pay?

R: They have to pay to play ball, because I have nephews out here, and they have to pay five dollars to play basketball, and I think that is ridiculous, you know. I think they need to open it up. They pay security or somebody to be up there, you know, where these kids play. The government, they got money; they can do that. They just sitting back right now, but they can make it real possible for our youth, 'cuz this our next generation, so you know a lot of them are getting killed. But if they open up and let some of this money loose so these kids can go in these places or build districts for them, you know, communities or clubhouses where they can go play in, then I think it would be a little less killing and fighting. Because they have something to do. Government, get the security, pay money for these people to watch these kids. So yeah.

A: Does working hard guarantee success?

R: Working hard . . . no, I don't think it does. Working hard, you're going to kill yourself. I feel it's only what you make it. And working hard, no success . . . you making the company successful. They don't care nothing about you. I experienced that with my job. They just let me know them companies don't be behind you. So you work hard because you want to work hard. Only going to do what I'm supposed to. I'm not going to kill myself, which I did do, so I experienced that before. So no. It partly depend on what employer you work for. You know. But who I worked for, no. And I worked hard. And this what came out of it; I'm still injured, and I'm still going through this case with them.

A: You going through a case with who?

R: East Lake.

A: Like workers' comp or something like that?

R: Mm-hmm.

A: Has CHA done enough to help you?

R: No. 'Cuz I have been interactive with CHA about getting my daughter and her son an apartment, and he got acute bronchitis where he sleeps on the floor, and since they moved us over here three years ago, we never had the central air. And I believe being on that floor, he never had bronchitis, too, till we moved here.

A: Why is he on the floor?

R: Where he gonna sleep?

A: What do you know about the Plan for Transformation?

R: Actually, I don't know a whole lot about it. I only know from the things from what I hear, and I don't know if that's true. You know you hear things on the street.

A: What kind of things do you hear on the street about it?

R: Well, I'm hearing they missing $99 million they done put into the development! Now, I don't know how true that is! And then I hear they supposed to hire Section 3 people, which would be like our children in the neighborhood. But like I say, they go they picks, the few they picks. Management stealing the money, yeah. That's what I hear. I don't know how true it is, but that's what I hear.

A: Do you think you and other people in public housing have any impact on these issues?

R: I think we do. We complain about no jobs and this and that, but they not going to listen to people like us. I just really never thought that they did. I just never really thought it. And then being Black [*chuckles briefly*]. I just always thought that.

Because CHA residents sometimes work within the private management companies or have resident positions on CHA committees like the Board of Directors, in 2011 there was a powerful whisper network throughout the CHA public housing developments. These whisper networks regularly reported on the mismanagement of funds within the CHA much earlier than the major newspapers. Being privy to those whisper-network reports, in addition to regularly attending public CHA meetings, meant that Regine was acutely aware of the CHA operating budget; its public federal, state, and local funding; and the ways CHA spent that money. During our interview, she was clear that the poor should receive substantially more resources. Regine had a variety of ideas about how local tax dollars should be spent: more money should go to departments like parks and recreation so that city kids could have more access to healthy outlets, CHA residents should have the right of first refusal for all construction jobs on the developments, more money should go to public education, and more money should be used to get residents through higher education (or trade certification).

Indeed, Regine's political viewpoint became increasingly more radical over the course of her years on the development. One example is Regine's admission that it was up to her and the other Altgeld residents to provide meaningful and safe resources for the children who live in the development. Her willingness to look to extrasystemic strategies to meet her needs and those of her neighbors and their families is especially notable. Ultimately, it was Regine's pushback against capitalist logics that insist "productivity" is the only means to moral goodness and a meaningful life that clarified her growing *liberatory PPS*.[55] She understood hard work does not always result in a just reward. Regine had clear-eyed expectations around what you will receive from a corporation (or government bureaucracy) regardless of your work ethic. Between the relationships within Altgeld Gardens that helped develop her cognitive liberation, and her personal experiences with injustice at the hands of CHA and other government bureaucracies throughout Chicago, her sociopolitical viewpoints skewed to the far left of the U.S. political spectrum.

Political imagination is not a static quality in individuals. Throughout the interviews, respondents recounted their experience of moving from a low to a neutral and eventually a high level of political imagination. Black feminist theory was central to parsing out how Black women could go from apathetic or alienated to a political imagination that allowed them to consider unconventional and more radical sociopolitical ideas. As Zenzele Isoke depicts throughout her work, Black women can develop higher levels of political imagination through a relational process focused on cognitive liberation via the creation of accessible home, social, and educational spaces:[56]

> Black women in American cities form sister-circles, girls' groups, book clubs, create formal and informal networks in their schools and workplaces, and they open their homes, knock on doors, and send emails to form community organizations and unlikely community coalitions. . . . I argue that in communities that are struggling with racialized poverty, open and hostile misogyny and homophobia, and urban economic containment . . . they are intimate spaces that build the will to resist structural intersectionality. These are intimate spaces that make sustained public resistance possible. These are places where young black people (male, female, transgender, and non-gender identifying) learn that their voices and perspectives are valid, that their commitment to social justice is needed, and their sacrifices for political struggle are appreciated. Most importantly, these are spaces where they learn they are not crazy, but that their feelings of discontent, despair, and frustration have been produced by an extenuated living history of black racial subjugation and gendered racialization and not by individual deficiencies in mood, temperament, and bad (read pathological) behavior.[57]

It is by developing relationships with their neighbors, attending community meetings, and cultivating a sense of belonging within a community, that the Black women in my study could develop a capacity for radical political imagination. The second axis of the PPS matrix is a visual representation of the spectrum of reported belonging to a sociopolitical community. On the low end of the spectrum of sociopolitical belonging are individuals who are completely, or almost completely, cut off from geographic or even digital community. These are people who have few to no friends or family members nearby and who spend most of their time alone or with a romantic partner or children (if they are not working).

People who had a general interest in sociopolitical issues and consumed news media, volunteered in their sociopolitical community, or took advantage of opportunities for political education had a neutral to high level of political imagination, despite their isolation. These folks could move in any direction on the PPS matrix as their sociopolitical belonging or political imagination grew. Respondents who could grow in political imagination but not sociopolitical belonging engaged in varying levels of political activity that focused on their unique and individual interests. On the other hand, people with high belonging and low political imagination would find work within their sociopolitical community especially salient or helpful. People with a visionary PPS were open to radical political ideas but were rarely substantially involved in the issues beyond political debates and discussions. As I will discuss later in the chapter, structural issues throughout Altgeld had a significant impact on which residents developed a sense of sociopolitical belonging in the Altgeld sociopolitical community.

The Spatial Realities of the PPS

The relationship I found between individuals with a more alienated PPS and spatial characteristics further illustrates the flexibility of the framework. The PPS framework might allow political scientists to explore how the politics of various groups are affected by traditional stimuli like political advertisements and nontraditional stimuli like music, dance, theater, or murals. The ability of the PPS model to explain how spatial characteristics affect the politics of an individual facilitates a fuller understanding of the politics of the Black women at the center of this study.

My data indicated that regular incidents of neighborhood violence or the chronic neglect and mismanagement of building infrastructure can skew the individual PPS toward the more disengaged end of the spectrum. The mechanisms of this process range from isolation that happens when a resident is afraid to leave their home, emotional fallout that leaves people too tired to even consider the future, and a singular focus on leaving public housing altogether, a focus that leaves no time for cultivating belonging or political imagination. Other spatial qualities, like the creation of apartment blocks near the bus route, the CHA administration, and businesses, can skew the individual PPS toward the more engaged end of the spectrum. These areas seemed to experience less violence because of the presence of rule-enforcing infrastructure. Violence generally was not performed near CHA bureaucracies because residents did not want to get kicked out of public housing.

Residents who lived in safer spaces, both old and new, veered toward the more engaged end of the spectrum. Their sociopolitical tools included activities like cleaning up their blocks, holding protests, planning community-wide programs, pushing back against the CHA, and planning field trips for the young people who lived in the development. The women who lived in these blocks were friends with a handful of neighbors and would bring newer neighbors along with them to community events. In short, something seemingly simple, like your apartment placement within the development, could have a radical effect not only on your sense of belonging but also on your emotional capacity to cultivate political imagination. It is important to note that there were women who had visible political engagement and lived on the more violent blocks within the development.

Other aspects of space, like the aesthetic qualities of the apartments and neighborhoods, can have a dramatic impact on how residents conceptualize and discuss their sense of political power. *Redefining the Political* examines what it means when residents understand power to be singularly organized in their individual body, and specifically what this means for the development of their PPS. Among the most significant conclusions of my project is that space matters deeply for the development of political identity and political engagement.[58] The impact of space goes beyond sociodemographic variables and reaches into those less easily quantified characteristics such as geographic boundaries, structural maintenance, benign neglect, aesthetic appearance, and interpersonal relationships, with both neighbors and various bureaucrats.

It is important to consider seriously the relational nature of politics, specifically in political engagement. It does not matter if we are discussing a traditional or quotidian idea of politics; generally, to participate within a sociopolitical community, you must be present; on the phone, in person, online, or in some other manner. Participating within a sociopolitical community is a key criteria for political engagement within Black feminist political frameworks.[59] The increasing potential for grassroots political work to facilitate access for all bodies of all abilities via material space and online and social media space means that politically necessary presence has an exponentially increasing number of forms. However, it is nearly impossible to be present if you do not feel safe. A loss of safety means you often no longer feel capable of speaking within, participating in, or being a part of the sociopolitical community.

A Black feminist criterion of the political requires an extrasystemic view of politics. It understands politics as something that can happen outside of traditional structures and institutions. Extrasystemic politics can include gossip about a particular manager resulting in their power being undermined. It could include a refusal to obey Robert's Rules of Order in a public board meeting to strategically draw attention to your cause. It could even include planting rosebushes with thorns in a development that has banned resident gardening. A Black feminist conception of extrasystemic politics understands everyday habits, speech, and patterns as being a part of the broader makeup of an individual's PPS. For an individual's political engagement to be visible—and beyond that, politically meaningful—they must be able to interact with others. Isolated and paralyzed political engagement is absent any form of power.

Given that sociopolitical tools require interaction with others, when an individual suffers a violation that creates difficulty communicating with people in their sociopolitical community, not only does it cause a gross loss of integrity but sometimes it disables their sociopolitical tools altogether.[60] To put it succinctly, when you live among violence, your sociopolitical tools can become less and less visible until its existence becomes debatable. For people living in violent homes, neighborhoods, states, or countries, a significant part of their life is transformed through the loss of integrity; they no longer feel safe. Losing safety means that, politically, there are entire groups of people who no longer feel like they can have visible sociopolitical tools. A democracy with segments of the population restricted in this way is not a fully functioning democracy.

My interview with Kate, a new resident of the Altgeld Gardens and Murray Homes, offered an example of how violence can foreclose on individual potential for local community belonging. Months before our interview, Kate's son was jumped and beaten up by more than twenty children. Kate also witnessed multiple shootings and beatings around her home. Because of these violent experiences, she requested an emergency transfer to move her and her children out of the Altgeld Gardens and Murray Homes. Without a transfer approval from the CHA, Kate couldn't move to another public housing development in Chicago. Because of those violent experiences, she fell into a deep depression and could not find steady work after she moved to Altgeld. Although she requested help from CHA multiple times, nothing was done about the physical and emotional violence she and her family encountered. As a result, Kate felt stuck in a neighborhood where she felt unsafe in almost every way.

Violence can shut down individual capacity for political engagement. As Katherine McKittrick argues, "Racism and sexism are not simply bodily or identity based; racism and sexism are also spatial acts and illustrate black women's geographic experiences and knowledges as they are made possible through domination."[61] The violence is inscribed into the geography of the neighborhood, which works to restrict and reshape the political habits of the people who live there. When an individual is entrenched with fear that they can or will be harmed at any moment, even attending to basic needs like getting food and going to work can be strenuous. Women I interviewed spoke about having bullets fly through their homes and police running through their houses in pursuit of a suspect. The home space was not a guaranteed place of safety or sociopolitical belonging.

Women who were aware they lacked a sense of belonging and support seemed to be isolated and expressed a diminished quality of life. Because Kate experienced multiple forms of violence, was relatively new to the development, and was without sociopolitical community or institutional support, her sociopolitical tools were on the less visible end of the spectrum. However, her PPS was not absent political imagination.

A: Do you vote or participate in any political activities?

K: I vote. I haven't participated in any political activities out here. I haven't gotten involved in any political activities out here, and I don't know if it's because they . . . well, that's not true. The LAC, the Advisory Council, has little forums and things, and I just attended the CHA listening forum they had. . . .

A: So do you think you would participate in LAC activities again?

K: Well, they address the concerns of the residents and . . . I don't know how many times they may post it for what they're doing. But they do send out things saying what they—like this past summer they sent out something that they had wanted Comcast . . . they were monopolizing us with just Comcast, and so they want another hearing for us to be able to choose the providers. And so they wanted us to come out for that, but I didn't go because I don't have cable. And I won't be interested in having cable any time soon, so I didn't participate in that. But normally I pick and choose.

A: Just according to what you think fits your life and applies to you?

K: Yes.

A: You said you didn't get involved in any political activities here, but have you done political activities elsewhere?

K: I helped a friend of mine. He was running for Illinois state representative.

A: OK, and what was that experience like for you?

K: It was interesting. Kind of get to see the inside of how it operates. You know, you're normally on the outside being a voter, but this way you're communicating with people, you're asking them to be involved, and you're asking them to sign petitions and things like that. So just more community activity.

Kate chose to not involve herself with political activities in the development. She generally didn't speak to her neighbors or go to community events. However, as Betsy Sinclair noted in her study, friendship networks outside of the residential neighborhood often facilitate political behavior.[62]

Because Kate kept in contact with a friend who ran for Illinois state representative, she took part in some get-out-the-vote activities. In various ways, Kate could be defined as alienated because her political engagement did not include most of the traditional political participation behaviors. However, her PPS (see Figure 2.1) occasionally participated in traditional political activities when asked by friends. Significantly, she also envisioned

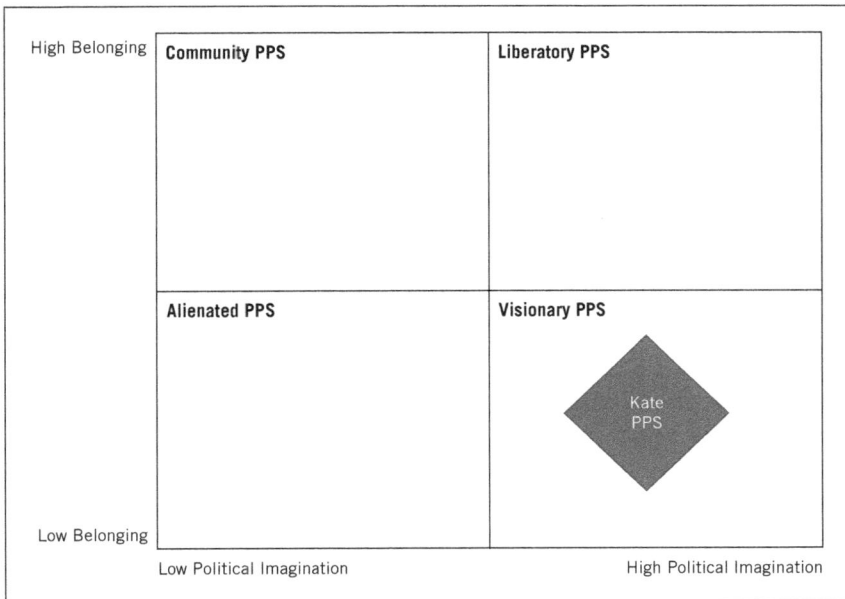

Figure 2.1 Kate's Political Possible-Self

herself capable of one day leaving public housing and changing public housing policy for the better.

Political Imagination and the Ability to Cultivate Political Possibilities

The Black feminist definitional criterion (BFDC) of politics and the political put forward in this book centers the effort to create sociopolitical possibilities as a core component of recognizing the political from the nonpolitical. As I noted in the Introduction, the Black feminist definitional criterion of politics understands politics *as the work of trying to create (or limit) possibilities (for better or worse) within or around the substantive reality of the world around you.* By centering the creation of sociopolitical possibilities, the Black feminist foundation of this project helps us understand political imagination as vital to any politics or political work. Nina Eliasoph defines political imagination as "a quality of mind necessary to grasp the constant interplay between our personal lives and the political world."[63] To create sociopolitical possibility, one must do the critical work of imagining those possibilities.

When Nina Eliasoph points to political imagination as the key to understanding that "the personal is political," she is reminding us that political people, structures, and institutions only have power because of the sociopolitical norms (embedded within everyday life) that make that power seem normal, palpable, and sometimes even desirable.[64] It is via the work of building points of connection and belonging to sociopolitical community, as well as developing political imagination, that the individual can move through the political domains making up the PPS matrix. The Tenant Services meetings within the CHA provide a good example of political imagination and political belonging as central to political identity formation. Frequently, residents used the meetings as a space to protest potential amendments to housing policy or injustices that touched their lives. For example, observed differences between the treatment of residents who lived in high-rise developments and those who lived in walk-up developments (like the Altgeld Gardens Developments) were frequently brought up during these meetings.

According to tenants at Tenant Services meetings, high-rise residents were under a higher degree of surveillance than tenants who lived in other types of developments. Below is a vignette from my field notes from a CHA CAC meeting in April 2011:

At this point, the floor is opened up to tenant questions and concerns. There seems to be a [consistent] issue with destruction of property [within CHA public housing developments]. As a result, a resident [justifiably] asked "what happens when somebody breaks the rules?" The response from Mr. Smith [an unidentified person who seemed to be in charge] was that "residents don't have the privilege of knowing what the punishments are, but they do happen." Needless to say, this struck me as a dodge, and the meeting attendees were visibly unsatisfied with this response, but there is no further explanation of the issue. It strikes me as strange that there are no clearly defined set of punishments for broken or stolen property within the ACOP (the CHA public housing development rule book) rules. Notably, actually getting a copy of the ACOP was a fruitless endeavor for me and many of the CHA residents I spoke to. It seemed that this pretty much allowed the CHA to do as little or as much as they want for any individual case with little to no oversight.

The next tenant had a concern with the exclusion list at Lake Park Place.*

According to the resident, if one person is evicted from the development, their entire family can no longer enter any CHA buildings. According to this tenant, an eight-year-old girl, whose mother was evicted from a CHA development, was banned from visiting her friends [the children the little girl grew up with]. The situation was so extreme that the little girl was asked to leave a slumber party being held by one of her friends, in the middle of the night. The eight-year-old had to wait across the street from the development for her mother to come pick her up. The resident reporting this incident was incredulous this happened and found it completely ridiculous. Mr. Smith directed Jane Doe, of CHA Asset Management, to answer this question (interestingly, she was the only CHA staffer fully introduced to the room, I wondered why that was. Was she the only person CHA wanted individuals to be able to access and contact?) Doe said that "the reality is, if you are kicked out, you cannot be on the property." Smith followed up by saying, "adults make decisions that affect children and cause them to suffer all the time, the adults need to be more responsible." This struck me as incred-

---

* In high-rise developments at CHA public housing, "exclusion lists" determined who was banned from the apartments.

ibly paternalistic and cruel. There was lots of grumbling from meeting attendees, once again, they were visibly unhappy with an answer from CHA.

Lake Park Place was a high-rise public housing development, I was surprised to realize CHA did not demolish all of the high-rise buildings, as they were reputed to have done.

The tenants then began to discuss the differences between the treatment of high-rise residents [like Lake Park Place] and walk-up residents [like the row houses of Altgeld Gardens, where residents had private access to their apartments and their guests did not have to show ID]. High-rise residents were under a higher level of surveillance, they had to go through intense security to enter and leave their homes, the high-rise residents believed this was unfair.

Interestingly, the CHA seemed to be highly invested in monitoring the social behaviors of residents, but they did not want to take responsibility or liability for the maintenance of property, resident safety, the quality of apartment rehab or repair, etc.

High-rise residents (and their guests) were required to show government-issued identification to enter the building, and in the absence of identification, guests could not visit resident apartments. High-rise residents consistently complained that this was unfair, that it constituted unnecessary surveillance, and that they should have greater freedom to come and go as they pleased. While on first pass this seems to be a relatively minor issue, it is an example of Eliasoph's public-spirited conversation.[65] The residents were concerned with how these surveillance policies affected them individually, but they were also concerned with how they affected everyone who lived in high-rise public housing in Chicago. When residents discussed these issues, they almost always framed them as issues of justice: as legal lease holders, they should have full access to their places of residence in the way they deem appropriate.

Over time, I observed the Tenant Services meetings to be a space of political learning and political engagement for the people who live in Chicago public housing. The meetings served as a sociopolitical training ground for residents: they learned how to speak in front of large groups of people and which communication strategies worked to effectively shift policy. During public discourse at CHA public meetings, residents tried to meet the expectations of both white and Black middle-class CHA Board members. The meetings served as spaces where residents from a wide spectrum of neighborhoods learned about the issues and concerns they shared. Many residents became regulars at the meetings and showed up early to take part in networking and informal information dissemination, where they made plans and strategized. Individuals shared stories with other residents about effective political strategies when combating the management companies, security guards, or even CHA itself.

After consistently taking part in the meetings, residents could make linkages between their individual struggles and the political power they held. Bearing witness to residents from other developments as they articulated their vision for a healthy and whole life within their public housing developments, helped new and old residents develop sociopolitical possibilities for their developments. By observing the creation of sociopolitical possibilities—that is, articulating their grievances, expectations, and dreams about life in the development—residents cultivated one another's political imagination. Political imagination allowed them to see how the connection between their quality of life and the political world could make a better daily life possible.

For some residents, attending public CHA meetings deepened their sense of belonging to Chicago public housing sociopolitical communities. The experience of attending public CHA meetings sometimes led to an increased capacity for political imagination. As a result, over the course of the year I was in the field, I watched a handful of Black women who were residents at Altgeld Gardens move across the PPS matrix as their sociopolitical identities shifted, changed, and sometimes even grew. Some women went from a "nonvisible politics" to a "community politics." Other women went from the "alienated" PPS domain to a "visionary" PPS domain. As scholars of women's community organizing, public housing activism, and Black women's political organizing have consistently shown, individuals often develop political capacity and political identity when they feel they belong to sociopolitical community and are given the tools to develop political imagination.[66]

Applying the PPS Matrix

Central to the PPS framework is its capacity for movement and flexibility. It presents political identity and political participation as a spectrum rather than a set of fixed binary choices. But within the spectrum of choices, the matrix also allows the individual PPS to grow and change. Someone like Kate, for example, could start with a *visionary PPS* and move toward a *liberatory PPS*. If Kate continued nurturing her political imagination and developed a sense of belonging to her neighborhood community, her desire to transform the violence in her neighborhood could absolutely push her into a resistance-oriented liberatory PPS. But potential changes with-

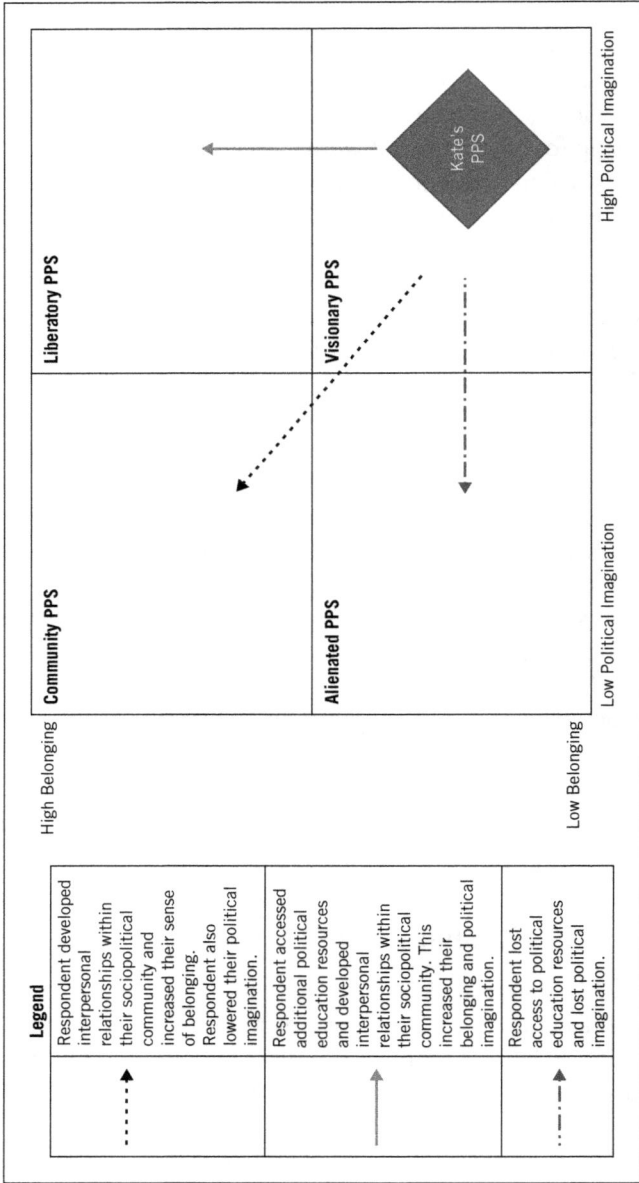

Figure 2.2 How Kate's PPS Could Change over Time

in the PPS are not limited to the horizontal or vertical axis. A transformation could also happen on a diagonal axis. If we use the example of Kate again, her PPS could transform from a *visionary PPS* to a *community PPS* (see Figure 2.2).

Kate could become particularly inspired by a political campaign (for example, when former president Barack Obama, who was once a volunteer in Kate's neighborhood, Altgeld Gardens, endorsed Joe Biden during the 2020 U.S. presidential campaign). If Kate volunteered for Obama organizers or the Biden campaign, she would spend time with other people from her residential neighborhood, as well as the wider South Side of Chicago. Acquiring new exposure to different people and places, as well as volunteering for a successful U.S. presidential campaign, could be enough to increase Kate's sense of belonging and commitment to the community of Chicago. An increase in her sense of belonging and a decrease in her political imagination would move Kate diagonally into a *neutral PPS*.

Becoming involved with traditional political engagement activities (volunteering for a political campaign, voting, etc.) could decrease an individual's political imagination. Individuals who consider engagement with the state to be the only legitimate form of political engagement, limit their political engagement accordingly. Those who are solely invested in traditional political engagement cannot, and will not, imagine radical alternatives beyond the state. By definition, their political imagination is limited. A decrease in an individual's political imagination, alongside an increase in political belonging, would make their PPS neutral (as illustrated in Figure 2.2).

It is possible that after the 2020 U.S. presidential election Kate could have lost interest in national politics because the person who drew her in (former president Obama) was no longer a national politician. It is possible to see how, without the push and pull of a national U.S. presidential election, her political imagination could continue to decrease. But if she developed relationships with her neighbors while she was volunteering for the Biden campaign in 2020, it is possible that her sense of belonging could increase. A high sense of belonging and a lowered political imagination could ultimately leave Kate with a *community PPS*.

Conclusion

The movement and flexibility of the PPS is made possible by the clear articulation of the connection between each domain of the PPS matrix and (1) local (or sometimes digital) community and (2) state power. The theory of the PPS is built on a foundational understanding that the politics of any individual, *A*, within any context, *B*, cannot be understood without a clear picture of *A*'s relationship to *B*.

Women who had higher levels of belonging expressed more neutral levels of political imagination. Women who had a more liberatory PPS had higher levels of belonging and political imagination. However, there were few respondents in this category. Individuals with a high sense of belonging tended either to be very social and extroverted or to have lived in the development for ten or more years. A person with a community PPS developed a higher sense of political imagination by joining local organizations, volunteering in their local community, signing up for political education, being mentored by elders in their community, or participating in social, political, or capital protest.

The growth of individual political imagination is facilitated by the growth of cognitive liberation. An individual develops a liberatory PPS when their political imagination understands community-based political power. The PPS matrix allows for a holistic political understanding of the individual. Over a lifetime, individual political identity and individual political engagement will shift, change, and grow. By making flexible movement throughout the PPS matrix possible, the PPS framework allows for a more holistic political picture of marginalized individuals, and marginalized groups writ large.

3

Black Folks in Chicago

Introduction

When I was a child growing up in Detroit, Michigan, my parents would read to my sister and me before we went to bed. In the 1980s and 1990s, my mom went through significant pains to collect Black American, African, and Caribbean folktales from throughout the Black diaspora. Stories like Anansi and Brer Rabbit taught us about the value of intellect and resilience. But the myths that stay with me to this day are stories emphasizing the collective power found within community. As I've grown older and transitioned to reading Black science fiction from throughout the diaspora, I have been struck by the way ideas about community link Black diasporic stories together. When I began collecting interviews from Black women who lived in the Altgeld Gardens and Phillip Murray Homes, I was not surprised to recognize the thread of community weaving through their stories as well.[1]

Black feminist social scientists and writers have consistently argued that community is a central and defining feature of Black sociopolitical life throughout the United States. I build upon their work by developing a Black feminist definitional criterion (BFDC) of politics and the political, which helps political practitioners recognize the unique features of sociopolitical life within Black marginalized groups. A clear understanding of respondent spatial context, as well as their sociopolitical community, is foundational to these theoretical criteria. As I will continue to argue throughout this book, a clear and holistic understanding of the politics of a Black marginalized population cannot be achieved without first understanding their spatial context, their sociopolitical community, and the public spheres they have access to. In this chapter, I begin by pinpointing how and why sociopolitical community, the public sphere, and spatial context function as theoretical mechanisms within the BFDC of politics and the political. From there, I focus on the sociopolitical context and spatial context of the research undergirding this book. I then go on to describe the methodological process that made this book possible. Finally, at the end of this chapter, I discuss a broader history of Black women's organizing within public housing and the impact of neoliberalism on the sociopolitical work of Black marginalized communities more broadly.

The Black Public Sphere(s) of Chicago Public Housing

Many scholars argue that the public sphere is a requirement for the existence of democracy.[2] They believe that public sphere(s) exist to cultivate a sense of community, so the community can take care of itself. Nina Eliasoph's work on citizen apathy provides an important framework for understanding how residential spaces can shape the political behavior of individuals.[3] In *Avoiding Politics*, she argues that public spaces that allow citizens to "talk politics" are critical for learning democratic principles and social responsibility as well as for generating power. For this reason, Eliasoph believes associations and groups are critical to the political learning of citizens; accordingly, "associations form the public sphere."[4]

> The public sphere is, theoretically, defined as the realm of institutions in which private citizens can carry on free and egalitarian conversation . . . it is not just a closed, hierarchical workplace, and not just family but is a third setting for conversation, with three main characteristics: participation is optional, potentially open to all and potentially egalitarian.[5]

Within Eliasoph's framework, the purpose of the public sphere is to cultivate a sense of community so people care more about the world around them, as well as to become a source of "meaning-making power."[6] One of the primary ways the public sphere achieves meaning-making power is by cultivating political imagination in individuals.[7] This imagination helps citizens develop an awareness of "the constant interplay between our personal lives and the political world."[8] Through talking, reading, and otherwise interacting, citizens are able to grasp the critical nature of politics and thus begin to care about, and become motivated to address issues in, the wider world.

Eliasoph argues that this kind of meaning-making political talk happens best within the privacy of homes and neighborhoods.[9] Otherwise, individuals and groups often fear being judged by outsiders (or in the case of Black marginalized populations, surveilled by the state). One of Eliasoph's most critical contributions is her conceptualization of "public spirited conversation." She contends that public-spirited conversation enables the public sphere to function. She goes on to define public-spirited conversation as "a process of giving voice to a wide circle of concern—a public spirited way of talking . . . public spirited conversation happens when citizens speak in terms of 'justice.'"[10] Significantly, Eliasoph's concept of public-spirited conversation provides a critical contribution to my Black feminist political criteria because it reaches beyond simple definitions of political talk. The concept of public-spirited conversation illustrates the mechanism through which an individual's politics goes from intellectual work to political work.* Put another way, public-spirited conversation helps an individual develop an expanded view of politics, a politics capable of considering the way public spheres, and indeed democracies, can operate as tools of collective power. Public spheres and sociopolitical communities function to legitimize and provide space for public-spirited conversation. Public-spirited conversation gives birth to political imagination and eventually political power.

However, the work of public spheres as spaces where political power can be generated brings to light a critical issue. As Catherine R. Squires makes clear, a lack of access to the public sphere has a substantial impact on marginalized Black sociopolitical communities:[11]

> Unfortunately, participation in public discourse is not always so accessible or vibrant. Not every group or individual enjoys the same access to public spaces, media resources, or other tools to participate in discursive activities. Particular groups may be targeted by government officials for censorship and have a harder time distrib-

---

* As discussed in the Introduction, according to my Black feminist theoretical framework of politics and the political, two or more people are required to cultivate community-based power. When individuals think about politics but do not communicate those ideas, they are engaged in intellectual work, not political work. This could be due to an individual concern for their own self-interest. For further discussion, see the introduction to Chapter 4.

uting their ideas. Furthermore, prevailing social norms may instill fear in citizens of marginalized publics that their ideas would at best be met with indifference, and at worst violence.[12]

A lack of access to the public sphere creates a lack of access to political power. As I point out in Chapter 2, the creation of political power requires multiple people coming together to create (or limit) a political goal. However, if Black marginalized sociopolitical communities are barred access to spaces or modes of communication where they can engage in public-spirited conversation, then those communities are effectively blocked from cultivating political power. Political scientist Traci Burch argues that one example of a structurally constructed denial of political power is the disenfranchisement of many formerly incarcerated people (a large number of whom are low income).[13] Without this basic right, formerly incarcerated individuals are unable to participate in the democratic process, which has a substantial impact on the neighborhoods they go back home to.[14] Many others living below the poverty line simply become so alienated from the government, they no longer see the point of participating in traditional forms of politics, like voting.[15] Thus, their needs often go unmet on the federal policy level.[16] But it is not just the larger public spheres that block the sociopolitical development of Black marginalized communities. Since the long civil rights movement, Black political discourse within the United States has been dominated by the mainstream Black counterpublic—a counterpublic Black people living below the poverty line have infrequent access to.[17]

Catherine R. Squires argues that not only are there multiple public spheres but there are multiple Black publics:[18]

> I propose we speak of multiple Black publics. Thus, a Black public is an emergent collective composed of people who (a) engage in common discourses and negotiations of what it means to be Black, and (b) pursue particularly defined Black interests. This definition, although still wedded to the idea that there is a Black social group, does allow for heterogeneous Black publics to emerge, and also for people who do not identify as Black, but are concerned with similar issues, to be involved in a coalition with Black people.[19]

When I use the phrase "mainstream Black counterpublic," I am using Squires's definition of the Black counterpublic. Squires defines the counterpublic as the Black public "which can engage in debate with wider publics to test ideas and perhaps utilize traditional social movement tactics (boycotts, civil disobedience)."[20] For the purposes of this book, the "mainstream Black counterpublic" refers to the Black middle-class counterpublic focused on respectability politics. As Frederick C. Harris and Cathy J. Cohen show in their work, this "mainstream Black counterpublic" currently dominates the Black American political agenda in the United States.[21]

That said, the absence of marginalized Black people from traditional politics does not mean that people on the margins opt out of politics altogether.[22] They simply use their sociopolitical tools within separate political spheres.[23] Marginalized Black populations like poor Black women have access to what Squires calls an enclave public sphere:[24]

> Oppressed groups often do not have the choice of picking safe spaces for themselves. Marginalized groups are commonly denied public voice or entrance into public spaces by dominant groups and thus are forced into enclaves. At different times in history, African Americans have been forced into enclaves by repressive state policies and have used these enclave spaces to create discursive strategies and gather oppositional resources. . . . The enclave is signified by the utilization of spaces and discourses that are hidden from the view of the dominant public and the state. These clandestine places and communications are dedicated to Black interests and needs. . . . Thus, an enclave public sphere requires the maintenance of safe spaces, hidden communication networks, and group memory to guard against unwanted publicity of the group's true opinions, ideas, and tactics for survival.[25]

Chicago public housing is one such "Black enclave public sphere." This Black enclave public sphere allows residents to develop their PPS through public-spirited conversation and also troubles firm divisions between ideas of "public" and "private" space.[26] As Squires notes, a Black public can "enclave itself, hiding counterhegemonic ideas and strategies in order to survive or avoid sanctions, while internally producing lively debate and planning."[27] In other words, the Black enclave public sphere facilitates concealed ingroup conversations, hidden from the surveillance of the state and mainstream Black counterpublics, what James C. Scott calls hidden transcripts.[28] Many respondents discussed hidden strategic methods for thwarting welfare street-level bureaucrats to gain access to key household goods and resources, strategies they often shared within the Black enclave public sphere.[29] The sociopolitical community should be considered a diverse network of individuals linked together by a shared residential neighborhood, a workplace, or even a grassroots organization. A Black enclave public sphere is a larger formation of individuals or groups who generally share one or two identities (race, gender, socioeconomic status, or even city) but do not necessarily have to.

For example, a Black enclave public sphere (made up of public housing residents within the United States) could comprise several sociopolitical communities from public housing developments all over the United States. Squires goes on to specify further that "this definition, although still wedded to the idea that there is a Black social group, does allow for heterogeneous Black publics to emerge, and also for people who do not identify as Black, but are concerned with similar issues, to be involved in a coalition with Black people."[30] Black feminist scholars note, talking and interacting with one another allows members of the sociopolitical community or Black public spheres to grasp the critical nature of politics.[31] Most importantly, public-spirited conversations within sociopolitical communities and public spheres facilitate the development of political imagination and political power.[32]

> As Baker (1995) puts it, the civil rights movement was a product of the *"active working imagination"* of a Black public sphere (p. 16). Today, such *imaginative work*, in concert with the political and economic action Dawson calls for, is still urgently needed. In the absence of the obvious target of Jim Crow and in the midst of entrenched economic problems and conservative backlash, Blacks are in the process of *reimagining their struggle*, their relationship to shared aspects of Black heritage and identities, and their future as a social group in the post–civil rights movement era.[33]

This is the central takeaway: every formation of community serves to stimulate individual and group political imagination and provide crucial forms of political education. Without public-spirited conversation and the resulting political imagination, political identity, political groups, and political power cannot be created.

Public housing and its Black enclave public sphere are politically important, as they straddle the line between private homes and publicly owned property the state has full control over. Like the home spaces Black feminists describe in their work, public housing is a public and a private home space for residents.[34] As in the work of Kevin Fox Gotham and Krista Brumbley, for residents I interviewed, each apartment constituted a private home, and for Black political women operating within the Black enclave public sphere and the Altgeld sociopolitical community, those homes were also spaces where they engaged in the politics of homemaking and sociopolitical community work.[35] Throughout my many conversations with Black women living in the Altgeld Gardens development, the sanctity of their homes, as a personal space and a sociopolitical space, came up again and again. Through the politics of homemaking, many respondents used the relative safety they created within their homes to facilitate public-spirited conversations. Those conversations helped their neighbors learn about the politics of negotiating public housing and welfare bureaucracies while also developing political imagination and collective power. In the following section, I provide an example of one of those public-spirited conversations at Altgeld Gardens and the political power it created.

An Example of Black Enclave Publics Developed to Fight Welfare Street-Level Bureaucrats

When I met Sara, she had moved into Altgeld five months prior. She did not enjoy living there, but at forty-eight years old, Sara had been on the brink of homelessness before CHA called her daughter about living in Altgeld. Sara had four daughters, all adults, as well as several sisters who mostly lived in Chicago. But Sara was pointed about not allowing family to come visit her at Altgeld. While she described her life as active—she frequently volunteered and participated in community organizations—Sara also lived with significant fear.

Sara worried a lot about robbery and rape at the hands of the young men who lived in the development. Without a doubt, if she could have lived elsewhere, she would have. But in the face of that fear, Sara's interview is an example of why traditional forms of political assessment miss important forms of political advocacy. Although she voted regularly, there were additional ways she advocated for the people in her neighborhood. Sara harnessed her "meaning-making" power by using her knowledge of the entitlements bureaucracy to help herself, her family, and others.[36] She engaged her community via public-spirited conversation, which created political power capable of helping women who struggled to take care of their families.

A: How has the government treated you?
S: Oh, they been good to me, because see, I get mines. I get mine,
     I get my daughter's. . . .

A: And how do you do that?

S: . . . I go to the aid office. I be on the caseworkers. I said I know what they qualify for and I know what [I] can get.

A: So how do you educate yourself? How do you find all of that out?

S: I read. I talk to people when I go up to there. It's a supervisor; her name is Jones; she tell me everything; she gives me pamphlets. But it's who . . . you have to interact with people to find out what's going on, because it might be a person that's been getting stuff from them for years, and they be sitting in there talking to people. This one lady asked me, she was like, "How you get [Medicaid]?" and I told her! She be like, "I didn't know that." I said you not going to know until we start asking questions. We sitting up here six hours anyway, so why not talk to each other, find out what's going on. Just like they told this one lady she wasn't going to get her stamps for two months because they were backed up forty days. . . , that ain't our motherfucking fault you backed up forty days. She supposed to get her goddamn stamps. I said, "so get a supervisor down here 'cuz I want to know why." And that wasn't even my business. And the lady was so grateful.

A: So it got worked out?

S: She got her stamps in two days.

A: Oh, wow.

S: See, if she had sit there and listened to this new caseworker, she'd have been waiting . . . hell, she'd have been starved to death. Ask for supervisors, ask for managers, ask questions. . . .

A: Can you remember when you started learning how to do that and advocating for yourself in that way?

S: Long as I can remember, I've been advocating. My grandma, she was born and raised in Mississippi. She used to have a truck; she would go around and see about the older people. Take 'em biscuits and meat and cook, make them cakes and pies, tea cakes. And we'd just ride on the back of the truck. And she'd get out, "Come on," and she'd go talk to them, see what they need . . . well, Ms. Jones, she need this, and she need . . . and she did this. And I seen my grandmother get these did. So if you don't talk for yourself, I tell [my daughter], you can't keep waiting for me.

Almost every aspect of residents' lives and their politics inhabited both public and private space. The welfare office is a public sphere where entitlement beneficiaries must advocate for the "private" need of feeding their families.

As a result, residents throughout the development cultivated a Black enclave public sphere invested in making sure residents could get the resources they needed to survive. At its core, this fight for survival, for fair resource distribution, was a political one.[37]

One way Sara protected herself was by using this Black enclave public sphere to educate herself and her neighbors about the entitlements policies they were eligible for. Sara was consistently public spirited in her advocacy for herself and others.[38] Eliasoph argues that the concept "public spirited" emphasizes an individual's concern for a broader world beyond their own. To be public spirited is to promote a view of politics beyond simple self-interest.[39] This view of politics considers how the various public spheres and democracies can function to support the greater good.[40] Sara's demand that the welfare office educate her and provide other women like her with what they were owed (in this case food stamps) was a fight to support the greater good. At their basest level, political fights are centrally concerned with the equitable distribution of resources.[41] As I show in the upcoming discussions of the spatial context of this study (Chicago, Illinois), ultimately, the fight for safe, accessible, healthy, and publicly owned housing is no different.

Public Housing in Chicago

Chicago has, and has had, the distinction of being one of the most segregated cities in the United States.[42] Many African Americans, Latinx, Asian Americans, and whites live in distinctly different neighborhoods and communities. As a result, racial groups have vastly different lived experiences in the same city. Many Black Americans have little access to healthy food options, and many Latinx lack access to basic social services. White neighborhoods on the North Side are beneficiaries of the heavy economic and social development city officials hoped would bring increased tourism.[43] Because the city is so segregated, many job opportunities bring minority residents into contact with white Americans of considerable social and financial privilege. Black folks living below the poverty line have a heightened awareness of the lack of investment their neighborhoods receive from local, state, and federal governments.* This inequity deeply affected the sociopo-

---

* In *Feminist Theory: From Margin to Center*, bell hooks argued in the first edition preface that "to be in the margin is to be part of the whole but outside the main body. . . . We could enter that world [the white wealthy world], but we could not live there. We had always to return to the margin, to beyond the tracks, to shacks and abandoned houses on the edge of town. There were laws to ensure our return. To not return was to risk being punished. Living

litical development of the Chicago public housing residents I had the opportunity to interview during my time there.

A History of Chicago Public Housing

Many Black Americans who migrated from the Deep South in the mid-twentieth century saw Chicago's housing projects as a refuge. Built originally to house World War II veterans and the increasing numbers of southern migrants to the Midwest, these urban communities gave working-class Americans of all races a jumping-off point for their new urban lives.[44] From the beginning, there was resistance to public housing across the country, mostly because of homeowner resistance to public housing being built in their neighborhoods.[45] Sudhir Venkatesh (2002) argues that

> the location of public housing in neighborhoods of highest poverty concentration is the result of federal toleration of extensive segregation against African Americans in urban housing markets, as well as acquiescence to organized neighborhood groups.[46]

As in most urban cities throughout the United States, the placement of public housing in Chicago directly reflected the desires of its white citizens and their socio-political-economic interests. Scholar Jessica Trounstine argues that these processes of neighborhood segregation have "profound political consequences."[47] As she points out, segregation wasn't merely the project of a few racist "citizens' committees" throughout the suburbs.

> Segregation is not simply the result of individual choices about where to live. Neither racial antipathy nor economic inequalities between groups are sufficient to create and perpetuate segregation. The maintenance of property values and the quality of public goods are collective endeavors. And like all collective endeavors they require collective action for production and stability. Local governments provide this collective action.[48]

---

as we did—on the edge—we developed a particular way of seeing reality. We looked both from the outside in and from the inside out. We focused our attention on the center as well as on the margin. We understood both" (hooks, xvi). This awareness that Black folks have of the inequities between the places where they live and the white spaces where they must work creates a hyperawareness of inequity. I argue that this hyperawareness can act as both a politically edifying force and a politically alienating force in the Black public sphere—particularly in the Black public sphere of communities living below the poverty line.

By facilitating and affirming the practice of local segregation, housing authorities all over the United States facilitated the systemic residential and economic marginalization of Black Americans who sought to use public housing as a pathway to build generational wealth. Because of white backlash, the City of Chicago often placed public housing in poverty-stricken Black neighborhoods.[49]

Early on, most public housing residents were white. However, white Americans also had access to housing markets, facilitated by legislation like the New Deal. Subsequently, it was easier for white Americans to eventually access homeownership.[50] "There were chronic shortages of decent housing for Black Americans in most cities. Consequently, most applicants for new public housing projects were Black."[51] Public housing played an important role for Black Americans escaping the South during the Great Migration. As J. S. Fuerst noted:

> Public housing once served as an engine for upward mobility and as an incubator of the middle-class, a fact largely ignored today. Early Chicago Housing Authority projects like Ida B. Wells, Altgeld Gardens, Dearborn Homes, Cabrini Homes and Leclaire Courts, to name a few, helped thousands of Chicagoans escape slum-housing conditions and enter a world that offered first-rate housing, a close-knit community, and the positive pride that comes from a shared experience.[52]

Scholar Edward G. Goetz noted that by the 1960s whites were leaving public housing in "even greater numbers," until over time, public housing was occupied almost entirely by people of color across the country.[53] In 2017, out of 16,150 total households in Chicago public housing, 12,211 heads of households were African American, 1,729 were Hispanic, and 938 were Asian.[54] "The popular image of public housing changed when its demographics changed."[55] Throughout the 1980s and 1990s, a Reagan-era moral panic about gangs, drugs, and inner cities caused the public to turn against the broader aims of the New Deal. Soon Americans believed welfare, public housing, and other forms of public aid only served Black Americans.[56] Racism, fueled by a lack of public support, allowed officials to justify chronic mismanagement of public housing all over the country, and as a result, public housing became plagued by violence, mismanagement, and disrepair.[57] This violence, alongside the government's chronic neglect of public housing neighborhoods and buildings, had a significant impact on the political strategies used by CHA residents, particularly residents at hyper-isolated public housing developments like the Altgeld Gardens and Phillip Murray Homes.[58]

The Site of the Study: Altgeld Gardens and Phillip Murray Homes, Chicago

In the summer of 2011, when visitors drove within a block of the Altgeld Gardens and Phillip Murray Homes, smells from the nearby sewage plant typically overwhelmed them.[59] As the weather got warmer, the smell got stronger. Originally, the entire area was covered by swamp. In the early twentieth century, Pullman Factory used the swamp as an industrial waste site.[60] Decades later, the City of Chicago filled the swamp and built the Altgeld Gardens Murray Homes to house low-income people of color.

> Altgeld Gardens was surrounded by industry and built on a toxic waste dump and sewage farm that had been created by the Pullman Palace Car Company decades earlier. The far south side of Chicago has been a dumping ground for industrial waste since the late nineteenth century, and it became officially sanctioned as the waste site for the whole metropolitan area when the city opened a large municipal dump there in 1940, five years before Altgeld Gardens opened. [At one point], about 250 underground chemical storage tanks actively leaked into the groundwater. Altgeld Gardens was also surrounded by approximately 50 landfills. . . .
>
> The Chicago Housing Authority, which owned and operated Altgeld Gardens, made resident exposure even worse by ignoring what toxins were coming from the former waste dump underneath Altgeld Gardens, using building materials containing asbestos and dumping PCB waste at the site.[61]

Across the street from the Altgeld Gardens and Phillip Murray Homes were several abandoned steel mills; the area is an industrial site.[62] Down the street from the old mills was a toxic landfill.[63]

Because of the odor and the toxins emitted, residents frequently complained about the chemical fumes from the old mills and the illnesses that they caused.[64] As a result, in October 1999, fifty former and current residents of Altgeld Gardens filed a lawsuit against the CHA.

> Plaintiffs assert that CHA built the Altgeld Gardens housing development "in an industrialized area, in and around a former sew-

age waste site," (Fourth Amended Complaint to Aaron et al. v. Chicago Housing Auth. (hereinafter, "Aaron FAC"), Ex. 5 to Defendant's Corrected Answer to Plaintiff's Complaint for Declaratory Relief, pp. 7), that CHA "knew that certain contaminants, toxic substances and chemicals, including but not limited to PCBs, PAHs, selenium, arsenic, lead, mercury and pesticides were introduced, released and allowed to remain in the environment in Altgeld Gardens by the surrounding industrial plants, abandoned factories, toxic waste dumps, landfills and a Metropolitan Sanitary District plant, and their agents and employees," (id. Pp. 24), that CHA "caused and was responsible for introducing, releasing and allowing PCBs and PAHs to remain in the environment in Altgeld Gardens," (id. Pp. 25), and that CHA failed to "advise, warn or educate the Plaintiffs of the full nature and extent of the presence and existence of the PCB[s] and PAHs[,] the risks associated with such, or the precautions that the Plaintiffs could take."[65]

According to residents, because of their exposure to such a broad range of toxins over the last twenty years, there were abnormally high rates of cancer and asthma in young people who grew up in the development.[66]

Residents of Altgeld Gardens received a $10.5 million settlement after they filed a class action lawsuit against CHA, accusing the agency of exposing them to medical risks linked to PCBs, which were released after employees dumped oil as they took copper from electric transformers. The settlement money went toward CHA tenants' monthly rent.[67]

In 2003, past and present residents of Altgeld Gardens won the class action lawsuit against CHA because of CHA's failure to notify residents of the toxic PCBs below their homes.[68] Altgeld Gardens "sits in one of the city's most isolated areas. The nearest supermarket is miles away, only one bus route serves the development."[69] In 2011 and 2012, generally the development looked abandoned; there were rows of abandoned or boarded-up homes on the development. Notably, in 2009 the crime rate at Altgeld was double the city of Chicago's crime rate.[70] The spatial realities described here, particularly the varying forms of residential violence (which includes environmental and bureaucratic violence) witnessed and experienced by residents, deeply affected the mental health and physical well-being of many Black women throughout Altgeld Gardens.

The CHA and the Neoliberal Plan
for Transformation

Over fifty years, the CHA developed a reputation for mismanaged and di-lapidated public housing systems. In 1995, the Department of Housing and Urban Development (HUD) took control of CHA to "salvage public hous-ing."[71] Chicago local government resumed control of public housing in 1999, and that year, the CHA began the Plan for Transformation. "The $1.5 billion Plan for Transformation [called] for the largest reconstruction of public housing in the nation's history. All but one of its 52 high-rise build-ings [were] leveled."[72] The central narrative around the Plan for Trans-formation was that the old Chicago public housing policy design facili-tated concentrated pockets of poverty that "exacerbated the problems of unemployment, substance abuse and crime."[73] Therefore, advocates of the new policy argued that the Plan would allow for a transition from clumping poor residents in high-rise buildings to instead integrating them into mixed-income neighborhoods.*

> In 1998, nearly 19,000 of the Chicago Housing Authority's (CHA's) units failed viability inspection, meaning that under federal law the CHA was required to demolish the units within five years. As a re-sult, the city put forth a plan to "transform" the CHA's enormous high-rise developments into smaller mixed-income communities of town homes and low-rise buildings. The CHA *Plan for Transfor-mation* calls for the demolition of 51 gallery high-rise buildings, as well as several thousand mid-rise and low-rise units. The CHA will redevelop or rehabilitate 25,000 units of public housing; however, the plan calls for a substantial reduction in family public housing units (a net loss of 14,000 units). The original plan called for the re-location of as many as 6,000 families with Housing Choice Vouch-ers (Section 8 vouchers). This plan, including relocation and revi-talization, is estimated to cost $1.5 billion over 10 years.[74]

Advocates of the Plan for Transformation argued that if families had the option to relocate using Housing Choice Vouchers (which allowed fami-lies to enter the private market or live in new CHA developments), resi-dents would be increasingly likely to become economically self-sufficient.

---

* Susan J. Popkin et al., "The HOPE VI Program: What about the Residents?," *Housing Poli-cy Debate* 15, no. 2 (2010): 385–414, https://doi.org/10.1080/10511482.2004.9521506.

The overarching goals of CHA's relocation services were to help participants make good housing choices for themselves and their families; help participants make a successful transition to the private market; and prevent the creation of clusters of relocatees in other high-poverty neighborhoods.[75]

Soon after, CHA addressed what they viewed as the central problem of public housing, the high-rise project buildings.[76]

The Plan for Transformation represent[ed] the most ambitious effort in the United States to remake public housing. [Originally] scheduled for completion in 2015, the Transformation [was supposed to] result in the demolition of approximately 22,000 units of public housing, the rehabilitation of over 17,000 units, and the creation of over 10 new mixed-income developments containing a mix of public housing replacement, affordable and market-rate units.[77]

The Plan for Transformation was a CHA policy proposal adopted in 1999 to redevelop the entire Chicago public housing system. The idea was to place CHA residents in middle-class neighborhoods to facilitate additional opportunities for residents.

To put it plainly, the Plan for Transformation was designed around the idea that placing low-income residents in middle-class neighborhoods would "improve" them both socially and economically.[78] The Plan for Transformation was aggressively publicized throughout Chicago as a progressive plan to "transform" the lives of public housing residents for the better. However, HOPE VI policies, like the Plan for Transformation, are neoliberal projects in sheep's clothing.* Scholar Jason Hackworth argues:

Though it is the second-largest housing authority in the United States, overseeing 34,699 physical units and 33,582 Section 8 vouchers, the Chicago Housing Authority (CHA) does not have the wider political support enjoyed in New York or Seattle. Chicago's history as a cauldron for land-use disputes associated with the siting of public housing is an important reason for this. Public housing has been and continues to be a deeply divisive issue in Chicago, and

---

* HOPE VI is a federal neoliberal policy that offers grants to public housing authorities who are willing to demolish some, if not all, of their high-rise public housing stock (see Hackworth, *Neoliberal City*).

its provisioning approach during the past fifteen years reflects this acrimony. The HOPE VI program offered city officials the opportunity to put aside this unparalleled acrimony by simply putting aside public housing. Rather than choose a retention, or mixed-income approach, the CHA has used its six grants during the 1990s largely to divest itself of its physical stock.[79]

However, many CHA residents did not leave Black low-income communities. Most significantly, despite the vilification of housing project spaces that went on to justify this million-dollar spending project, the Plan still called for one in every ten CHA residents to be housed in a housing project in the city limits, Altgeld Gardens.[80] At the completion of high-rise housing demolition, thousands of CHA families were dispersed or displaced all over the city of Chicago and its suburbs. To date, many CHA residents have not been able to return to Chicago public housing because of the organized housing stock shortage.[81] Simply, CHA demolished a significant amount of housing stock and has not replaced it. This "organized housing scarcity," or what Ruthie Wilson Gilmore calls "organized abandonment" via the state, has forced many poor Black Chicago residents out of the city entirely.[82]

Neoliberal public housing transformation plans nationwide are marketed as policy focused on residents' well-being and their ability to "choose" where and how they live. However in practice, neoliberal impulses have facilitated the continuation of moral-respectability policing of Black women living below the poverty line by equating poverty with moral ineptitude.[83] As Black feminist political scientist Cathy J. Cohen argues:

> New ideological narratives that emerge under advanced marginalization highlight the formal equality achieved by marginal groups, while actual inequalities are overlooked and avoided. Marginal groups looking for formal recognition and rights under advanced marginalization must embrace a model of inclusion premised on the idea that formal rights are to be granted only to those who demonstrate adherence to dominant norms of work, love and social interaction. Marginal group members are forced, therefore, to demonstrate their normativity and legitimacy through the class privilege they acquire, through the attitudes and behavior they exhibit, and through the dominant institutions in which they operate.[84]

Ultimately, as Hackworth made clear, in Chicago, the Plan for Transformation has signaled a full embrace of policy informed by respectability politics.

HOPE VI thus represents much more than a basic divestment of the housing stock. It also represents a more transparent roll out of neoliberal policy in practice. It has been linked . . . to the "work responsibility" acts discussed earlier, and the program's promotional material is rife with the language of economic "self-sufficiency." Increasingly, tenants must behave in "acceptable" ways to continue their housing benefits. PHAs [Public Housing Authorities] have been given new powers to evict for behavioral or even economic reasons.[85]

CHA diverted the management and maintenance of some public housing stock to private housing managers, moving many former public housing residents to Section 8 housing owned by private landlords. Subsequently, CHA scattered an active multigenerational resident sociopolitical community all over the metro Chicago area.[86] Ultimately, CHA transferred their mandate to care for the most vulnerable and destitute to the private market.

Whether the Plan achieved anything is a matter of perspective. Researchers at the Urban Institute argue that "most CHA families now live in better housing, in safer neighborhoods."[87] While voucher programs placed some residents in safer neighborhoods, it also isolated them from family, friends, and support systems. Ultimately, the consequences of Section 8 dispersal programs were financial, social, and political.[88] By transferring residents all over the metro Chicago area, the CHA could break up important political communities. It has become much harder for tenants to advocate for themselves to the CHA or the private management companies CHA empowered. Scattering residents across the region has also undermined the ability of tenants' rights groups within the Chicago public housing space to organize around broader political issues they share with Chicago locals living in poverty.

Ultimately, Chicago public housing has been through a tumultuous half century. While the social and political impulse of many is to place public housing on the outskirts of the city to keep the poor out of sight, this is not a decision without real consequences for the public sphere.[89] Given that local, state, and federal governments have so much power over the everyday lives of public housing residents, we must take seriously whether politicians and bureaucrats are creating residential spaces that provide dignified, sanitary, and safe living conditions for marginalized communities. By falling far short of these minimum qualifications, the U.S. political-industrial complex has helped birth a generation of citizens who have cocreated political identities—and resulting political strategies—

that fall outside of what many traditional political practitioners recognize as political. If we are to understand who poor Black women are as citizens, we must look carefully at their lived environments.[90]

Does Neoliberalism Shape What Kind of Politics an Individual Will Have?

Neighborhood placement and design have a profound impact on political development.[91] Each neighborhood or residential space teaches distinctive lessons about what a member of the sociopolitical community could and should look like, as well as what citizens can reasonably expect from the state over their lifetime. White American individuals living in impoverished rural areas within the United States learn completely dissimilar lessons about what membership in the sociopolitical community looks like (as compared to Black people within the United States who live in urban public housing while also living below the poverty line).[92] Despite their poverty, white people in the United States receive messages affirming them as voters and as hard workers.[93] This political affirmation happens via media but also through institutions (e.g., this can be as simple as the availability of voting places that do not seek to impede their access).

Black people who live in poverty in the United States are frequently treated like badly behaved, neglected children. As scholars have indicated, poverty entitlement programs throughout the United States denigrate, disempower, and humiliate those seeking aid.[94] They are as intentionally difficult, complicated, and discouraging as possible.[95] Not only are public housing buildings intentionally neglected and ignored until they fall into complete disrepair, but U.S. public housing policy treats residents similarly.[96] This policy of intentional neglect is what geographer Ruthie Wilson Gilmore calls "organized abandonment" by the state.[97] As Osama Tanous and Rabea Eghbariah explain:

> Her analysis of organized abandonment and organized violence explores how states simultaneously use these two tools to further dispossess and control the already impoverished and marginalized. Her work tracks how the state disregards its obligations toward certain people, households, and communities in what Gilmore calls "the anti-state state" and provides unequal levels of support and protection. These same communities that are subjected to organized abandonment are criminalized and marked as undeserving and ineligible for social programs.[98]

The scholarship is clear: U.S. policy has a deep and sometimes lasting impact on the sociopolitical tools accessible to marginalized political communities (e.g. Black people living below the poverty line). Through policies of organized abandonment, the state can expose marginalized populations to disproportionate levels of violence and an artificial scarcity of housing, safety, education, and food.[99] In short, the government can use policy to create sociopolitical communities that appear to be politically disenfranchised. However, as other scholars have made clear, these same circumstances have also historically created a vibrant and powerful extrasystemic politics within Black Afro-diasporic communities globally.[100] Like Eliasoph, I argue that people learn what sociopolitical tools look like via their experience within neighborhoods.[101] This is reinforced through government institutions and street-level bureaucrats like CHA, welfare bureaucracies, resident interactions with the police, and entitlements policy writ large.[102] But sociopolitical tools are also reinforced via the social networks and communities of care developed by public housing residents over generations.[103]

I should clarify that the argument I am making about the impact of built structure on political engagement is separate and apart from the "failed architecture" and "broken windows" arguments, popular among the proponents of the 1990s HOPE VI HUD policy.[104] Similar to Hackworth, I argue that the 1990s policy to demolish high-rise public housing and build new mixed-income townhomes as a corrective to the issues within Chicago public housing, muddied more urgent issues present in many of the demolished public housing buildings.

> The "failed architecture" argument has also been harshly criticized by a group of housing scholars who argue that the overwhelming focus on design obscures more important causes of "failure," such as congressional funding levels, federally imposed design restrictions, and pressure from homebuilding lobbyists to make public housing "stand out."[105]

Public housing is in crisis throughout the United States, but it is not because public housing developments in places like Chicago, New York, and Detroit were high-rises. Instead, as Hackworth and D. Bradford Hunt make clear, the failure of public housing in the United States is because of federal, state, and local governments' choice to neglect and abandon the poor.[106]

As the Plan for Transformation slowly gathered steam, some Altgeld Gardens residents knew they were being moved to a rehabbed apartment. Other residents knew that new people were being brought in and out of Altgeld Gardens, seemingly on a whim. But residents seemed to lack the formal political capital that would give them transparent access to information about the Plan or allow their needs to be heard by those in power. After all, in 2011 residents frequently lacked internet access and transportation. As a result, getting information about CHA policy could be challenging.[107] One of the primary mechanisms the CHA used to perpetuate the political invisibility around its housing policy was neoliberalism and the ongoing privatization of its housing developments. When private companies began managing CHA public housing, the extent to which residents could go to their management company for information about the larger policy projects of CHA was often unclear, maybe intentionally so.

Iris Marion Young argues that "interest-group pluralism . . . perpetuates a depoliticized public life that fragments social life and privatizes citizens' relationship to the state."[108] This is especially clear within the privatization of the welfare state as facilitated by the neoliberal turn, particularly as it pertains to public housing.[109] When private business represents the government's interests within public housing, it perpetuates the idea that public housing residents are clients, not citizens.[110] Within this framework, only the residents with the greatest amount of social and financial capital, as determined by street-level bureaucrats, got their needs met.

> The depoliticized process of policy formation in welfare capitalist society, thus makes it difficult to see the institutional rules, practices and social relations that support domination and oppression, much less to challenge them.[111]

When Young mentions the "depoliticized client-consumer citizen characteristic of welfare capitalist society," she is describing neoliberal policy.[112] The financial interests of privatization can obscure the legal rights of residents who live on public property. The welfare-industrial capitalist complex and its ensuing neoliberal privatization can prevent residents from seeing or understanding that privatized interests within public housing perpetuate domination and oppression.

The housing policy of organized abandonment directly affected the Black women I interviewed during this study. Political empowerment within their sociopolitical communities facilitated respondents' capacity to engage in what Zenzele Isoke (2011) calls "a politics of homemaking."[113] In several ways, their political empowerment was shaped by the infrastructures they lived in and called home. This was especially true for respondents who grew up in one Chicago public housing development and still lived there at the time of the interview. But frequently the Black women who took part in my study were unsuccessful in their attempts to get their needs met by CHA or any of the welfare agencies in Chicago. Various street-level bureaucrats of all races, who believed that the women in the development had nothing to offer the community, frequently gave the residents lectures about their unwillingness to "work hard." Scholars have consistently found middle- and upper-class Black bureaucrats to be some of the most aggressive proponents of neoliberal policies that frame Black women on welfare as being *counterproductive* to the race.[114]

But despite the neoliberal effort to re-create poor Black people in its own image, policy feedback scholarship has clarified that experiences with the state have had a different set of political consequences than intended.[115] While welfare recipients may not always see traditional forms of political engagement—such as voting or writing to a senator—as particularly useful, they do in fact engage with and make claims on the state.[116] Soss argues that "welfare institutions have become key sites of political action for many people in the United States."[117] Throughout my interviews, a repeated theme was the importance of "knowing what you are doing" when engaging welfare agencies. Several respondents spoke about learning to navigate the welfare and public housing bureaucracy system via their mothers, friends, or neighbors. Negotiating entitlement benefits, and navigating government bureaucracies more broadly, became a highly valued political skill in the lives of public housing residents. It was also a skill passed down through informal information dissemination among public housing resident sociopolitical communities and their larger Black enclave public sphere.[118]

A History of Black Women's Organizing within Public Housing

Informal information dissemination focused on successfully navigating welfare and public housing bureaucracies is one of several extrasystemic sociopolitical tools I noted while in the field. Scholars of public housing argue that poor Black women who engage with the state are part of an important and ongoing political movement happening behind closed doors all over the United States.[119] According to Lisa Levenstein, there was "a mass movement of African American women to claim the benefits and use the services of public institutions."[120] Both Rhonda Williams and Levenstein point to the way "the government's subsidy of low-rent housing implied a right to decent living conditions for U.S. citizens."[121] Engagement with the welfare state is a legitimate political strategy in its demand that the U.S.

government live up to its promises.[122] By grounding my project within public housing scholarship, I continue the effort pointing to the urgency of this political work.

There is a long history of Black women in public housing who organized their sociopolitical communities in meaningful ways. Ethnographies answering the question of how public housing can and has developed the politics of residents across time and place have been incredibly important to the development of this project.[123] Historian Rhonda Williams (2005) points to the spaces and places that shaped poor Black women's politics and explores what forced them into militant protest to get their basic needs met. Williams's insistence that we take seriously the need for "activism at the point of consumption—that is, around housing, food, clothing, and daily life in community spaces"—is a prescient reminder that politics exist beyond electoral fights for power.[124] For Black women living below the poverty line, politics are a fight for the essentials of basic survival.

> Although poor people and black women had to contend with onerous and intrusive regulations as public assistance recipients, many low-income black women received a political education through their engagement with the welfare system. The federal government's subsidy of low-rent housing implied a right to decent living conditions for U.S. citizens. From the beginning, this implied right highlighted poor people's low citizenship status and politicized groups of tenants. For poor women, in particular, subsidized housing created a sense that the previously private sphere of home had become public and political space.[125]

Like the respondents who participated in my research, the Black women Williams describes in *The Politics of Public Housing* clarified how the infrastructure, resident communities, and representatives of the state all serve as mechanisms through which resident politics are developed. Black women living in poverty within state-owned public housing experience street-level bureaucrats as an obstructive, if not violent, force in their lives. In public housing there is no clear dividing line between public and private. Public housing residents have little agency over when, how, or where street-level bureaucrats enter their homes for welfare checks, Child Protective Services monitoring, food stamp monitoring, or public housing inspections.[126] While this had severe consequences for their privacy and sense of personal autonomy, the Black women in Baltimore public housing interviewed by Rhonda Williams and the women in Chicago public housing that I interviewed, had access to a political education about the inner workings of government few citizens ever had.[127] Residents used the social networks within their neighborhoods to educate one another via informal information dissemination.

Social Networks as a Sociopolitical Tool

Monthly CHA meetings are a good example of how social networks frequently functioned while I was in the field. Tenant Services meetings or CHA Board meetings drew public housing residents from all over the city. A consistent topic at those meetings was the demolition of high-rise public housing throughout Chicago and the subsequent destruction of the sociopolitical communities who used to call those buildings their homes. Given recent trends in public housing policy over the last twenty years (e.g., mass demolitions of high-rises), some public housing residents are being placed in developments or mixed-income housing that isolate them from friends, family, and job opportunities.[128] The social networks of those receiving public assistance are being tremendously—and forcefully—transformed. Political scientist Betsy Sinclair's framework is a key component needed to understand the connections between social networks and political identity development.[129] I extend her argument by arguing that the social networks of individuals receiving various types of social welfare are defined and developed by the state and its representatives.[130] The power of the state to shape, define, and erase the social networks of its dependents living in poverty has urgent ramifications for their political development and the state of democracy in the United States, writ large.

The potential impact of state-run institutions on the makeup of neighborhoods is critically important when you consider arguments made by scholars like Robert Huckfeldt, whose work considers the importance of neighborhoods in the development and maintenance of social networks.[131]

> Neighborhood residents can seldom escape interacting with people who share the same living space. These social interactions take different forms: standing in line at the post office, getting together with friends, talking across a backyard fence or on a street corner, sharing the same public facilities—supermarkets, gas stations, laundromats. None of the interactions are politically neutral. Politics, especially urban politics, is not merely a function of individual characteristics and predispositions, it is also shaped by the social context within which it occurs.[132]

For Huckfeldt, neighborhoods are not a politically neutral space individuals choose to live in, depending on racial, economic, or religious preferences. Instead, they are a highly politicized space where individuals are constantly interacting with and learning from one another. Similarly, multiple scholars have thought about the importance of the residential neighborhood as a politicized space.[133] It is important to keep in mind, then, that the choices the government makes around who should live where, and with whom, have significant implications for the political development of people who live in neighborhoods below the poverty line.[134]

Methods, Theory, and Questions of Political Definition

A growing and substantial body of scholarship within the academy has carefully documented the massive amount of political work Black women, and in particular, poor Black women, have been doing since Reconstruction.[135] Central to this growing body of work is the ever-increasing number of political scientists who use a diverse methodological toolkit to get at the diverse political experiences of Black women living in the United States.[136] It is critically important to use qualitative data, ethnography and in-depth interviewing specifically, to capture the political engagement and political identity formation of marginalized groups. As I mentioned in the Introduction, groups like poor Black women are often missed in large surveys because of the well-recognized problem of incomparability between survey questions because of differing interpretations of variables related to cultural context.[137]

Scholars of race, ethnicity, and politics continue to point out characteristics unique to the political engagement and political identity formation of various marginalized groups (e.g., Afro-Cuban immigrants, Black trans women, and DACA students seeking citizenship). Survey data frequently misses intersectional and secondarily marginalized groups like poor Black women in the United States.[138] We know they are being missed because of the extensive qualitative data (and quantitative data) showing marginalized populations and their ongoing resistance to the power and politics affecting their everyday lives.[139]

Over the course of a year (2011–2012), I conducted twenty-nine in-depth interviews with Black women who lived in Altgeld Gardens and two in-depth interviews with Black women who had recently left the development. I also followed various respondents around the development and attended several political meetings and community events. Throughout my time at Altgeld Gardens, I asked respondents how they defined the political and whether they considered themselves to be politically active. I compared these responses to my observations of their actual behaviors and reported activities. As a result, I collected concrete data that assesses and engages with the traditional measures of politics, political engagement, identity, efficacy, and alienation used by political scientists. I use this data as the jumping-off point for developing conceptual categories that provide a stronger and more substantial theoretical framework that can recognize and understand the politics of marginalized individuals living in the United States.

By using qualitative methods, I can specify the mechanisms at work when respondents react to indicators that ultimately cause researchers to label them as cynical or efficacious. The hallmark of this project is a specification of the language respondents used to describe themselves as members of sociopolitical community.[140] I entered this project by asking methodological questions: What combinations of these broad concepts do people use to describe themselves? How do individuals understand their efficacy and cynicism (for example) working together? Most significantly, how do individuals understand their own holistic political identity? Ultimately, these questions concern political imagination. How do individuals' conceptions of their political placement within the public sphere affect how they engage the sociopolitical community? I argue that the individual engages the state based on how they understand their political possible-self (PPS; that is, what they believe to be politically possible for themselves as a part of sociopolitical community). How a person understands their PPS is based, in part, on how the state treats them.

Methodological Choices

I used the case study method to examine whether public housing shaped the political identities of Black women living within CHA housing developments. Robert K. Yin argues the case study is useful when observing context is especially important.

> In other words, you would use the case study method because you wanted to understand a real-life phenomenon in depth, but such understanding encompassed important contextual conditions—because they were highly pertinent to your phenomenon of study.[141]

By using the case study method, I observed the shifting political identities of CHA tenants. Case study also allowed me to observe respondents' lived experiences, spatial context, and understandings of themselves as members of a sociopolitical community. In this study, the context cannot (and should not) be separated from the case itself; the case study method facilitates the "study [of] a case when it itself is of very special interest. We look for the detail of interaction with its contexts. Case study is the study of the particularity and complexity of a single case, coming to understand its activity within important circumstances."[142] I argue that we cannot separate the influence of the material structure of public housing on the political lives of residents from their lived experience within the housing developments.[143]

Data Collection

As is typical in the case study method, I triangulated the data with three sources of information. I used in-depth interviews, participant observation, and archival analysis to examine my questions. In this study, I conducted in-depth interviews with thirty-one Black women who were past and present residents of Altgeld Gardens. These interviews allowed me to slowly get to know the women and the nuances of their lives within the housing development and surrounding neighborhoods. I asked questions about how these women understood politics and whether they considered themselves to be members of a sociopolitical community. Most significantly, the in-depth interviews examined how the women felt about the public housing space and the presence (or nonpresence) of government actors in their lives. While each in-depth interview was based loosely on the same interview guide, the questions were open ended to allow each individual woman's narrative to develop. It was not my goal to shape how the respondents told their stories. It was my goal to get as close to an authentic self-description of their politics as possible. All interviews were audio recorded and transcribed.

I used participant observation within the Altgeld Gardens and Phillip Murray Homes so I could pay especially close attention to Altgeld Gardens and the people who live there. I attended Altgeld-Murray LAC meetings, CHA Central Advisory Council meetings, and CHA Board of Commissioners meetings, as well as local community organization gatherings, events, and other spontaneous or planned political gatherings on the development. Spending time within the housing development itself, as well as observing CHA meetings and gatherings, facilitated a greater understanding of the discourses within public housing spaces and the residents they affect, but also to examine how the space shifts and changes over time to fit the needs and desires of those in power.

Procedure

Before entering the field, I designed the interview protocol around the research questions. These questions were open ended in design to allow respondents to answer as they saw fit. I tested the interview protocol in the spring of 2011 during the initial pilot study in the Altgeld Gardens and Murray Homes. Throughout this period, I refined the protocol until it yielded consistent and reliable results. I began my study by attending as many public meetings as I could. What I found during my months of observation at those meetings was the intensity with which tenants fought for basic necessities. The meetings were always scheduled for midmorning, so often only a handful of residents could actually attend. This meant that older residents (in terms of both natal age and number of years lived on the development) held most of the tenant leadership positions and advocated on behalf of all residents, new and old. As a result, there was a fracture between residents who'd lived in CHA for over ten years and residents who were relatively new to the developments (less than five years).

Each interview was held in the respondent's home, the only exceptions being when multiple respondents were interviewed in one day or when the respondent was uncomfortable having me in their home. I interviewed individuals in their homes to facilitate their comfort and to build trust. I did not want to bring respondents to the University of Chicago or the CHA offices, where potential negative bureaucratic associations might exist. By interviewing respondents in their homes, I minimized the inconvenience posed to them. However, meeting individuals in their homes also allowed me the opportunity to further study their relationship to their place of residence, as well as document the aesthetics of their lived experience.

I paid each respondent twenty dollars for their participation. I paid in cash because of the remoteness of the Altgeld Gardens and Murray Homes from any major retail establishments. The closest shopping centers were at least thirty minutes away by bus, and many of the women did not shop online. Interviews, on average, lasted about forty minutes to one hour. However, individual interviews ranged from three hours to twenty minutes. The shorter interviews were with women who were elderly or battling various addictions or illnesses. I kept the shorter interviews in my dataset because they offered differing perspectives important to my study.

Sampling and Recruitment

I defined the case by a sample of thirty-one Black women who lived within the CHA development, the Altgeld-Murray Homes. All respondents were over eighteen years old, and I strove for a diversity of age ranges from young adult to senior. To create diversity in my sample, I recruited poten-tial respondents by posting flyers throughout the housing development. Essentially, there are two units of analysis in my project, the individuals and the development itself. Within the individual unit of analysis, there are actually three different populations: those who were new to public hous-ing, those who were new to Altgeld Gardens, and those who had lived in Altgeld Gardens for a significant period (ten or more years). Since my pri-mary interest was in the ways public housing shaped the political identity of its residents, the diversity within the individual units of analysis provided me with the purchase I needed on the core conceptual questions. Given this, I shaped my subject pool around these three population groups.

I used a snowball or convenience sampling method. I interviewed the women who volunteered for the study and who met the specifications of my sample. From there I asked my respondents to recommend other women for the study. This sampling method enabled a better understanding of the community and of the political and social networks of the respondents. As has been noted time and time again in studies of political participation, an individual's political and social network has one of the largest impacts on their ever-evolving political identity.[144] Understanding the broad net-works of the respondents gave me better leverage when constructing a the-ory of political identity development. Within the context of public housing, it is also critical to consider how demolishing high-rise communities that had existed for at least forty years shifted, and sometimes even destroyed, the social networks women in public housing depend on.

Conclusion

In this chapter I've argued that the spatial conditions of public housing shaped the politics of residents who lived in CHA developments.[145] Neo-liberal policies of the 1990s and 2000s have meant that the CHA has systematically been removing itself from management and the basic infrastructure maintenance of the remaining Chicago public housing de-velopments.[146] But despite almost constant surveillance by street-level bureaucrats and worries about state and residential violence, Black com-munities living within public housing still develop political strategies to nurture themselves, their families, and their community.[147]

II

Recognizing Extrasystemic Politics outside Academia and without Polling

4

THE VISIONARY AXIS OF POLITICAL
IMAGINATION

Introduction

Throughout my time at the Altgeld Gardens and Phillip Murray Homes development in Chicago, many of the Black women I interviewed were engaged in a politics of homemaking.* This politics devoted itself to creating a safe space within their homes where neighbors and friends could engage in public-spirited conversation. By creating a place where they could engage in such conversation away from state surveillance, Altgeld residents were able to provide one another with a political education that facilitated the development of political imagination and, subsequently, political power. In Altgeld Gardens, a respondent's home demarcated the choices government bureaucracy (the CHA) distributed to the

---

* "The Politics of Homemaking" is a theoretical concept developed by Zenzele Isoke ("Politics of Homemaking"). Isoke defines the politics of homemaking:

> Homemaking, as an affective form of resistance, involves more than just being attentive to and providing care to individuals. It also requires building an enduring affective relationship to the physical environment. It is the imaginative political work that transforms the built environment of the city into a home: a place of belonging, a place of remembrance, and a place of resistance. Homemaking, then encompasses black women's efforts to build the will to resist the alienating and dehumanizing practices and ideologies that continue to ghettoize and minoritize black people in Newark's Central Ward. It involves making people—or bodies—care about space. (Isoke, "Politics of Homemaking," 119)

leaseholder. The aesthetics of public housing served as a sort of canary in a coal mine.

I visited most of my respondents in their homes, and as I discuss throughout this chapter, how they related to and spoke about their home told me a quite a bit. In particular, respondents who felt they had control over what happened within and around their home were frequently those who engaged in political work throughout their sociopolitical community. Unsurprisingly, the respondents who felt empowered and safe within their homes were frequently (but not always) confident they could convince CHA to attend to whatever maintenance needs they had. Respondents who felt powerless often had apartments that fell into disrepair, usually because they did not believe that CHA's maintenance team would attend to their needs, no matter how severe the issue. In short, respondents who gave up hope, in themselves, their neighbors, their sociopolitical community, CHA, and Altgeld Gardens itself, often had apartments that reflected that reality. Sadly, as Sofia's story (later in the chapter) makes clear, this frequently happened after multiple experiences of being disappointed or abandoned by CHA.

However, this should not be confused with broken windows theory.[1] Scholars of the broken windows theory mistakenly interpret the structural neglect of buildings and neighborhoods as an indicator that residents are apathetic about the state of their community.[2] What broken windows scholarship fundamentally misunderstand is that the benign neglect of the structures and spatial realities within low-income neighborhoods is not an indicator of how the residents feel about their homes, lives, and communities.[3] The neglect of neighborhoods is actually an indicator of what the state, government bureaucracies, and street-level bureaucrats think poor Black people deserve.[4] Respondents regularly reported that the benign neglect, which became a hallmark of Chicago public housing, reminded them each and every day how little the government cared for them. As a result, the aesthetics residents imagined for themselves within and outside of their homes became a powerful sociopolitical tool. Residents who were able to keep their block clean, or plant illegal rosebushes with thorns (to get back at maintenance people who repeatedly neglected a resident's home), cultivated political imagination, and with it political power, in creative and subversive ways. Aesthetics came to represent a portion of the breadth and heft of the sociopolitical freedom residents imagined for themselves. Political imagination, as an aesthetic, physically manifested itself in the material appearance of public housing, which, in the context of individual row homes, was understood by residents as a representation of their relative control within their everyday life.[5]

Black feminist geographers and political scientists have made important interventions in our understanding of how the neighborhood and the home can shape the sociopolitical tools of Black women living in the United States. Black feminist geographer Katherine McKittrick argues that "geography is not, however, secure and unwavering: we produce space, we produce its meanings, and we work very hard to make geography what it is."[6] For McKittrick, geography is more than the material ground we walk on and experience, with its various nations, states, and continents. Instead, geography is a series of spatial realities constantly being interpreted and reimagined via social practices and geographic dominations. McKittrick argues that geography transforms the legacy of Black women's oppression into a material reality.[7]

The Afro-diaspora must contend with the connection between Blackness and spatial dislocation as a mode of racial domination.[8] When McKittrick asserts that "Black lives are necessarily geographic," she is pointing to the decisions of multiple European nation-states to kidnap millions of Black Africans from their continental homes.[9] The dislocation of Afro-diasporic people and the dismantling of Black sociopolitical communities seem to be foundational features of the structural architecture of white supremacy. Whether it is the transatlantic slave trade, the demolition of Seneca Village, or the destruction of Cabrini Greene, geography, white supremacy, racial capitalism, and the spatial dislocation of the Afro-diaspora seem to be intrinsically intertwined.[10] For hundreds of years, the state has used its ability to overdetermine who lives where, and when, to manage their citizens and those citizens' political power. In the United States, geographic dominance over marginalized populations has looked like racial and economic segregation, as well as state-sanctioned and extrasystemic violence.[11]

How Political Imagination Informs the Development of the Political Possible-Self

In the first three chapters, I explained the thinking behind the political possible-self (PPS) and the Black feminist definitional criterion (BFDC) of politics and the political. I developed these ideas with the hope of aiding the recognition and accurate description of the sociopolitical lives of marginalized Black populations living in the United States. I hope the ideas developed in this text can be useful in the research of other marginalized groups. But ultimately, the concepts and frameworks developed in this book were created to support a holistic sociopolitical understanding of

Black women who live below the poverty line. The BFDC of politics and the political, as well as the PPS, take a step closer to a better understanding of the extrasystemic politics, sociopolitical tools, sociopolitical communities, and Black enclave public spheres of Black women. However, this small step forward in the sociopolitical research of Black women living below the poverty line comes with the full awareness and recognition that the best research on this sociopolitical community can only come from writers and researchers who are poor Black women living in the United States. As an outsider to this sociopolitical community, I can only hope to be a respectful observer and make good on the confidence and encouragement given to me by the women who lived in Altgeld.

In the next two chapters, I discuss what the PPS looked like in the context of the Altgeld Gardens sociopolitical community. I use each of these cases, not as empirical evidence, but as conceptual studies that illustrate the theoretical frameworks I've developed in this book. Each chapter will focus on a particular axis of the PPS matrix. Chapter 4 focuses on the axis of political imagination and the roles pleasure, intellect, and alienation play in understanding the individual PPS. Chapter 5 discusses the belonging axis and explores in-depth the centrality of interpersonal relationships to individual sociopolitical development. I argue that political imagination absent interpersonal relationships connecting the individual to their residential sociopolitical community seemed to result in an individual politics disassociated from the public sphere. Among the women I interviewed at Altgeld Gardens, people who landed on the more visionary end of the PPS spectrum seemed to experience social isolation or alienation. However, the same respondents tended to have higher levels of creativity or intellect, which appeared to fuel an imaginative and at times even visionary internal political life. This disassociated internal political life seemed to deal almost exclusively in the realm of words, beauty, alienation, and ideas.

This particular group of respondents were people I, as an academic, felt a certain kinship with. After all, everyone at some point in their lives has retreated into the world of books, beauty, film, TV, games, or other art forms when the outside world became too much.[12] Scholars have shown that the intersection of poverty and trauma often results in significant psychosocial disconnection and alienation.[13] Many respondents directly credited their total socioemotional disconnection from Altgeld Gardens as the thing that kept them alive and safe. It is not a strategy without merit.[14] However, it is a strategy often absent political power in the political context of the United States (at least in 2011–2012, and now in 2024). As discussed in the Introduction via the BFDC, politics requires two or more people to cultivate community-based political power. When individuals think about politics but do not communicate those ideas, they are engaged in intellectual work, not political work. Ultimately, a disassociated internal politics seemingly correlated with the isolated and violent spatial realities of government-subsidized public housing is a major problem for democracy.

Resident Case Studies

As I mentioned in the Introduction, I use Chapter 4 to provide further insight into the political imagination axis of the PPS framework. To be more specific, all four cases presented in this chapter fall along an *x* axis that goes from alienated to visionary within the PPS matrix (as shown in Figure 4.1).

The political imagination axis represents the first step toward generating community-based political power. My data showed again and again that, without a belief in the possibility of successfully achieving whatever goal the respondent or their community had in mind, political power could not be attained. Respondents who had the capacity to believe in new possibilities within their substantive realities were frequently able to rally other residents to their cause.[15] At Altgeld Gardens, this was most pronounced with the infamous and successful Gautreaux court case.[16] Gautreaux started

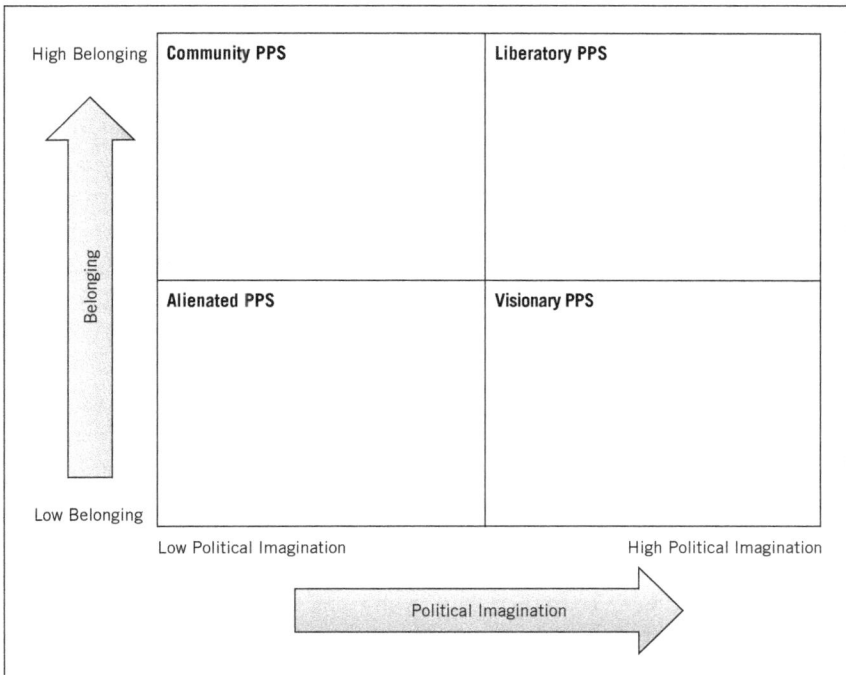

Figure 4.1 Political Possible-Self Matrix: Axis Overview

at the behest of Altgeld Gardens residents and forever changed Chicago public housing policy.[17] The power of birthing new possibilities was also clear when Harriet Shaw, a longtime resident of Altgeld Gardens, gave birth to the environmental justice movement and U.S. understandings of environmental racism.[18] It was Ms. Shaw's ability to imagine a safer and cleaner Altgeld Gardens that inspired residents to join her organization, and ultimately, they successfully sued the CHA for exposing them to environmental toxins.[19] My ethnographic and archival data are clear: residents with the capacity to imagine sociopolitical possibilities and teach other residents about those political possibilities via public-spirited conversation created, and then strengthened, long-lasting sociopolitical communities with political power. Black women's ability to exercise political imagination has everything to do with their capacity to think of themselves as having power—power over themselves, power over what happens to their life (broadly conceived), and power and influence over the institutions who attempt to exert power over their lives. Knowing this, I am starting Chapter 4 with an acknowledgment that the four cases featured here are centrally concerned with Black women's relationship to power. Because ultimately, power is inextricably critical to their ability to have and grow into greater political imagination.

Alienated

When I interviewed Ceely in 2011, she was twenty-four years old. She originally signed up for CHA public housing in 2007. After a four-year wait and some negotiation, Ceely moved into a large three-bedroom apartment in Altgeld Gardens with her son in 2010, two and a half years before I interviewed her. Initially Ceely had reservations about moving to the development; Altgeld's reputation was well known to her. When I asked her what it was like living in Altgeld Gardens, she said:

> You know what, it's really quiet out here. I was kind of skeptical about moving out here at first because, like, all the rumors I heard and how walking around used to be like to terrible out here. But when I moved out here, it's just, it's quiet. It's like your own town.

Ceely described Altgeld Gardens as a "pretty cool" opportunity, a place where she could keep to herself. When she was allowed to view the apartment, Ceely decided she had the skills and wherewithal to manage what seemed like a relatively quiet block within Altgeld. However, she kept the warnings about Altgeld in the back of her mind. Ceely's initial reticence was caused by what she described as "terrible rumors" about Altgeld. Within the sociopolitical community of her former residential neighborhood, Altgeld was known as a place where

> a lot of drugs, a lot of drugs. . . . Your house get broke into. They used to tell me, like, when you move out there and if you buy a TV, don't bring the box 'cuz soon as they see the box, they're going to break in your house and steal the TV, you know, things like that.

Ceely's primary goal was to finish school and buy her own home. As a result, she tried to remain out of sight while moving through the spatial realities of Altgeld Gardens.

> C: No one bothers me. My neighbors are quiet. On my block is a lot of kids around here. I mean, I hear about other blocks, but it's pretty cool.
> A: What do you hear about other blocks?
> C: Well, how they shooting all the time. I think like twice I heard gunshots, twice, the whole two years I stay here, I heard gunshots twice. A lot of people ask me, like while I'm on the bus and everything, they're like, "I never saw you out there before. Do you like it?" and I'm like, "Yeah, I love it. It's quiet," and people are like, "What? It's quiet? Where do you live?"

But in subtle ways, she expressed a reserved sort of enthusiasm about Altgeld, even when describing circumstances others might have found troubling. For example, in the above transcript, Ceely discussed Altgeld's somewhat infamous reputation throughout Chicago, especially in a post–Cabrini Greene and Robert Taylor Homes world.* However, she did not

---

* Cabrini Greene and Robert Taylor are two former CHA high-rise public housing projects. Both high-rises had reputations for violence throughout Chicago. Amidst tremendous controversy, they were demolished during the Plan for Transformation. Because of this forced spatial dislocation, CHA residents spoke frequently about gangs whose members were scattered across Chicago in the aftermath of the Plan for Transformation. In the early 2000s, a Chicago gang's power was traditionally delineated along geographical boundaries. Gang members who formerly lived in Cabrini Greene and Robert Taylor (among migrants from other forced CHA dislocations at other CHA high-rise demolitions) were living far and wide across Chicago and the surrounding suburbs. Some respondents speculated that the recent murder at Altgeld Gardens was a result of a conflict between rival organizations trying to

express worry over the shootings.[20] Instead, she was pleased she only heard gunshots twice during her two and a half years at Altgeld. I conducted this interview at Ceely's home, two months (to the day) after four people were murdered and two were wounded in the Altgeld Gardens store, the Connect.[21] The murders were a topic of conversation among several Altgeld residents I interviewed.

A Cabin in the Woods

But Ceely discussed her apartment at Altgeld Gardens within the context of her life experience. She only mentioned the 2011 murders in her interview once, very briefly at the end. Ceely did not seem moved by the two incidents where gunshots were audible from her apartment. She stressed throughout our conversation that her apartment was on a quiet block she enjoyed. This was most emphasized when I asked her what she liked about living in Altgeld.

> A: What do you like about living in Altgeld?
> C: It's quiet and it's away. It's away from, like, everyone else. When you come out here, it's like, it's like you stay out of town. It's like I'm Indiana, and it's like, you know, over there is Calumet City or something. It's like it's so different.
> A: Do you even feel like you're a part of the city?
> C: No, not until I hit 95th. And that's when I say OK . . .
> A: I'm back in Chicago. [*Laughter.*]
> C: That's the borderline.
> A: What don't you like about living in Altgeld?
> C: Hmm, the workers out here, their attitudes.
> A: People who work for CHA?
> C: Yeah, people who work for CHA, the office people. Their attitudes aren't terrible, but their attitudes are like, they act like they gave us this. They act like they pay our bill and . . . because I had a problem when I first moved out here. I did have a problem.

Ceely identified her biggest challenge as negotiating the sociopolitical dynamics within CHA. Throughout the interviews I collected, respondents reported that Black CHA street-level bureaucrats insisted on treating CHA residents as a nuisance at best and a scourge of the earth at

---

manage the spatial dislocation of their members across the "territories" of Chicago-based gangs (Goetz, *New Deal Ruins*).

worst. The secondary marginalization respondents experienced at the hands of Black CHA street-level bureaucrats took a number of different forms depending on the resident.* Ceely's particular challenge with the politics of the CHA bureaucracy was negotiating and advocating for her needs in CHA and welfare meetings. But in the midst of that, I was struck by the way Ceely talked about Altgeld, especially when I asked her what she liked about it. Take a look at this transcript segment again; the extremes of how Altgeld was described by everyone on the development are interesting. But even within the context of our interview, Ceely would at one moment describe Altgeld as a hyperviolent space she needed to hide from and then in the next try to liken Altgeld to a suburban development.

C: It's quiet and it's away. It's away from, like, everyone else. When you come out here, it's like, it's like you stay out of town. It's like I'm Indiana, and it's like, you know, over there is Calumet City or something. It's like it's so different.

A: Do you even feel like you're a part of the city?

C: No, not until I hit 95th. And that's when I say OK . . .

A: I'm back in Chicago. [*Laughter.*]

Ceely talked about Altgeld almost like it was a cabin in the woods where she was solitarily working toward her goal. She seemed to appreciate Altgeld's location on the very edge of Chicago's South Side. When Ceely described Altgeld as "quiet and it's away. It's away from, like, everyone else," her words immediately brought to mind the many artists and writers who've found their deepest solace and creative expression when they've run away from the world for a time. Lorraine Hansberry would go to upstate New York, James Baldwin went to the Middle East, Maya Angelou went to Ghana, and Malcolm X went to Mecca. But most of us never have the opportunity to break away from everything and anything to be able to think. However, there were important moments during our time together

---

* Cathy J. Cohen defines secondary marginalization as the oppression and exclusion experienced by people with multiple sites of marginalization. Specifically, when marginalized identity groups stigmatize more marginal group members. In other words, secondary marginalization is usually referring to the oppressive experiences of people with multiple sites of high-stigma identity. In this manuscript, I describe Black communities living below the poverty line as marginalized Black communities. Secondarily marginalized populations, like Black women living in Chicago public housing, are consistently targeted via government, bureaucratic, and residential violence because of the stigma attached to their intersecting sites of marginalization.

where the cracks of her idealized presentation of Altgeld Gardens showed through.

> A: Do people in government care about the people who live in Altgeld Gardens?
>
> C: I feel like what they . . . no and . . . really no, 'cuz I feel like they really just stuck us out here. To me, this is no man's land. You don't have no stores; you don't have nothing out here. You have a clinic. The dentist is inside the clinic. You know, you got a library, a liquor store, of course. And if you want to go somewhere, you got to go all the way out. You got to go on Roseland or you have to go on River Oaks or something like that. So I think they just stuck us out here in the middle of no man's land. Then it's like, they send us letters about the water and chemicals. Then I heard a rumor, like, years ago that people was getting sick out here, you know. Yeah.
>
> A: Can you trust the government?
>
> C: No. No, I mean . . . I don't know. That's a good question. I say no because I'm the type of person, I don't trust anyone.
>
> A: Why is that?
>
> C: I don't know, 'cuz you know, I watch so much on television, I hear so many stories from people, and I see what a person would do to you. I'm like, oh no, I don't trust nobody, no. I trust my family and stuff like that. But as far as other people outside us, no.

Ultimately, the truth was probably complicated. The desire of respondents to please the interviewer is a very real factor in any form of research. However, what was consistent about Ceely's interview was her capacity to articulate reality and to repackage what she saw into a different form. Ceely was clear that her "cabin in the woods" was a dream created out of neoliberal nightmares.

Ceely was able to use her sociopolitical imagination to create the life she needed. She paid eighty-eight dollars a month for rent and paid no heat or gas. Living in Altgeld allowed her to go to school for her master's and take care of her son. At the outset of this chapter, I argued that spatial dislocation has become a key identifying feature of the children of the Afro-diaspora. But people with vivid sociopolitical imaginations, people like Ceely, were able to transform the alienation neoliberalism handed to them via spatial dislocation. Ceely had the internal capacity to see Altgeld Gardens as a moment in time where she could finish her education. Seeing it as a temporary stopping place, she felt she had the capacity to escape Altgeld, CHA, and poverty as long she did not allow herself to become a part of the Altgeld sociopolitical community. Like many respondents, Ceely saw invisibility as being central to her capacity to escape Altgeld. For residents like Ceely, becoming part of Altgeld would create a weight they insisted would render them immobile.

An Alienated Sociopolitical Life

However, while she was alienated from the larger sociopolitical community of Altgeld Gardens, Ceely did have the sociopolitical tools to manage life there. When she encountered issues with an Altgeld Gardens street-level bureaucrat, she called downtown and advocated for herself. When I interviewed her in 2011, she was living in one of the largest three-bedrooms I saw within Altgeld Gardens throughout 2011–2012.

A: Why did you move here?

C: 'Cuz of my own place. [*Chuckles.*] You know when you get your own place, this is my own place, and everything was reasonable. My rent is like eighty-eight bucks, and I'm not paying gas and heat.

A: You are or you're not?

C: No, I don't have to. I don't have to pay like no utilities at all. Like I'm saying, my rent was eighty-eight dollars. It's my own.

A: How would you describe your attitude towards life in Altgeld?

C: I stay positive because I know I'm not going to be out here too long because a lot of people, when I do bump into people and I have a conversation with them, people been out here for years, you know, and they have that mentality like this is the best it get. You know, I had heard people say that before, you know, like this is where I live and this is where I stay; I'm from here. A lot of people [get wrapped up in] the Gardens, you know. Me, I don't see myself staying out here long. I'm getting my master's now, so once I'm done and find me a nice job, I'm going to be heading for the border for a house.

A: What are you getting your master's in?

C: Business.

Throughout my interviews, there were consistent warnings about "people who get wrapped up in the Gardens" or "people who got caught up" while living in Altgeld Gardens. The ideas and warnings crammed into the short phrases could warrant a chapter in and of themselves, but scholars of Chicago gangs like Laurence Ralph are a good resource for a more through engagement with the social-spatial dynamics within Chicago neighborhoods that led to violent conflict among residents.[22]

Many Altgeld respondents were worried about becoming absorbed in the various sociopolitical dramas and conflicts among residents, particularly because some conflicts ended in violence. The mixture of limited resources and limited opportunities to leave the development safely often led to a sense of unease among residents, particularly during hot summer months. Suffice it to say that in any public sphere, there may be countless sociopolitical communities. Within the public sphere of Chicago, Altgeld Gardens is a sociopolitical community, Hyde Park is a sociopolitical community, and University of Chicago is a sociopolitical community. Each sociopolitical community has their own vision of politics and a firm idea about which sociopolitical tools are accessible to them (and appropriate to use). With that in mind, every sociopolitical community attempts to find a way to advocate effectively for power and a way to disperse that power throughout its membership. Even spatial residential (political) communities (like your local neighborhood association or your teenager's high school and its school board) are constantly negotiating and managing power.

Members of a sociopolitical community may vary in their level of commitment, interest, and engagement with the larger politics and sociopolitical tools of their political communities. My childhood friend Perry's mother was not at all interested in the parent-teacher association at our middle school and tried her best not to "get caught up" in the politics of whose kid got any particular opportunity. My mother, on the other hand, was very interested in the PTA, the school board, the city council. You name it; if there was a system of power in Detroit, my parents wanted to understand it. Similarly, this very dynamic happened within Altgeld Gardens. Some residents (as you will see) were very caught up in Altgeld's sociopolitical community. Other residents, like Ceely, could not care less about the sociopolitical community of Altgeld Gardens. As far as Ceely was concerned, the sociopolitical community of Altgeld Gardens held significantly more risk than reward.

Figure 4.2 illustrates Ceely's approximate position within the PPS matrix. Because she described herself as having no friends, family (beyond her children and partner), or any other connection to Altgeld Gardens (or anywhere), she falls on the zero point of the belonging axis. When a respondent described themselves as belonging to no community, inside or

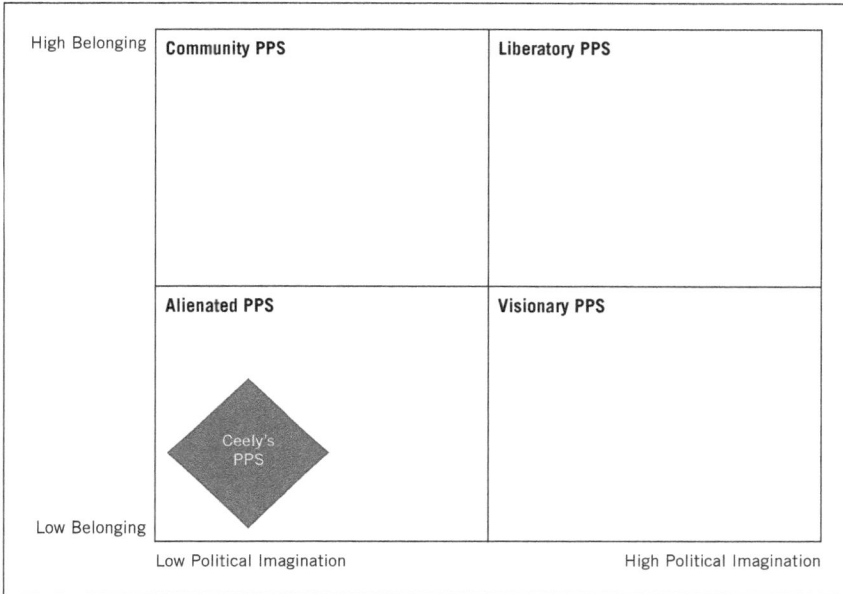

Figure 4.2 Ceely's Political Possible-Self

outside of Altgeld, I placed them on the zero point of the belonging axis. Ceely also described herself as being completely disinterested in politics, whether neighborhood, city, state, or even national politics. Beyond focusing on the immediate safety of her family and their general well-being, she never articulated much hope, let alone a vision, for the future. As a result, I placed her on the zero point of the political imagination axis.

Ceely's primary goal for her family was for them to have a small impact on their spatial-social environment so none of them would draw attention to themselves. Ceely thought that if they could avoid struggles for power, maybe the violence would not touch her or her child. When I asked her, "What kind of folks are the people that you have conversations with?" I was asking her to describe her social support system, or even a loose network, within Altgeld Gardens. But Ceely told me, "You know what? I don't know anyone out here. I know the lady at the Laundromat. I see her, and she's pretty nice. She's like my mom age, probably around forties, but I really don't communicate with anybody. I go in and I leave; I come back. I probably see, like, my neighbors next door, some teenagers. I wave at them, and I keep moving." In this way, verbally at least, Ceely separated herself from the people who live in Altgeld, and she did so consistently throughout our interview.

A: Do you have any friends out here at Altgeld?

C: No, I don't know anyone out here at all.

A: Are you married, dating, or in a relationship?

C: In a relationship with my son's father. We been together since 2006.

A: I know you have your son. How old is he?

C: He's two, yes.

A: What's your experience like raising him here?

C: It's no problem because he's young. I don't want him to grow up here.

A: Why is that?

C: 'Cuz he don't need to stay in the Gardens when he get older. I want him in a house, nice community, nice school, you know, not here. Not here. I don't like it that much.

Consistently, respondents with an alienated PPS emphasized a distinct separation between themselves (and their family) and everyone else in Altgeld. Ceely had enough sociopolitical imagination to navigate the bureaucracies of CHA when her family required it. But outside of advocating for her family, Ceely preferred to keep to herself. Even when I asked her if she had any friends in the neighborhood or anyone she ever spoke to, she said no. While Ceely reported volunteering at her former school (at a fundraiser for kids in her former community), she was not involved with any community activities at Altgeld.

A: Do you go to CHA meetings?

C: No. No, I never been to a CHA meeting.

A: Why not? You just not interested?

C: Yeah, I be like, whatever. My attitude with them be like, hey, whatever. I do what I'm supposed to do. I just don't . . . I really . . . because CHA have a lot of stuff going on out here, for the people out here. That's another thing why I like out here too. But I just never [have] time to participate in anything.

A: Yeah, it can be time consuming.

C: Yeah, it is, and I be like, I'm not wasting my time . . . but I'm probably not wasting my time. I think I should go, now that you brung it up, but no time.

A: Do you ever go to CAC, LAC, or any of that kind of stuff?

C: No. No, I don't go to any of those. I be so busy at school and take care of my son. It's like they be my main things, so when they do send out things like that and they be, like, trying to stress it out,

like come out here, voice your opinion, and everything, I just
don't go.

Like other respondents with an alienated PPS, Ceely discussed a family
member who was involved in politics (she reported that her father worked
for an alderman) and said that as a result she would occasionally engage
in his election campaigns. However, she had an on-again, off-again interest in traditional political news media; when I interviewed her in 2011, she
had never voted. However, given her recent move to Altgeld Gardens, she
was excited about voting for the first time on behalf of former president
Barack Obama in 2012.

If Ceely were assessed for efficacy and cynicism using traditional political science measures, she would certainly be described as politically alienated, much in the same way as she is here. After all, it would be easy to just
dismiss Ceely as completely alienated and leave it at that. However, I argue
that respondents like Ceely are precisely the people who can teach political practitioners the most. What matters, when examining Ceely's PPS,
is not where she ultimately placed on the matrix but instead what scholars
can learn while attempting to figure out her precise relationship to belonging
and political imagination. As a political scientist, I know quite a bit about
how to label an individual, a community, or even an entire population as
having one political identity or another. However, I needed to explore more
of how and why those political identities come to be.

Interviewing respondents like Ceely helped me to understand the sociopolitical realities of marginalized Black communities. Yes, collecting
the total sum of people who are efficacious versus cynical is important work.
But there is also significant value in interviewing and observing people
within their real lives, their spatial contexts. Doing so can help us develop
a firmer understanding of who people and their communities actually are,
beyond the political labels we assign them. Considering how an individual
thinks about and imagines power tells us a lot about their political imagination. Asking a respondent about how they understand their relationship
to, or sense of belonging with, a particular sociopolitical community provides an opportunity to learn much about the individual person I am engaging with, as well as their entire community.

Fully developing Ceely's narrative as a case study within this larger project was critical, whether or not she understood herself to have a fully
formed political identity. Her story is not simply a point of comparison;
it is a beacon of how much work there is to do. Her case forces us to seriously reckon with the reality of material, social, and political life for some
Black women living in Chicago public housing. Further, it forces us to ask

ourselves, Will we simply study these women's stories? Or is there something to be done?

Less Alienated

After the initial research pilot, Nettie was one of the first Altgeld Gardens residents I interviewed. She was a thirty-year-old Black woman who lived in Altgeld Gardens for two and a half years. Notably, she was one of a handful of respondents whose child required special education services. Nettie's son attended a public school close by (outside the Altgeld development). Although she had recently quit her job so she could care for him full-time, overall, Nettie felt that their transition over the last two and a half years had been smooth.

> A: What is it like living in the Altgeld-Murray Homes? How would you describe your experience here?
> N: So far, it's been pretty good. I hear of, like, different incidents, like with violence, but for the most part I have a very positive experience living out here. I have nothing bad to report. Like, if something is wrong with my apartment, maintenance is pretty good with coming out and fixing things. And for the most part, it's been very positive. Nothing bad so far, because I've been here [for two years], and for the most part everything has been pretty good. So I have nothing bad to report.

It is important to note the similarities and the differences between Nettie and Ceely on the PPS matrix. While Nettie had a more neutral relationship to the Altgeld sociopolitical community, Ceely was more alienated. However, they were similar in their relative nonchalance about the violence on the development. I interviewed Nettie a month before the shooting at the Connect.* However, there were reports of violence throughout the development. Strikingly, Nettie said she was having a "very positive experience living" at Altgeld. Like Ceely, she was aware of the violence but only passingly referenced it in her interview.

---

* For more (brief) details, please see page 118.

You Get What You Pay For

A consistent theme throughout my interviews with women on the more alienated end of the spectrum was the belief they could not expect more in regard to the maintenance or spatial realities of the development. A consistent indicator of a more alienated respondent was the sense that they needed money to leave CHA if they wanted to feel 100 percent safe. The more alienated respondents accepted violence and absent building maintenance as immutable reality for those who "choose" to live in public housing. The violence, gunplay in broad daylight, buildings in disrepair all over the development, isolation from grocery or big-box stores, and environmental issues were chalked up as the price of living below the poverty line.

> A: Who do you interact with the most [within the Altgeld Gardens development]?
>
> N: My neighbors sometime. If I see them, I just say hello. Right next door and the door right after that, they're mostly in their midthirties, I think.
>
> A: What's your relationship like with your neighbors?
>
> N: Not that much. I just say hello, goodbye, but never like friendship or nothing. Just saying hello and seeing what's going on in the neighborhood. But nothing like really close, but just saying hello, being friendly. And that's it.
>
> A: How come nothing close?
>
> N: Because I'm, like, hardly around. My son is at school, and sometimes I'm at school helping out with his classroom or, like, looking for a job, 'cuz I quit my job in April, April of this year, so I could take care of my son full-time. Prior to that I was working at [a nonprofit], and I was working at [an association]. So, with my job and helping out with my son's school, and that's about it. I'm just like a real, like, you know, I'm not very social, so I just try to help out with my son's school or with my job. But at home I just like peace and quiet. I don't like all that drama and stuff.

Nettie repeated a popular sentiment within the interviews: she kept to herself because she did not want to get caught up "in the drama." What this meant for each respondent varied slightly. But generally, it meant the respondent avoided any conflicts that could escalate to violence. It also generally implied that they did not want other Altgeld Gardens residents to know what kind of electronics, clothing, or shoes they had in their home. For Nettie, "no more drama" was a mantra she repeated over and over through her life, at every opportunity.

The Politics of Invisibility within a Sociopolitical Community

I walked away from Altgeld asking myself, What are the politics of invisibility?[23] Who has the freedom to speak, be loud, and be seen, without social repercussions or threats of physical harm?[24]

> As marginal group leaders pursue the goal of expanded access and integration, part of their strategy may become portraying their community as representing and adhering to values and norms as defined by dominant groups. It is difficult for these indigenous leaders, who gain part of their authority and legitimacy by conforming to dominant values, to continually and actively challenge these same norms and values as unfair criteria upon which to judge individual merit. Thus, by accepting the dominant discourse that defines what is good, normal, and acceptable, stratification among marginal group members is transformed into an indigenous process of marginalization targeting the most vulnerable in the group. This process [is what] I label *secondary marginalization*.[25]

In *Boundaries of Blackness*, Cathy J. Cohen argues that *secondary marginalization* is not simply about the hierarchies within legacy organizations or the decision of who gets to contribute to public policy targeted at Black American communities (although local, state, and federal policy is critical).[26] The stakes are much larger than those concerns. According to Cohen, *marginal group members* "are forced, therefore, to demonstrate their normativity and legitimacy through the class privilege they acquire, through the attitudes and behavior they exhibit, and through the dominant institutions in which they operate."[27] In the U.S. context, dominant mainstream Black communities are the ones who decide what the dominant values and norms are. Marginalized group members like Black women living in Chicago public housing are consistently targeted via government, bureaucratic, and residential violence because of the stigma around their sites of marginalization. Within the mainstream Black counterpublic in the United States, the battle is around which Black communities are able to adopt a politics of recognition and which Black communities must utilize a politics of invisibility.*[28] In *Democracy Remixed*, Cohen defines the politics of invisibility:

> I believe that significant numbers of Black youth, at least prior to 2008, have used the limited agency available to them to stay under the radar. These young people have chosen a politics of invisibility disengaging from all forms of politics and trying to remain invisible to officials who possibly could provide assistance but were more likely to impose greater surveillance and regulations on their lives. They have focused and relied on their own social worlds instead. Of course, the danger of a politics of invisibility is that the voices of young black Americans, especially those who are most marginal—and whose voices are very critical in a representative system that is based on the articulation of wants and needs by the populace—are muted.[29]

The politics of invisibility asks a simple question: Where is it safe to be seen and heard? For poor Black women living in the United States, their very presence elicits violence from the state, Black men, mainstream media, and academics who still make arguments about "welfare queens" of the "underclass."[30] The humanity and political power of Black women is removed when their survival is tied to their successful self-erasure.[31] The opposite and life-affirming political placement is within a politics of recognition.[32] In *Sister Citizen*, Melissa Harris-Perry argues that Black women's membership within sociopolitical communities is primarily a quest for recognition.[33] She goes on to note that binding the mainstream Black counterpublic with recognition ultimately allows that counterpublic to give birth

---

* When I use the phrase "mainstream Black counterpublic," I am using Catherine R. Squires's definition of the Black counterpublic. In "Rethinking the Black Public Sphere," Squires argues that there are multiple Black public spheres: "I propose we speak of multiple Black publics. Thus, a Black public is an emergent collective composed of people who (a) engage in common discourses and negotiations of what it means to be Black, and (b) pursue particularly defined Black interests. This definition, although still wedded to the idea that there is a Black social group, does allow for heterogeneous Black publics to emerge, and also for people who do not identify as Black, but are concerned with similar issues, to be involved in a coalition with Black people" (Squires, 454). Squires goes on to define the "counterpublic" as the Black public "which can engage in debate with wider publics to test ideas and perhaps utilize traditional social movement tactics (boycotts, civil disobedience)" (Squires, 448). For the purposes of this book, the "mainstream Black counterpublic" refers to the Black middle-class counterpublic focused on respectability politics. As Frederick C. Harris and Cathy J. Cohen show in their work, this "mainstream Black counterpublic" dominates the Black American political agenda in the United States (F. Harris, "Rise of Respectability Politics"; Cohen, *Boundaries of Blackness*).

to a political sense of well-being, which provides not only Black women but all human beings with access to discussions around the meaning of justice, order, and right doing.[34] Without acknowledgment as human beings with value, the challenge to become recognized—and furthermore, to become members of their sociopolitical community and the Black mainstream counterpublic, who can safely and effectively assert power—continually grows larger.[35] Unfortunately, Black women living below the poverty line in the United States rarely have access to the Black mainstream counterpublic or the larger U.S. public sphere.[36]

However, it is important to note that Nettie and Ceely expressed no desire to access the mainstream Black counterpublic or the larger U.S. public sphere.[37] As far as Nettie and Ceely were concerned, success meant no one knowing they lived in Altgeld. For women with an alienated (Ceely) or more neutral (Nettie) PPS, their sociopolitical goals were inverted. They exchanged the possibility of political power and recognition within a bigger counterpublic for the perceived safety of invisibility.[38] Ultimately, the women of Altgeld raise a meaningful question: Is it safe to hold political power?

Figure 4.3 illustrates Nettie's approximate placement on the PPS matrix. Like Ceely, Nettie did not have close relationships with anyone at Altgeld Gardens. However, she knew who her neighbors were. Nettie believed that having a passing familiarity with who lived on her block, and who did not, helped in her effort to keep her and her family safe. Nettie's tenuous tie to the neighborhood sociopolitical community was not one of belonging, but it did seem to signal an acceptance of Altgeld as a place she had intentionally made her home. Therefore, I placed her on the matrix as having a low sense of belonging to Altgeld Gardens and a neutral sense of political imagination.

As I mentioned in Chapter 2 within the PPS text matrix (Table 2.1), people with this placement generally understand the potential benefits of political, social, and civic engagement. However, respondents like Nettie typically did not engage in many visible or public sociopolitical activities; in fact, according to her interview, it was pretty rare. Nettie did not participate in sociopolitical activities at Altgeld Gardens or within the CHA. However, she voted regularly, and she volunteered at her child's school. Notably, she supported disability advocacy organizations in Illinois. While Ceely seemed completely alienated, Nettie had other spaces and places outside of Altgeld Gardens where she engaged in public-spirited conversation. She valued her occasional political work within a sociopolitical community that focused on neurodivergent children living in Illinois. Her political imagination was neutral in the sense that she did not have a

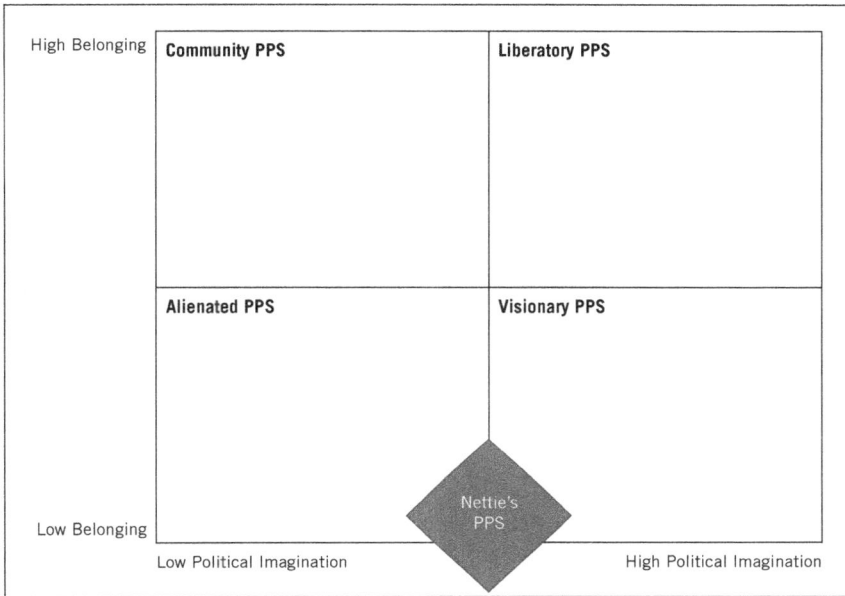

Figure 4.3 Nettie's Political Possible-Self

significant amount of cynicism regarding government, politics, or socio-political life more broadly conceived, but she also did not express a strong sense of efficacy in any of the aforementioned categories.

In Chapter 2, I argued that respondents can move up and down the belonging and the political imagination axes as a result of socio-political-civic education of some sort or another. Nettie's case study clarifies how that can happen along the axis of political imagination. Ceely knew no one within her community and did not seem to have many relationships outside of Altgeld. As a result, she had no access to resources or people who could help her develop the sociopolitical skills needed to navigate even basic welfare or CHA bureaucracy. Nettie was further along on the political imagination axis because of the sociopolitical education she received while volunteering at her child's public school. Working with the special education program led to volunteering at a state disability advocacy organization. She accompanied this organization to Springfield, Illinois, so she could help the organization protest at the state capital. Along the way she learned quite a bit about civic and political advocacy. As a result, Nettie had hope for the future. She imagined her future self as someone who could eventually grasp at some form of power within a community context and advocate for herself and others. Throughout the ethnographic data I collected at Altgeld Gardens, I found that respondents were able to move around the PPS matrix as a result of increased sociopolitical relationships or increased socio-political-civic education.

Frequently, respondents accessed socio-political-civic education by building new relationships, often within their local sociopolitical community. Nettie's familiarity with her neighbors was a meaningful difference from Ceely's lack thereof. Nettie seemed to think a passing familiarity with who lived in Altgeld, and who did not, kept her safe. Ultimately, she wanted to be able to recognize if a stranger or a teenager from elsewhere in the development was standing in front of her walk-up.

> A: How would you describe your attitude towards life in Altgeld?
> N: It's OK. Sometimes, like, you know, it's like sometimes I want to get a job and stuff, but it just makes it so easy. [*Laughs.*] It seems like it's so easy to just sit around, but for the most part, I like it. I like it. Yeah. But I still want to get a full-time job, but right now is just not the time. I've got to take care of my son. He has special needs. He has autism. So I think right now this is what I need to be doing. I need to take care of my son. But for the most part, I have no complaints about living out here so far. . . .
> A: So, what do you think keeps you from being more involved with people here at Altgeld?
> N: It's just me because I'm not a very social person. I just like peace and quiet. I don't like no drama, no conflict. I don't like all that gossiping stuff. So I just keep to myself. If I want to find out about anything that's going on in the world, I look on the internet or I look on TV. But for the most part, I mostly keep to myself because I like peace and quiet in my household. Like, it's mostly quiet. I don't have a lot of people running in and out.
> A: So nobody bothers you?
> N: No. Yeah, so that's the way I prefer it because at the end of the day I don't want all that conflict and drama. So I try to stay away. I be social when I can, like say hello to my neighbors. I try to look out and see who's living around me. But for the most part, shoot, I stay to myself. Yeah.

Nettie structured her entire life, her work, and even her education around her son. With consistent help from her parents, Nettie spent most of her days making sure her son had what he needed. However, living in Altgeld meant that in addition to the labor required as a single parent with a neurodivergent child, she also had to negotiate parenting in one of the most dangerous public housing developments in Chicago. As a result, whenever he wanted to play on a local playground or go outside for an activity, Nettie would take her son outside of Altgeld and Riverdale proper.*

Moving to Altgeld with
One Foot out the Door

Many respondents believed keeping their children safe meant keeping them separate and apart from the spatial realities of Altgeld Gardens. The children who were born in Altgeld and understood its social rules and logics were frequently described by the mothers who were newer to Altgeld as a violent mob lacking all reason.

A: When you tell other people you live in Altgeld, how do they respond?

N: For the most part, they're like, OK, I'm kind of vague; I don't tell them exactly where I live. I just say I live close to Riverdale, you know. But for the most part, if I say I live in Altgeld Gardens, it's really no bad response. I just always tell them I live I in CHA, and I just tell them it's a good neighborhood. Like how it used to be, like it used to be really a violent neighborhood. But now, it's not that bad. So a lot of people, they're more receptive, and they're willing to come to my house. So for the most part it's not that bad, like when I tell them where I live.

A: So, none of the violence or anything, you don't experience any of that?

N: No, because for the most part, like me and my son, whenever we have free time, we go downtown; we go to museums and stuff. We try to get outside the neighborhood. Like, we really don't . . . I go to the Laundromat or to the store, like the little local store at 131st and Ellis, sometimes.

A: The Rosebud or the liquor store?

N: Yeah, the liquor store and Rosebud. I go there sometimes. But for the most part, we mostly out the neighborhood when we have free time. We mostly go outside the neighborhood.

---

* Riverdale is the name of the closest neighborhood to Altgeld on Chicago's South Side.

Rosebud was a local grocery store directly outside the Altgeld Gardens development. Rosebud was a controversial topic on the development. They were known among Altgeld residents for price gouging because they were one of the only grocery stores within walking distance. Strangely enough, Rosebud did not accept WIC or SNAP. This obviously created a problem for residents, given that many of them received some form of welfare entitlement. As a result, a month after my interview with Nettie, there was a multiday protest at the Rosebud grocery.[39] It is unclear if the protestor demands were met, but residents did meet with the owner of the Rosebud store. Since Nettie did not communicate with many people on the development, she often missed opportunities for clothing, toy, or food giveaways, as well as job opportunities and educational grants. While Nettie tried to keep her ears to the ground, her politics of invisibility were not without consequences.

> A: Do you go to CHA meetings? What are they like? What do you think of them? What are the people like?
>
> N: No, not yet.
>
> A: How come?
>
> N: A lot of times they give us short notice. They don't really tell us about things that are going on. Like, if I do see anything, it's mostly at the Laundromat on that little bulletin board. So it's like really short notice. They tell us at the very last minute, so that's the only reason why I don't go.
>
> A: Do you ever go to CAC, LAC, or commissioners' board meetings? Why? Why not?
>
> N: No, not yet, but I do want to go.
>
> A: Has Altgeld changed since you first arrived?
>
> N: No. But a lot of people that I talk to, like sometimes, they always say how bad it used to be. But I never had that problem. Sometimes in the Laundromat you hear gossip about shootings or different violence, but I never see that along this block. So for the most part I haven't had any bad experience out here.

Every once in a while, I would be listening to one of the women in the study, and I knew immediately they were saying something untrue. This always left me in an uncomfortable position, but I was clear from the beginning of the project that I would never "confront" someone I interviewed about a "lie." After hundreds of years of training scientists to believe that positivist methods are what differentiates science from fiction, academics in the social sciences have become so consumed with collecting "objective facts" that they often miss the truth.

In *Interpreting Racial Politics in the United States*, Robert Schmidt rightly points out that objectivity is a myth. We often miss what we are looking for by obsessing over tiny details. There were important contrasts between what I found beautiful and what was beautiful to the residents. Similarly, there were differences between what I knew as the truth and where their truth lay.[40] What differentiated Nettie, as someone with less alienation and less visionary qualities, is that she was not alienated across every area of her life. While she did separate herself from the political community of Altgeld Gardens, Nettie participated in sociopolitical communities in other Chicago neighborhoods.

A: What kind of activities do you participate in? Are you involved in any groups, volunteer work, or organizations?

N: Well, sometimes, if I have the free time, I go to this website called Volunteer Corp, and they do, like, different volunteer opportunities. Like, they help out at the Food Pantry Inc., or they help out at the park. I like that because you don't have to commit, like, a certain amount of time. Whenever they have that's available, you can always volunteer. So I like volunteering through Volunteer Corp. I help out at my son's school, and that's about it.

A: Do you vote or participate in any political activities?

N: Yes, I do vote on a regular basis when they have the voting. The last time I participated in something political was . . . it was a couple of months ago because we actually went down to Springfield, and I talked to my state representative . . . oh, I forgot his name . . . I forgot his name! [*Laughing.*] Oh, damn, if I had that book . . . so we actually went down to Springfield, and we talked to, I forgot who the state representative was, but we talked to a senator, and we were talking about having him do more for the disabled community. Because my son is a special needs child, so that's really important to me. Yeah. So, I just was asking him can he do more for the disabled people. He was really receptive. He was a really nice person. And so was the state representative. He was also very nice because he was telling me that his mom was actually doing home health care. So he was really receptive. Both of them were very nice people.

A: Do you see yourself doing any more of that political advocacy work in the future?

N: Yeah, it was very interesting because they just want the facts. They don't want nothing objective. You just got to state the facts. Like this is what happened on this visit; this is what happened on that visit. So I just liked stating the facts. You don't have no feelings involved, just, like, state what happened on each visit. So I enjoyed the work, yeah.

Throughout the interview, Nettie emphasized the relationships she had with sociopolitical communities in other parts of the city.

A: I noticed the "We call the police" on your window. What made you put that up?

N: Because I had it. I went to a CAPS meeting in my old neighborhood, so they were giving out the "We call the police," so I have one in my front window and back window, and I have one on my side window. I just put it up in there, you know. But yeah, I will call the police if something's bothering me.

A: Have you had to do that since you've been here?

N: No. I just try to let stuff go, like I don't take things personally. You get what you pay for. It's like reduced rent. Everything's, you have the lights, gas, water. So for the most part, it's kids that run across, but I don't let that get to me. But if somebody's trying to get into my house, yes, I will call the police!

A: Have you been to a CAPS meeting out here?

N: No, I haven't, but there is a police station, I think, what street is it on? It's, like, on 131st Street. So there is a police station out here, and they're actively involved. It's a lot of police out here. You can really see the police presence. So I feel safe for the most part.

A reoccurring sentiment across respondents newer to Altgeld Gardens came up again in Nettie's and Ceely's interviews: "you get what you pay for," "we pay reduced rent," with a kind of shrug and sigh. The idea is that if you are not wealthy, you cannot expect to live in a safe neighborhood. Nettie did not have any dreams for her community. Ultimately, she simply hoped to one day afford a two-bedroom house for her and her son, as well as a car. But unlike a more visionary PPS, Nettie's neutral PPS resulted in a sociopolitical imagination focused on survival within the spatial realities of Altgeld Gardens.

Less Visionary

As I noted when discussing Nettie's approximate placement on the PPS matrix, an individual can move up, down, across, or even diagonally, depending on the increase or decrease of their belonging or political imagination. This becomes clearer via Shug's case study. Shug was significantly more connected to the sociopolitical community within Altgeld Gardens than Ceely or Nettie. She prided herself on being a community resource for residents at Altgeld, in terms of information, as well as basic household items. I interviewed Shug a little over a month after the Connect shooting. At the time, she was thirty-nine years old. Shug moved to Altgeld Gardens in 2008, and while she was a bit less isolated than Ceely, she had more political imagination than Nettie. Shug's family was originally from the South. When her mother was sixteen years old, Shug's father (twenty-two years old at the time) moved them both to Chicago. Both lacked a formal education, and her father was illiterate for most of his life. But despite these challenges, Shug reported that her father maintained his own business for most of his life. Shug was the eighth of their nine children and proudly referred to herself as "the smart one" in her family. She dropped out of high school in the twelfth grade, but twenty years later she completed her GED. Shug was a proud woman; after describing her educational journey, she told me, "Yes, I ain't never been a dummy." It was clear from the beginning of the interview that she had a lot of experience when it came to finding her way through the world.

A Less Alienated Life in Altgeld

Shug grew up in Chicago, but as an adult she moved to North Carolina with her younger brother. Unfortunately, Shug was forced to leave North Carolina because her younger brother became addicted to crack cocaine and living with him was untenable. She had three daughters, who were thirty-one, twenty-six, and sixteen. Shug and her sixteen-year-old daughter packed up their things, came back to Chicago, and moved in with her middle daughter (the twenty-six-year-old) across the street from her mother. Unbeknownst to her, Shug's oldest daughter put her on the CHA waiting list. Months later, Shug fell out with her mother, and once again she needed a new place to call home. Fortunately, six months after her application was originally submitted, CHA called her in for an interview. When her CHA application was approved in late 2008, Shug moved to Altgeld Gardens.

A: What is it like living in the Altgeld-Murray Homes? How would you describe your experience here?

S: Different. I would describe my experience as being different from what I'm used to. I participate a lot with the children, as you see. All the children love me 'cuz it's like I'm the mother over here, because I see a lot of children are lost out of here. And I'm not used to that. I'm not used to children running the household and parents trying to be their children friend instead of parent. So I see so much chaos between a mother and daughter or mother and son out here, and it's different to me. I describe this as being different.

A: What do you like about living in Altgeld?

S: The rent. I can afford it. I like the fact that I can afford the rent for me and my fifteen-year-old. She'll be sixteen tomorrow. And, ah, I like the housing. It's just the people. Yeah, I like the housing. It's not the apartments; it's the people.

Shug, like many respondents, centered the low rent as the reason she lived in Altgeld Gardens. Quite honestly, the rent seemed to be the only thing she liked about Altgeld. Despite that, Shug was more open to interacting with her neighbors within Altgeld than Nettie and Ceely were. She paid close attention to the comings and goings of the neighbors who lived in close proximity to her home. She was particularly invested in getting to know some of the children within the development and supporting them in small ways here and there. Despite that, Shug made it clear throughout our interview that she did not consider herself to be in a sociopolitical community with her neighbors. She described her attention to who-was-who and who-lived-where as being a strategy she engaged in to support her and her family's survival.

Less Community and Fewer Politics

Shug's disconnect from her neighbors and the Altgeld sociopolitical community writ large was also reflected in her politics and sociopolitical tools. She understood herself to be a reluctant, if not marginal, member of the Altgeld sociopolitical community.

A: Do you vote or participate in any political activities?

S: Obama in there. I feel like if you ain't a part of it, you a problem to it. You need to go . . . people died for me to get that right. I would not ever miss a vote.

A: Do you think this makes a difference?

S: Yes, I do. Yes, I do! And people that didn't vote, I don't want to hear anything about the government, their Social Security check, the food stamps; you should have voted!

A: Right. What kind of skills and knowledge are needed to participate in politics?

S: Common sense. Common sense and to be aware, know what you
hear, don't believe everything you hear or see. Basically, common sense.

A: Do you have those skills and knowledge?

S: Of course, yes.

A: How do you define politics? When I say the word "politics," what
do you think of?

S: Hmm, votes. I'm just being honest.

I continued to interview the women of Altgeld, and along the way it became clear to me they had their own interpretations and understandings
of politics and the political. As time went on, I started to recognize that I
could not simply apply my understanding of the world to the sociopolitical context of the respondents in the study. After all, at the time of the interviews, I was a twenty-five-year-old Black girl who grew up in middle-class
Detroit, with a meaningful class difference and a contrasting set of spatial
realities. I was raised in a sociopolitical context that understood politics
and the political in terms of elections, campaigns, grassroots organizing,
and social movement organizing. But Shug associated the word "politics"
with voting and other systems beyond her reach. As my research went on,
I realized residents at Altgeld and I did not have the same definition of politics in mind when we discussed who they knew themselves to be and how
they understood their sociopolitical community.

A: Do you think you could make a difference by participating in
politics?

S: I don't know politics. I'm going to vote for Democrat; that's all
I want to do.

A: Why is that?

S: It seem like they make more sense to me, and it's not all about
money, you know. Most Republicans want to hang somebody.
. . . But I feel like they just, man, I don't know how they got all
the power. I really don't. I don't know why they got all the power.

A consistent theme throughout the interviews was inconsistency. Respondents would waiver on how they politically self-described throughout the
interviews.[41] Early on in our interview, Shug self-identified as someone
who knew, recognized, understood, and was capable of political partici-

pation. But later in the interview, she told me, "I don't know politics." Likely, as the interview progressed and I asked additional questions regarding "traditional politics," some respondents lost a bit of self-confidence about presenting themselves as politically knowledgeable and capable. It might have also been a result of having to answer more-detailed sociopolitical questions. But it could have been a consequence of questions some respondents found difficult to answer—in particular, the questions I raised about power and whether respondents thought of themselves as people with power in the context of their community and beyond.

> A: Who do you believe has the most power in this society?
>
> S: White people! I mean, our kids have to struggle . . .] All these people want to put this on Obama. This problem was here before Obama was even born! And I don't like it! Let me calm down. See, you getting me upset. 'Cuz there ain't nothing but common sense. You see straight through that.
>
> A: Do they have any power over your life?
>
> S: No, I fin to become insensitive to it. I make sure they don't have no power over me.
>
> A: Do you have power in this society?
>
> S: I seem to think so, especially in my neighborhood. 'Cuz as you see, they always come to me. I mean, I like to tell people the truth. I don't like to lie. You tell one lie, you got to tell a million more; you got to remember the lie you told. Just keep it simple. Keep it simple. And that's how I am. Through experience. I wasn't always like that. I was just like them. That's why I tell them you don't have to experience it; I experienced it for you. Hear the message.
>
> A: What does it mean to have power?
>
> S: I don't really know. I've never had that kind of power. I don't even think I would want it. I just want everybody to treat each other like they want to be treated. You know, treat me with respect; I'll give it back to you.

Throughout her interview, Shug continued to be consistently inconsistent.[42] At the beginning of the questions about power, she described herself as a person who intentionally developed a sort of immunity to the structural forces of whiteness. She went on to describe herself as a person with some power and some influence within the Altgeld neighborhood she lived in. But at the very next question, Shug described herself as someone who "never had that kind of power." Ultimately, I think Shug saw a significant difference between the power she exerted in the context of her residential community and the structural forces that exerted power over the Altgeld Gardens community.[43]

A: Do people in government care about the people who live in Altgeld Gardens?

S: It depends on who we talking about. Because to me, this was one thing, when I first moved out here, I had no other choice. Like I say, I was staying with family members. So to me I had no other choice. I needed my own roof over my head for me and my child. But when I got out here, I'm like, they just threw these people away out here. It's no stores. I'm used to stores on every corner, whether it's liquor stores, clothing stores, grocery stores. And there's nothing out here. You have to have a vehicle out here. They in the store, they call Up-Top, by where we pay rent at the CYC [Chicago Youth Center] building. It rains inside the store! Have you ever been in it?

A: The liquor store?

S: Yes! It rains inside that store! Drug dealers hang out there. I don't even go down there! . . . That store is more popular than that one 'cuz it's on the main street! So if I got robbed there, I'm damn sure ain't going down there!

A: Yeah, that makes sense. Do you believe you have any influence over what the government does?

S: No. Only if I . . . I'm more like a recruiting type person. You know, I like to try to get people to vote, get involved, you know . . . do something. Because if you're not part of the problem, you're part of the solution, one of the two. Real simple. So, whether you're going to help us . . . at least we did our part trying to make something! Like that store up there, the prices so damn high it don't make no sense. But that's got people trapped out here! I mean, four pounds of chicken, eight dollars, come on!

During the interview, I asked Shug if she thought the "government" cared about the people living within Altgeld Gardens. What is notable about her response is that right away she said, "It depends on who we talking about," meaning there are multiple possible answers to that question, depending on which aspect of the government we are discussing. Shug went on to note, "When I got out here, I'm like, they just threw these people away out here. It's no stores. . . . They in the store, they call Up-Top, by where we pay rent at the CYC building. It rains inside the store!" By "they," Shug was referencing the public housing authority. Immediately she equated the "government" with the CHA, the bureaucracy the federal HUD agency entrusted with the management of public housing within the city of Chicago.

The CHA owned the real estate within the Altgeld Gardens and Phillip Murray Homes development, including the buildings that housed the Up-Top liquor store and the CYC building. For Shug, the mismanagement and benign neglect of the Altgeld Gardens neighborhood and buildings made evident the lack of care the government had for everyone who lived within Altgeld's borders. Ultimately, Shug and Nettie said, "they just threw us away out here . . . [and] that's got people trapped out here." Shug saw her lease within Altgeld Gardens as evidence of her lack of sociopolitical power over the structural forces of the government vis-à-vis the CHA.

In 2011, Altgeld Gardens was located near the southern border of the city of Chicago, and there was only one bus to service the entire development. Respondents estimated their average trip to a big-box store, where they could get basic necessities like toiletries, food, and school supplies, at approximately two hours each way if they did not have access to a car. Given that Altgeld was built on top of land that formerly served as a dumping ground for toxic waste and that it was surrounded by former factories, as well as a landfill, it's easy to understand why respondents like Shug and Nettie likened themselves to mere things the City of Chicago chose to throw away. As a result, some respondents compared Altgeld to an open-air prison that was difficult to escape. These spatial realities clarified how the choices made by government bureaucracies like the CHA played a large role in the sociopolitical development of every citizen who lived within Altgeld for any significant amount of time.

Having said that, it is important to remember that the spatial realities of their residential neighborhood were not the only meaningful sociopolitical force in the lives of Altgeld residents. Residents with a sense of connection to the people within the Altgeld sociopolitical community used the safe spaces they created to engage in public-spirited conversation, where they could express their political cynicism while maintaining a sense of hope about the future. Their sense of belonging allowed those respondents to maintain a sense of sociopolitical capacity as they moved through their daily lives. Throughout the interview, Shug was very focused on her capacity to nurture her sociopolitical network. She also considered electoral politics to be a form of politics she had the capacity to use. In other words, political cynicism did not constrain Shug's capacity to understand her own sphere of influence and the power she wielded within it.

Less Visionary, More Violence

Throughout the interview, Shug spoke frequently about her relationships within the Altgeld Gardens sociopolitical community. Like Nettie, Shug found a lot of value in maintaining a distance from other residents within the development. However, while Nettie's PPS featured alienation and isolation from the residential neighborhood she lived in, Shug did have some relationships within Altgeld.

> A: [Who] are your friends? What kind of things do you talk about? Do you have friends in Altgeld?
>
> S: I have associates. I don't trust these people. I mean, any time your house is not in order, how do I trust you? If the mother's not caring about the child, the child not caring about the mother, what the hell are you going to care for me for? And I'm not related to you. No, I don't trust these people. Now, the one that live here with the kids, Whitley, I pretty much trust her. And Frankie, over any of them.
>
> A: So what kind of stuff do you guys talk about?
>
> S: I try to tell them when I was their age how I had nice cars, nice house, everything. And that they can get it and don't let no man use them. You can do better by yourself by putting it somewhere where rent is affordable, so if a man is living with you and he want to beat on you, put him out! . . . That's my motto, and I just say it as it is. . . .
>
> A: What makes you happy?
>
> S: Seeing smiles on kids' faces. And they know I got a Freeze Pop or something for them every day. The kids . . . it's the kids. Kids make me happy. The adults . . . I don't care about the adults. I ain't going to lie. It's the children. I want to save the children.

A number of respondents were reluctant to call anyone a friend. Instead, many used the language of "acquaintances" or "associates" to communicate a certain amount of socioemotional distance. But despite initially framing her relationships as dynamics that were without emotional closeness, Shug also described her world as focused on the children and the younger adults in the community. Her survival strategy involved creating a wide net of relationships.

Shug's PPS was less alienated than Ceely's or Nettie's and less politically imaginative within the visionary PPS domain. More specifically, Shug's

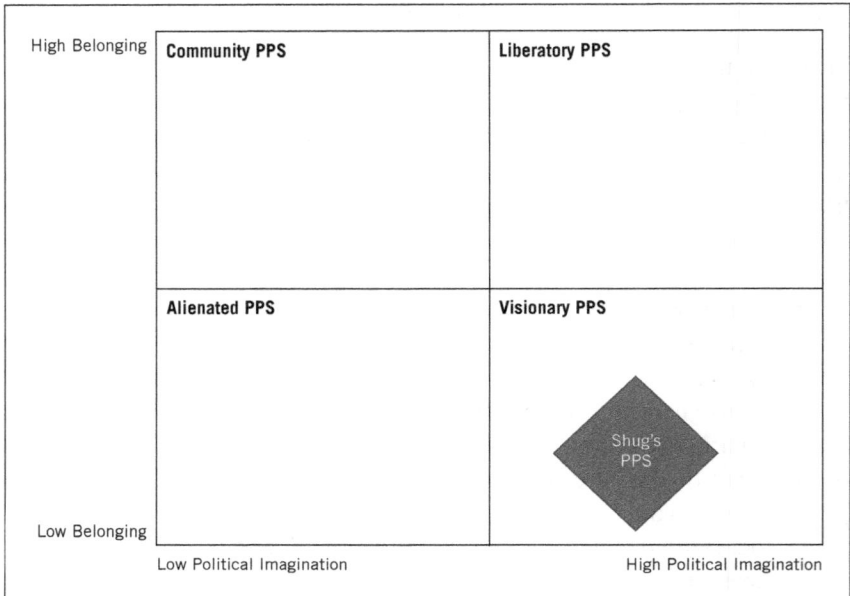

Figure 4.4 Shug's Political Possible-Self

PPS fell within the "neutral PPS" domain in the bottom political imagination section of the text matrix (see Table 2.1). As has already been noted, Shug had few sociopolitical tools and a range of shallow interpersonal relationships tying her to the Altgeld community. As discussed on pages 138–142, Shug had a solid understanding of the wider sociopolitical world. While her political point of view might have been cynical, it was firmly grounded in her lived experience. Shug's political imagination still had room to grow, as did her overall political knowledge.

However, Shug's lack of substantive political belonging meant she often went without a sense of safety and protection while she walked through her neighborhood in Altgeld Gardens. However, while Shug, Nettie, and Ceely all decided to protect themselves using varying levels of invisibility, Shug found value in finding means to make herself useful to residents in Altgeld. Over time, Shug developed a side hustle by becoming a resource of household items, as well as advice, for her neighbors.

A: So what don't you like about the people [who live in Altgeld]?
S: I don't like all the drinking because then, you know, that's when a lot of drama, chaos, neighbors fighting . . . see, I'm a neigh-

borly person. If you tell me you collect cans, I'll make sure you
get every can come through mine. I even pick them up on the
streets, like collecting plastic tops. That's why I had a plastic top
off the dishwashing liquid. You know, I'm a neighborly person,
and I don't see too much of that out here.

A: That totally makes sense. What has been your experience interacting with the people who work here? (For example, the management company, CHA, government offices, social welfare
offices, et cetera. . . .)

S: Oh, my case manager, Ms. Richards, she's nice. You know, I can
talk to her. . . . So now I start participating at the CYC, like I
go tomorrow and do poetry. And it's called Altgeld Talks, and
I done got involved in that. I been to the last four, and I'm going
to every one of them 'cuz I'm trying to make a change out here.

A: So what do they do at Altgeld Talks?

S: . . . Ask what they can do to better the place. And I was telling them
they need to enforce the rules, you know, when you have a teen-
age child, especially a son that's disrespecting your household as
well as everyone else, starting fights. They just beat this boy with
a golf club; they need to evict him. They need to enforce the rules,
evict him! If a mother cannot maintain her child, don't let them
contaminate the whole neighborhood! Get rid of them! Give her
a warning about it, and if she can't put him in somewhere to get
help and stop being in denial, "Oh, not my child," put him out!

Shug's relationships within the community, like all of our relationships,
were complex. While she found value in mentoring children and young
adults, she spoke frequently about "kids gone wild" throughout the development. This was a consistent narrative throughout the interviews I collected:
women spoke about children and teenagers who had no adult supervision
and were agents of chaos. Ultimately, it was hard to tell how much of their
fear of children and teenagers was warranted. After all, there were only three
respondents who reported violent encounters with preteens, teenagers, and
children. The rest of the respondents who reported being robbed, including
Shug herself, were robbed by adult men. The frequency of violence perpe-
trated by adult men is notable given that the majority of leaseholders in
Altgeld Gardens were adult Black women.

S: Oh, no, they was robbing the cable man, robbing us!

A: So they broke into your home?

S: No, I got robbed up there by the store. The first year I moved out here. Then they called this the "blind side." They robbed a cable man, the pizza man, the tenants.

A: Why did they call it the blind side?

S: Because, you know, we're the new site, and everyone over there pretty much lived out here, and they remodeled, and they brought them back. People like us, you know, we never lived out here. You know, we from Indiana or West Side, you know, Naperville. So, they called this the blind side because the police station and all that is across this big field out here.

A: Oh, so they can't see you.

S: Exactly. We have no help over here.

A: So you were walking from the store here . . .

S: Yes. And he had pulled a gun on me and cut my hand.

A: Oh, wow.

S: Yeah, 'cuz I threw my hand up, and he had a knife. I was like, you can have it; it's not . . . me and my baby just moved out here. So he just pushed me on.

The spatial realities of Altgeld Gardens meant some blocks were considered safer than others. Respondents noted that the blocks with CHA bureaucratic buildings tended to be safer. The Altgeld block that held the library was situated toward the front of the development and seemed to have fewer violent encounters, given that there were few places to hide, a number of security cameras, and a higher police presence. However, the Altgeld Gardens and Phillip Murray Homes development was large and incredibly easy to become lost in. A large number of one-way streets, the identical edifices of walk-up apartments, and the circular block structure meant I spent many days completely disoriented when trying to find a new respondent's apartment.

On the other hand, many of the development elders who grew up in Altgeld were placed near the back of the development. Given that there was nothing else in the back of the development besides athletic fields and parks, the elders were rarely bothered by gang clashes or robberies. At least one elder reported that she always left her doors and windows unlocked because the young people other respondents feared were incredibly protective of the seniors who dedicated their lives to the Altgeld community.

Shug, however, lived in what respondents called the "blind side." The blind side was made up of a few blocks that could not be seen from the front of the development, the police station, or the CHA buildings. According to respondents, it also had the largest number of new residents, many of whom were former residents of demolished CHA high-rises from across the city. This meant some gang members from the West Side and North Side of Chicago were suddenly living in South Side gang territory, which created an uptick of violence. Ultimately, the rate of violence in Altgeld Gardens reached 200 percent higher than the rest of the city combined. The structures of the built environment, a privatized neoliberal management structure, and decades of benign neglect created spatial pocket environments that varied in the violence or safety they created for residents.[44]

During our interview, Shug discussed violence and drug use as a pervasive force throughout the development. Shug was ardently clear; she would pack up and leave Altgeld the day her finances allowed it. Since leaving wasn't possible during the time I was visiting the Altgeld community, part of what helped Shug stay safe was her wide sociopolitical network across the community.

A: Do you go to CHA meetings?

S: Yeah, those are the meetings they setting up now.

A: What do you think of them?

S: I pretty much think that it's like they say one thing but do another. But now they say they getting on board. They fin to start enforcing these rules and things like that, 'cuz pretty much . . . then the lady [a CHA employee] explained it to me. She said, "I understand where you coming from, but we can't just put them out." It's a procedure, you know; they have to take them to court. So they say they fin to start enforcing it. Because there ain't no sense in putting the cameras up here and telling people what they can and cannot do and then when their children break into houses or beating somebody, or even shooting somebody! They're still here! Get rid of them! You didn't put them out; they put theyself out. They are the rules. And that's how I feel about it.

A: Do you ever go to CAC, LAC, or commissioners board meetings?

S: Yeah, this is basically all the same, what I'm talking about, the meetings that we started going to. And I been recruiting this and telling them to get involved 'cuz it's about trying to save the children.

A: And the people that organize and run those things, what are they like?

S: Well, I only met Ms. Khadijah James and Ms. Maxine Shaw, and the Muslim guys, yeah, they very nice. They're very nice; they very nice. I haven't seen my case manager at one, but Ms. Maxine Shaw and Ms. Khadijah James and them, they very nice. They always make me do poetry.

Shug's network of support allowed her to keep tabs on what was going on within the Altgeld development. Going to the Central Advisory Council, LAC, and commissioners board meetings allowed her to keep tabs on what was happening within Altgeld and in the larger CHA. Through talking to her neighbors, CHA staff, and the young people she mentored, Shug sometimes received a heads-up before policy changes were made, or fights broke out, in the development. As abolitionist and Black feminist Mariame Kaba often says, "We keep us safe." Shug understood that better than most. It was through her wide sociopolitical network that she was able to start performing her poetry as a form of activism. Shug was able to communicate her wider vision and the fullness of her political imagination via her art and poetry. Through this form of art making and performance, Shug found larger meaning in her life.

The Creativity of Political Imagination

Pleasure and intellect are key expressions of political imagination. Central to the push for structural change is the labor to imagine what change could look like. As several scholars within Black studies have shown, important political work has been done amid the aesthetics of artists, activists, and organizers.[45] When I use "aesthetics" as a political term, I am referencing what my respondents see as beautiful. In the article "Beyond Mysterium Tremendum," Omar McRoberts explains this view of the aesthetic:

> [The aesthetic approach to the study of religious experience] presumes that people who choose to practice religion find the more mundane aspects of that practice beautiful; it then sets out to understand experientially the stylistic aspects of religious experience.[46]

Public housing residents who spend their time painting their walls, planting thorny roses, or mowing their lawn "find the more mundane aspects of that practice beautiful," and in that beauty they find pleasure. However, I argue that aesthetic choices, and the circumstances facilitating those choices, are connected to residents' self-perceived political power. As McRoberts notes, whether aesthetic choices are important or beautiful to me as a scholar is beyond the point.[47] The home is central to our lives.

The women I interviewed found beauty, pleasure, and a personal sense of power in the daily mundane aspects of housekeeping many might otherwise dismiss or fail to take notice of.[48] Zenzele Isoke's work beautifully articulates the vision embedded within the politics of homemaking:

> Homemaking, as an affective form of resistance, involves more than just being attentive to and providing care to individuals. It also requires building an enduring affective relationship to the physical environment. It is the imaginative political work that transforms the built environment of the city into a home: a place of belonging, a place of remembrance, and a place of resistance. Homemaking, then encompasses black women's efforts to build the will to resist the alienating and dehumanizing practices and ideologies that continue to ghettoize and minoritize black people.[49]

Isoke's research explains sociopolitical tools like the stylistic aspects of home and community upkeep. The respondents I interviewed placed a strong emphasis on creating spaces that were beautiful, not only for themselves but for their neighbors and loved ones. The desire to make their neighborhood beautiful motivated their ongoing effort to transform Altgeld Gardens into a home space capable of nurturing their sociopolitical community. By creating beauty and pleasure, my respondents found meaningful sociopolitical tools.

> An ethnographer of religion can reasonably, if humbly, try to relate to believers who find aspects of ritual or doctrine beautiful or sublime, even though that ethnographer is not directly concerned with the transcendent realms to which those religious expressions ultimately refer. We can try to appreciate or get "it," at least try to write about what "it" is, then speculate about the social significance of "its" appeal to believers.[50]

Like McRoberts, as a participant observer of a community unlike my own, I can humbly relate to residents who find lawns, walls, kitchens, a clean room, an old fishbowl, or a new bed beautiful in a way I may not initially be concerned with.[51] I can try to appreciate the meaning-making practice happening with the object, or set of objects, at the center of the individuals' appreciation. By connecting to their appreciation, I can attempt to make the connection between the moment and its larger sociopolitical significance. The creation of a "home" is a project in creating beauty and pleasure, as well as sociopolitical community. It is an attempt on the part of the individual to connect to a place that would otherwise be empty, dull, and neglected. By turning attention to residents who created beauty and pleasure within their homes, the observer can witness the moment aesthetics become a material representation of self-imagined sociopolitical tools.

Visionary

The politics of the aesthetics surrounding each home within Altgeld Gardens plays a significant role in my analysis of the last respondent case I examine in this chapter. Throughout her interview, Sofia frequently discussed feeling as if the blocks throughout Altgeld Gardens were tumultuous and completely out of her control.[52] However, consistent with Zenzele Isoke's conceptualization of the politics of homemaking, Sofia's home functioned as a refuge and a community resource.[53] She was a woman whose PPS fell in the domain of the visionary PPS. Sofia spent a number of years in school, as well as in the Altgeld Gardens community, and as a result she had a tremendous political imagination. Sofia knew a number of people within the Altgeld development, although interestingly, she indicated that she tried to keep herself at a distance from other Altgeld residents. Like Nettie, Sofia was among the first handful of respondents I interviewed at Altgeld in 2011. When I met Sofia, she was thirty-four years old and had been living in the Altgeld Gardens and Phillip Murray Homes off and on for most of her life. Most recently, she had moved back to Altgeld Gardens in 2009 after her daughter was born. In total, Sofia had three children, including a three-year-old daughter and a twelve-year-old son. She also had a fifteen-year-old daughter who had moved in with Sofia's mother after running away from home. Sofia converted to the Nation of Islam (NOI) in 2004, and her faith was an important part of her life.*[54] Significantly, Sofia referenced her own religiosity, as well as the ostracization she experienced as a NOI Muslim living in Altgeld, at length throughout the interview. All things considered, the previous fifteen years or so had been hard on Sofia, and she struggled with depression regularly. To add insult to injury, like other respondents who spent their childhood living in the Altgeld development, Sofia described an intense nostalgia for the Altgeld of her past, a place she described as beautiful and community centered.

---

* In his book *Islam and the Blackamerican*, Sherman Jackson describes the NOI as a Black American "proto-Islamic" group created in the 1930s, whose founders "were not so much *interpreting* Islam as they were *appropriating* it" (Jackson, 43–47).

A: That totally makes sense. When you tell other people you live in Altgeld, how do they respond?

S: Whoo, girl! Yeah. Everyone, like, "That's the worst project ever!" And it has gotten worse. Like I told a lot of people, back in the eighties it was beautiful. I loved where I lived. I never had a problem with living in Altgeld Gardens. But this now, these last couple of years, I've never seen so much madness in my life. And they going to hell faster than you can say boo. I hate it there. It's not a place to raise your babies.

This nostalgia for the "old Altgeld" was a consistent sentiment among respondents who had been living in Altgeld for twenty or more years. Another resident used similar language to describe Altgeld's previous incarnations. Ms. Barbara was seventy-seven years old when I interviewed her in 2012. Ms. Barbara moved to Altgeld Gardens with her mother when she was fourteen years old, before the Phillip Murray Homes had been built. When the Plan for Transformation policy started offering longtime residents a Section 8 waiver so they could rent market-rate apartments, Ms. Barbara took the offer.[55] She remained close to her lifelong friends who still lived in Altgeld. So much so, Ms. Barbara rented an apartment close by and asked to do our interview in the apartment of one of her Altgeld friends.

A: What was it like living in the Altgeld [Gardens and Phillip] Murray Homes? How would you describe your experience here?

B: Oh, it was beautiful when I was out here. My mother moved out here when I was fourteen? Yeah, I was fourteen, and it was gorgeous out here. Murray . . . wasn't out here then. It was my oldest brother; he was in construction, and he helped build those Murray Homes. But when we first moved out here, it was just Altgeld.

A: OK, so it was a lot smaller then?

B: Same size that it is now except for the little bit they put up where the Murray Homes are. It hasn't changed that much. It pushed some of the space, you know, some of the, like over there across the highway, there, that used to be all swamp. That's the way it was before they put the Murray Homes up.[56]

A: OK. Can you describe the community here?

B: Well, when I was coming up, it was beautiful. I can't say too much about it now because I don't live over here. I know people from over here, all that haven't passed, but majority of my friends that I grew up with, they've passed on. So I can't really say too much about anything. And I just moved from over here, let's see, three years ago? Yeah, three years ago. I lived in, in fact I was raised in Block 2. And then from there when I was grown, married, I was in Block 3. Then I moved over, then they transferred when they started remodeling, rehabbing these apartments, they transferred me over to Block 8.

A: So what made you decide to leave?

B: Because they don't have washing machines. See, I'm old, and I can't be, they just put those Laundromats up about a year and a half ago. Ain't even been two years. And I'm not going to come out of my house to go do laundry. So that's the only thing I have against this project. Other than that, I'd be right out here now.

A: What is [your new] place like?

B: It's nice. It's quiet. It's nice, but see, they furnish you the washer and dryer. I had my own washer and dryer. I had to get rid of it. Had to get rid of my ceiling fan. Housing just made you get rid of everything.

A: OK, so stuff you'd had your whole life?

B: Yeah. Stuff that's hard to get a hold to. It's no easy thing to work and accumulate washers and dryers and ceiling fans and this, that, and the other. Then you had to get rid of all this stuff.

Ms. Barbara moved out of Altgeld permanently after being moved around the development by CHA and then being asked to throw away a number of major appliances she had spent a lifetime saving up for. But it is important to note that, had Ms. Barbara not been on the wrong end of new policy changes via the Plan for Transformation, she would have spent the rest of her life at Altgeld. After all, she moved close by so she could remain close to her family and friends. This was a dynamic borne out in many of the Moving to Opportunity studies (the program that offered Section 8 waivers to public housing residents willing to give their public housing apartments back to CHA).[57] Instead of moving to the wealthier segregated neighborhoods Section 8 proponents encouraged, many public housing residents decided to stay in neighborhoods nearby, or at least very similar to, those of their old public housing development.[58] A lot of this was due to the desire to stay close to family and friendship networks.[59] But it was also due to the discrimination and prejudice many former CHA residents experienced when attempting to move to wealthier segregated neighborhoods.[60] Ms. Barbara's case was not unique. Many former CHA residents desired to re-create their homes near the communities they had developed over the course of generations.

Octavia is another respondent who had pronounced nostalgia for the beauty of the Altgeld Gardens she grew up in. Octavia was a fifty-five-year-old woman who, at the time of our interview, had lived in Altgeld for forty-six years. She originally moved to Altgeld Gardens with her mother when she was a young girl.

A: What is it like living in the Altgeld-Murray Homes? How would you describe your experience here?

O: Well, when I first moved out here, it was, it was OK, because I was young, you know, because when I first moved out here I was like nine years old, and it was so beautiful when I first moved out here. I mean, the people was nice. You know, it's still all right to me. You know, some people might say the neighborhood got rough, which it did because of the years that you didn't go up out here. But since I been out here half my life, they don't too much bother me. . . .

A: OK. Do people in government care about the people who live in Altgeld Gardens?

O: Me myself, I don't think so because if they did, Altgeld wouldn't be like it is.

A: In what way?

O: OK, I put it like this: OK, if they had any say-so about what's going on in Altgeld, they would try to help. Because in Altgeld it's a lot of homeless people out here. And these empty apartments, if they came . . . they haven't really actually fixed up, they could put some homeless people in there. You know, 'cuz it's not just all these homeless people don't have skills. A lot of these homeless people got skills. They can put them to work and help them fix up some of these apartments. That way it won't be so many abandoned apartments.

One thing that still strikes me whenever I go back through the interviews and field notes I collected during my time at Altgeld is the sheer range of language used to describe the same neighborhood. Within one interview, respondents like Sofia would tell me how beautiful Altgeld used to be, how much she used to love living there.[61] Shortly thereafter, she would be telling me how deeply she hated Altgeld and how desperate she was to get out. Similar issues came up in my interviews with Octavia and Ms. Barbara. During our conversations, they both described how happy they were to move to Altgeld Gardens with their mothers forty, fifty years ago. Yet

154 / CHAPTER 4

both had significant sadness about what Altgeld had become. Ms. Barbara ultimately decided she could no longer make her lifelong home work for her. In 2011, Octavia was still trying to make Altgeld work.

Respondents made clear connections between the government and the conditions they suffered through in Altgeld Gardens.[62] This makes sense, given that public goods, like public housing, can shape and inform the set of politics and political identities residents feel are available to them. Michael Lipsky argued that government bureaucrats (whom he refers to as "street-level bureaucrats") are often the first, and sometimes the only, meaningful interaction with the state over the course of an individual's lifetime. He argued, "Citizens directly experience government through [street-level bureaucrats], and their actions are the policies provided by government in important respects."[63] He goes on to say that while in an ideal world people would feel comfortable lobbying government bureaucracies for whatever they need, they are often socialized to adopt a set of behaviors more acceptable or palatable to street-level bureaucrats, like the individuals who work at the CHA. Unfortunately, as Lipsky points out, sometimes no matter what they do, marginalized communities fail in their attempts to receive support from the state. In *Arresting Citizenship*, Amy Lerman and Vesla Weaver argued that interactions with government institutions not only provide political socialization but also systematically constrain and alienate the politics of marginalized communities:

> Recipients of these and other social benefits come to view their contacts with the state as "a microcosm of government," generalizing their experience within the program to the broader nature and goals of the political system. Lessons learned through contact with social programs are lessons learned about government writ large, as contact with one part of government forms a "bridge" to perceptions of other aspects of the state. . . . Interactions with the state influence individuals' perceptions of their own political standing, membership, and efficacy. Institutions allow us to observe how the state treats and responds to people "like us."

I suggest that residents' lifelong experience navigating public housing, public housing bureaucrats, and the infrastructure of the development itself shapes their politics.[64] For example, hypothetically, public housing residents could be pushed into a more radical extrasystemic politics because their experience within CHA teaches them that "following the rules," being polite, and being nonviolent does not work when you are trying to get the state to fulfill your urgent material needs. The B.F.D.C. illustrates how, if used en masse, extrasystemic sociopolitical tools (like a rent strike) could create quite a bit of collective political power. Other residents could become completely politically and socially alienated (like Ceely) as a direct result of their experience living in public housing and decide they do not want to have anything to do with anyone, government included.

When I asked Octavia if she thought "people in government care about the people who live in Altgeld Gardens," without skipping a beat she told me, emphatically, no. After all, for Octavia, if the government cared about the people living in Altgeld, the CHA would not have allowed the abandoned-building problem across the development to have become so bad. Furthermore, for all the talk throughout popular public housing and welfare policy about "putting people to work," construction and maintenance jobs never seemed to go to people who were unhoused or living in public housing.[65] Respondents like Sofia also had tremendous cynicism about government. She was skeptical at best when considering whether the street-level bureaucrats working for CHA cared about Altgeld residents.[66]

A: What has been your experience interacting with the people who work there? (For example, the management company, CHA, government offices, social welfare offices, caseworkers, et cetera.)

S: As far as management and maintenance, arrogant . . . so arrogant. So just, "I'm better than you; you're nothing." Everybody out there don't want to be out there [living in public housing] for the rest of their lives, you know, so don't treat me as though I [do]. . . . Treat me as though I have some form of education, which I do. We all hit a rough spot in life, and unfortunately, sometimes we got to digress before we can progress, you understand what I'm saying? . . . So, the management team . . . tend to just, like, degrade you at times. Like for instance, I wanted to beautify my block. . . . So I retilled my land, my yard, and I wanted grass seeds . . . so after a while they figured we're not going to give her any more grass seed; she did have enough. I said, well, let me put up a fence. That way . . . I'm on a corner, so you know how corners are. So I said, let me put up a fence, that way I could be able to try, you know what I'm saying? I'm the only one trying. I get out; I clean up my neighborhood. They done fired almost all the maintenance workers, don't want to hire anybody, so they have one guy, maybe two, but I think one guy manning all the blocks right now.

However, in spite of all her challenges, Sofia worked hard to make her home in Altgeld beautiful. As she mentioned above, Sofia was constantly fighting a losing battle to keep the exterior of her home attractive. She told me her row-house apartment was on the corner of her block. As a result, there was high traffic, and children, police, maintenance workers, and numerous others were constantly cutting across her lawn so they could arrive at their destination faster. CHA would not allow her to put up a fence around her lawn. So every time Sofia laid down grass seed, it was quickly kicked back up and rendered useless.

Sofia talked frequently about the pride she had as a former homeowner, and she expressed a sense of shame about her inability to keep her Altgeld lawn up to her standards. Although technically the lawn was not her responsibility, Sofia had all but given up hope in the maintenance staff hired by CHA.

> S: Yes! [They] don't want to hire anyone [CHA does not want to hire additional maintenance staff]. It's just, it's horrible. So I got to clean up my own yard, which I have no problem with that. . . . My issue is help me to help myself. Let me put up a fence! What's the problem with me putting up a fence? I'm trying to beautify. They [CHA bureaucrats] was snooty, snotty. . . . So if you would have came to my home, you would have seen that the inside is beautiful, beautiful. Keep my [home] inside clean, immaculate, but the outside [of my home], it doesn't reflect what I got going on in. And it's depressing. It's depressing. So I'm at the point of my life, I'm just ready to just go because I don't see myself prospering there [Altgeld Gardens], because they make it hard for you to prosper there.
> S: Very soon. I see myself getting out of Altgeld Gardens before I fall by the wayside or one of my children fall by the wayside.
> S: When you got so much negativity and energy pulling you down and nothing lifting you up, you lose hope. You lose hope. I lost hope in me. I lost hope in me.

Throughout her interview, Sofia told several stories about the way CHA bureaucrats mistreated residents.[67] In this particular vignette, she was telling me about the way CHA bureaucrats looked down on her. Sofia frequently mentioned that CHA bureaucrats assumed that she had no education, that she was lazy and wanted to stay in public housing. It was clear Sofia had absorbed all the negative sentiments spread throughout the larger public sphere, and political culture, about Black women who live below the poverty line.[68] Being seen as someone who was "clean" and took care of her home was of the utmost importance to her. When she said, "So if you would have came to my home, you would have seen that the inside is beautiful, beautiful. Keep my [home] inside clean, immaculate, but the outside [of my home], it doesn't reflect what I got going on," Sofia was telling me that the exterior of her Altgeld row home did not reflect who she was. "It doesn't reflect" what she actually had "going on." Sofia and innumerable other residents did not make such an effort to clean up their blocks and beautify their homes simply for their own sake. It was also a means of reclaiming their own aesthetic power and fighting back against a CHA that insisted they live surrounded by abandoned buildings deteriorating by the day.[69]

By creating beauty in their homes and providing resources for others, respondents like Sofia exerted a subversive political power, meant to heal their own heart and the hearts of others throughout their community.[70]

A: What do you like to do for yourself?
S: Pray. Study. I like to close up and pray and study. That gives me so much peace. I love praying and studying. I found my peace in praying and studying. I don't have any hobbies anymore. Like I say, my hobbies is doing for others. That's my hobby, doing for others. What can I go out to do today to help somebody else? But as far as me, I get my blessings in praying and studying. That's where I find peace. I like to sew, and I like to cook. I love to cook, to cook for others, feed others, cookies, homemade cakes, everything, just cook. When I feel depressed, I cook, you know, to feed people.

The profound sense of strength and imagination behind Sofia's vision for herself, her family, and her community jumped out at me during our interview. Although she frequently spoke about the isolation and depression she had been plagued with since returning to her community, Sofia also frequently discussed her desire to be of service to the community she grew up in. While Altgeld often enraged her, it was also the neighborhood and political community her mother had raised her in. Shame was lurking beneath my conversations with Sofia and many other respondents. The stigma and disdain the respondents experienced as a result of being Black women, living in public housing, receiving welfare, and living below the poverty line was tremendous.[71] Respondents frequently reported cruel and judgmental treatment.[72] As in Shug's interview, the fear of Black children born and raised in Altgeld Gardens rang throughout Sofia's interview. As Susan J. Popkin noted, there is a particular stigma applied to Black children who grow up in Chicago public housing.[73]

There was a strand of anti-Blackness weaving its way through Sofia's interview, despite her Black nationalist roots. Although she was clear in her critique of CHA street-level bureaucrats (especially Black bureaucrats) who were consistent sources of class-based anti-Blackness, Sofia simultaneously directed similar class-based anti-Blackness and misogyny at the very community she prided herself on being a part of.

> A: Use whatever language makes you feel most comfortable.
> S: Well, we taught not to use "nigger," but . . . I want, want, want, want, want, want. And because you ain't going to give it to me, I'm going to go to somebody else and, yeah, I'm going to do it in your face, so what is what is; live with it. And it's like my neighbor told me . . . my neighbor told me . . . she said she was getting $474 a month too. And that's the most hustling girl I ever seen. She pregnant right now, so she can't hustle as much as she want to. I've never seen the character of women . . . when a woman tell you I will kill, destroy, I don't care what I got to do as long as I get a couple of extra more hundred dollars in my pocket, I'm going to do it. If I got to sleep with this man, this man, prime example . . . starting dating. I hadn't dated in over two years when I moved back to Chicago. I was celibate for over two years, and I started dating, and the guy I started dating, he got in with God, of course, because that was the only way he could have got in. My neighbor, not knowing that my neighbor was talking to him too.

While Sofia admitted the impossibility of $474 per month covering all the bills, rent, food, clothing, and other expenses for a multiperson household, she still seemed to feel an immense sense of disdain for a number of people throughout her community. When she caught her ex-boyfriend sleeping with a young woman who lived next door, Sofia accused the woman of sex work, despite it being an honorable form of work, particularly when you consider the many structural barriers that prohibited Altgeld Garden residents from long-term employment.*[74]

My point is simple. In short, people are complicated, as are their sociopolitical worldviews. While most if not all of the respondents I interviewed could clearly articulate the class-based anti-Blackness they frequently expe-

---

* See Chapter 4, the end of the subsection "Less Community and Fewer Politics."

rienced as a result of living in Altgeld and receiving various forms of welfare, that did not stop many of them from holding their own anti-Black animus toward certain neighbors. Usually, respondent anti-Black hostility was directed at the people lacking housing who lived full-time in the abandoned buildings throughout Altgeld. But it was also occasionally directed at Altgeld residents with severe drug addictions who, for the time being, had successfully hidden their addictions from the CHA. Ultimately, the sheer force of anti-Blackness within, among, and directed at Black communities living in public housing is an ever-growing storm of harm.

A: What kind of activities do you participate in? Are you involved in any groups or organizations?

S: I used to. I was so, Frontrunner, PTA, LAC, this and that. All you could think of . . . community this and community that. Tutoring, mentoring. I lost the drive and the thrive to do anything in my community. I lost it.

A: Why did that happen?

S: When I tell you I'm so depressed right now . . . but I know God got me regardless. I know God got me. . . .

A: Do you think you ever will participate in any activities at Altgeld Gardens again?

S: I see myself leaving very soon. . . . Like I said, a bullet just came through my house Saturday night. I see myself moving very soon, and I'm making provisions to make that happen.

A: So that was just cross fire?

S: It was cross fire, but two more inches and just because of a cross fire, my son could have been dead. It came through his bedroom window. The shrapnel of the bullet wrapped in the same cover that he was in; the actual bullet ricocheted through my house into my daughter's bedroom. It's time to go.

A: That's terrible. Yeah. Do you vote or participate in any political activities?

S: I do vote. Like I said, the last couple of years I haven't did anything. I was actually thinking about running for mayor for Indiana. I was, when I tell you I was deep in the community, had meetings with the mayor, had cleanup meetings, doing tutoring, mentoring, PTA president, just doing so much, working doing grant writing because I grant write . . . when I came to Chicago I had a thrill, and I had a thrive, and I went full force, and it's like this door shut, this door shut, nope, nope, nope, nope, nope. I just, you know, you lose that thrive.

It made sense that Sofia struggled with anxiety and depression. Despite her capacity for profound sociopolitical imagination, which birthed incredible visions for the future, she also dealt with shame, abandonment, and a pervasive sense of being surrounded by danger. Sofia's home and her family carried meaning for her and over her life.[75] However, she was unable to protect her home and family from the violent spatial context of Altgeld.[76] A shooting broke out in front of Sofia's home the night before our interview, and we rescheduled our interview as a result. While we were eventually able to reschedule our interview (we met at a workforce training program Sofia was participating in), the memory of the shooting stayed with her for weeks.

Notably, when I asked Sofia about her political participation, one of the initial things to come to her mind was the bullet from the drive-by shooting that ricocheted into her children's bedrooms. It was clear to Sofia that, whatever power voting and other sociopolitical activities on the development were able to generate, it was not enough to protect her family from Altgeld's violence.

As I mentioned earlier, Sofia's PPS fell approximately on the far right end of the PPS matrix, within the visionary domain and just on the edge of the liberatory domain. Her placement there was in large part due to her immense sociopolitical imagination. Sofia described herself as immensely creative. She liked handcrafting, cooking, and providing advice to her Altgeld neighbors. She had a number of ideas on how the daily lived experience of residents at Altgeld could be changed. She described herself as adept at writing grants and navigating the complex bureaucracies wrapped around welfare and public housing resources. It made sense to place Sofia on the far end of the political imagination spectrum. As someone who grew up living within the Altgeld development, Sofia knew quite a few people, some of whom she remained in contact with. She was not placed squarely within the liberatory domain because she had been limiting her relationship to the wider Altgeld sociopolitical community for quite some time when I interviewed her. Years of negative relational experiences on the development had led her to believe her only chance at achieving her dreams was to leave Altgeld as soon as she could. Her feelings toward other Altgeld residents meant she rarely participated in community or sociopolitical activities held on the development. This resulted in a PPS that was highly efficacious and highly cynical.

I found that many respondents who either were alienated from the Altgeld Gardens sociopolitical community or had wide but shallow relationships throughout Altgeld Gardens tended to vacillate throughout the inter-

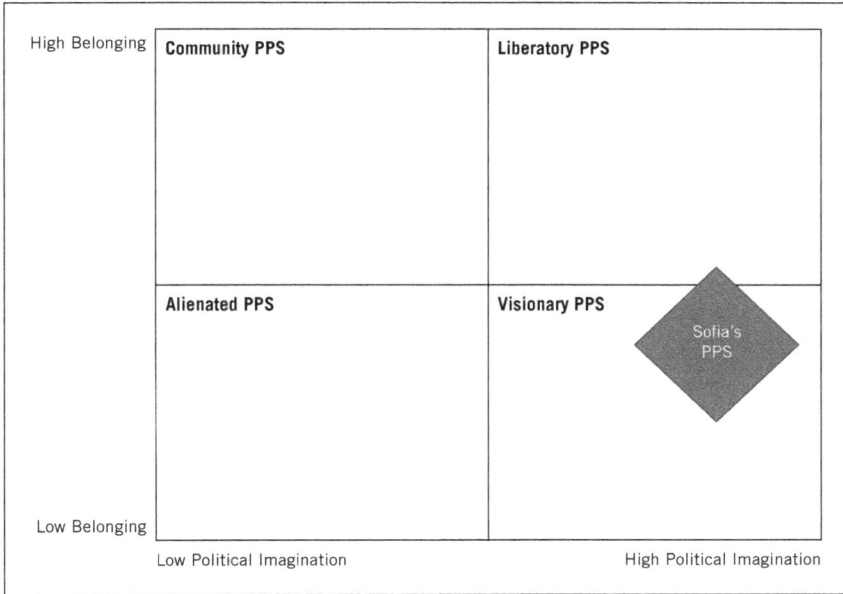

Figure 4.5 Sofia's Political Possible-Self

view about the true extent of their sociopolitical capacity. But there was also a rage burning beneath everything else.

A: Do you have friends at Altgeld?

S: Not anymore. I mean, there's people . . . I don't have no friends. I have associates. I socialize. Even my best friend from when I was in high school, me and her don't even get along, because I don't do what she do anymore. . . . Once in a blue moon, my uncle will come by whatever. . . . But literally I'm out there by myself. I'm out there by myself. . . . But I don't socialize. I stay to myself. I stay home most the time . . . I hate it there. I've never hated it there before. I used to love the Gardens. That's all I knew.

S: But it's time to go. I hate it there. Hate it.

There was a deep sense of hurt and betrayal throughout Sofia's interview. While she felt that CHA had done the right thing by allowing her to come back to Altgeld, she was clear that the government had abandoned her and everyone like her. Regardless, after a lifetime in public housing, Sofia knew quite a bit about how to find leverage within and around government bureaucracies. Her knowledge and expertise likely grew out of the cynicism she felt after watching the organized government abandonment of her community.[77] Ultimately, the complexity of Sofia's PPS went far beyond static definitions of alienation and efficacy. Her sociopolitical self-awareness was an ever-varying and malleable thing.

Conclusion

The sociopolitical tools communities access and use are not simple preferential choices.[78] Instead as Hanchard makes clear, the sociopolitical tools used by sociopolitical communities have everything to do with who they are, where they are, and what financial capital they have.[79]

> Resistance is often cast in terms of cultural practices, "weapons of the weak" (Scott, 1985), as if these were the sole modes of engagement with dominant social groups. Yet this response to oppression, I have argued, contains within it both the prospect of resistance as well as the logic of domination. How people resist, the "weapons" chosen, tell us as much about the nature and conditions of social and political struggle as specific acts of resistance themselves.[80]

When communities or groups are physically dislocated, the state illustrates its capacity to isolate entire communities from their friends, family, and social supports.*[81] In this way, "geography [is] a racial-sexual terrain."[82] In other words, geography becomes the space in which domination is exerted over marginalized Black people. In turn, geographies create limitations on, as well as unique opportunities for, marginalized communities seeking to exert their sociopolitical power.[83]

All political practitioners must be concerned with the sociodemographic features of the people who live within neighborhood sociopolitical communities, but we should also be concerned with the environmental, aesthetic, maintenance, and spatial realities of neighborhoods as well. To fully understand the sociopolitical identities of marginalized communities, scholars will need to clarify the ways that ecological, spatial, and geographic factors in turn shape the sociopolitical tools of residents.[84] In short, what neighborhoods look and feel like matters for democracy.[85]

---

* Here I am referring to the CHA's Plan for Transformation policy. This policy led to the demolition of most high-rise public housing buildings in Chicago. Some residents were moved to new neighborhoods, townships, or suburbs, during the Move to Opportunity CHA policy. This policy demolished public housing and moved some residents to the suburbs. For more information on the Plan for Transformation and the Move for Opportunity, please see Chapter 4.

5

THE LIBERATORY AXIS OF
POLITICAL BELONGING

Introduction: The Sociopolitical Communities of
Black Low-Income Neighborhoods

Throughout my research on the politics of marginalized Black communities, one truth consistently came to the forefront in discussions about political identity: it begins in the local community.[1] To be invested in national or even city politics, people need to feel they belong to a neighborhood or a group of people living in their local community.[2] Without a sense of belonging, some respondents haphazardly noted that, yes, they felt like an American or a Chicagoan, but it rarely seemed to result in visible sociopolitical tools. In *Avoiding Politics*, Nina Eliasoph clarifies the value of belonging to the development of sociopolitical communities. She asks, "How do citizens create context for political conversation in everyday life?" She concludes:

> Without a vibrant public sphere, democratic citizenship is impossible: there are no contexts to generate the kinds of selfhood, friendship, power, and relations to the wider world that democracy demands. The point is dual; participation in the public sphere helps cultivate a sense of community, so that people care more and think more about the wider world; and second, participation becomes a source of meaning-making power.[3]

164 / CHAPTER 5

In this chapter, I consider the role of public housing as a Black enclave public sphere and a sociopolitical community where some respondents felt they could belong. My work takes Eliasoph's framework and builds on it through an assessment of the intersections of multiple marginalized identities and their impact on a sense of belonging to the local sociopolitical community. Specifically, this chapter focuses on the y axis of the PPS matrix, the representation of individual sociopolitical belonging.

As I mentioned in the prior chapters, the vulnerability of CHA residents to the authority of the government occasionally destabilized their ability to establish and act upon a coherent sense of sociopolitical community.[4] However, residents were frequently able to retain their local sociopolitical communities or build new ones. Among the respondents I spoke to, a sense of individual belonging to their local sociopolitical community was frequently built from a shared identity of being poor, Black, and often, female. In other words, the shared experience of living with multiple intersecting high-stigma marginalized identities functionally reinforced their bonds with one another.[5] In the early years, Chicago public housing held a greater capacity to serve as a Black enclave public sphere where communities of residents could exchange ideas and social resources.[6] Unfortunately, the Plan for Transformation required a forced dislocation of many residents.[7] As a result, some residents' sense of self became more individualized and isolated from communitarian ethics. However, some women had relationships within their community and felt they belonged to their local sociopolitical community. This sense of belonging facilitated the establishment of networks that helped them feel safe.[8] Those social networks also seemed to facilitate the development of more visible sociopolitical tools. In the context of Altgeld Gardens, building community included making friends with neighbors or classmates and also creating resources and systems of support that reinforced an internal feeling of safety and security.[9]

Respondent Case Studies

As I mentioned in the Introduction, I am using Chapter 5 to provide further insight into the belonging axis of the PPS framework. To be more specific, both cases presented in this chapter fall along a y axis that goes from alienated to community within the PPS matrix (as shown in Figure 5.1).

The extent of a person's feeling of belonging to their neighborhood or their neighbors is an important contextual clue to discovering their relationship to their local sociopolitical community. Individuals who lack a sense of linked fate to their residential community are more inclined to avoid using any visible sociopolitical tools.[10] If a person experiences an

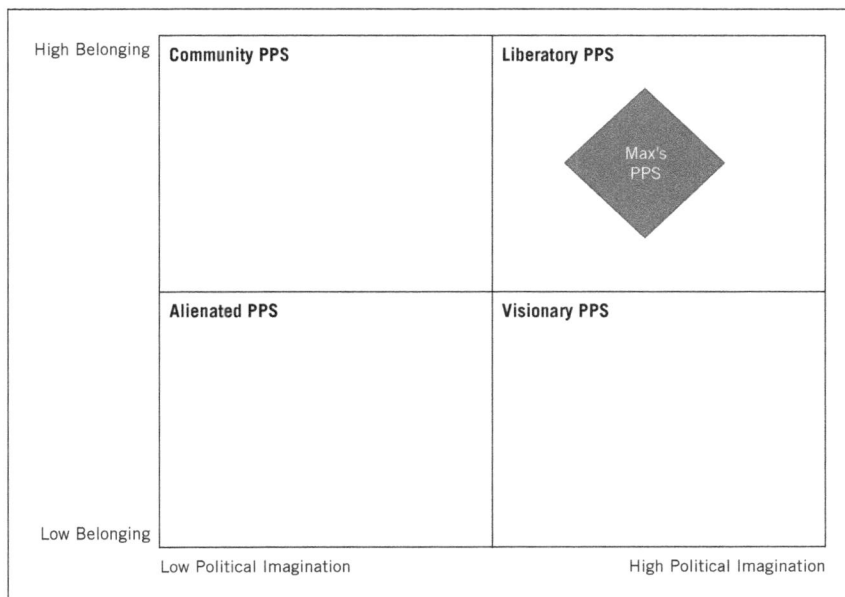

Figure 5.1 Max's Political Possible-Self

increasing sense of isolation from their local residential community, they may acquire a set of behaviors referred to as political "alienation."[11] Past research has consistently indicated that there is a relationship between spatial residential context and the cocreation of political identity.[12] Additional research has shown that social networks, as well as welfare policy, can shape individual politics and political behavior.[13] This chapter builds on that research by examining if the spatial contexts of public housing, as well as public housing bureaucracies, contribute to the formation of resident political identity, specifically via their impact on sociopolitical belonging.

Given the centrality of local sociopolitical community to individual well-being and sociopolitical development, I share a small example of a CHA housing policy that did not support the maintenance of multigenerational sociopolitical communities within Altgeld Gardens. The following vignette is from field notes I took during a Altgeld LAC meeting I attended in April 2011.

Khadijah James, the LAC president, ran the meeting according to Robert's Rules of Order. Ms. James mentioned they would not be doing an "old timers' picnic" this year. The old-timers' picnic was

> an event where former residents of Altgeld Gardens came back for a daylong picnic in the Altgeld Gardens Park. According to Ms. James, CHA took issue with this event, so CHA was trying to shut it down. The news was met with significant displeasure from the audience, in the forms of grunts and "humphs." . . . But Ms. James quickly let the audience know they would replace "old-timers' day" with "family day" to escape the suspicions of the police and CHA.

It was not clarified why CHA street-level bureaucrats did not want former residents to come back for a day of reconnecting with friends and loved ones currently living in Altgeld Gardens. But within the rationale for mixed-income public housing, I consistently noticed that policymakers seemed to believe keeping poor people away from one another was what was "best" for them.[14] When U.S. welfare and public housing policy analysts discuss what will "help poor people succeed," a core belief seems to be that economic success cannot happen if poor Black people develop, grow, and maintain multigenerational networks and communities.[15]

Amid debates about the "failure" of Chicago public housing, one of the key data points pundits refer to is the tendency of families to stay in public housing for generation after generation.[16] This point of view was consistently reflected back to residents via CHA street-level bureaucrats.[17] When I attended a CHA Central Advisory Council (CAC) meeting in April 2011, I noted the following vignette in my field notes:

> Another resident issue seemed to be that CHA residents were living in broken down and overcrowded apartments. Current residents were being made to wait, while new people were being moved into the new developments. The old residents were threatening to expose the CHA to the media around this issue. The resident who spoke on this issue said, "nobody cares about us, but us." Mr. Smith, a CHA street-level bureaucrat, said the following: "this project called public housing is meant to help families move on, not house you forever. . . . I know this is a tough economy . . . but it has also forced us to help more new families. . . . Public housing is not meant to serve the same families for the rest of their lives, we are trying to help families become self-sufficient and move on. . . . You are not going to get everything you want . . . you have to stop this 'us' vs. 'them.'"*

---

* Mr. Smith seemed to be a CHA street-level bureaucrat with a lot of authority. I saw him frequently at the public CHA meetings across the city that I attended in 2011 and 2012. However, he never once identified himself or his role in CHA.

Critics frequently cannot understand why individuals would want to stay in public housing, so they immediately point to laziness or some sort of cultural deficiency as the reason families living below the poverty line want to put down roots, develop a sense of community, and ultimately create a space and place they can call home.[18] But this way of thinking has never made sense to me. As sentimental as it may be, most of the people I have met and interviewed over the years desired a place where they belonged, a place that felt like home.[19]

Given the centrality of home to our social, political, economic, and even financial well-being, how do you develop a sense of belonging when your right to put down roots within your neighborhood and local sociopolitical community is constantly challenged? I argue that understanding how the sociopolitical bonds of belonging are created, solidified, and strengthened within the spatial context of Chicago public housing is critically important. It illustrates the sociopolitical importance of a sense of belonging to facilitating political empowerment within Black marginalized communities. Within the United States, whether we are allowed to participate in each election is directly connected to our ability to prove to state and local governments that we are residents of a particular neighborhood.[20] In practice, this facilitates political organizing, get-out-the-vote efforts, and political canvassing organized around the local sociopolitical communities of specific residential neighborhoods. As I will show throughout this chapter, a sense of belonging to specific sociopolitical communities and public spheres is truly foundational to the creation of political identity and sociopolitical tools in the U.S. context.

For many in the United States, having a place to come home to in a neighborhood we like and enjoy is something we take for granted. But for Black women living in public housing, this desire is often pathologized (as illustrated in the vignette above).[21] Many in the United States only confront the reality of people without housing, or without residential security, when walking past a soup kitchen or a shelter. But approximately 554,000 people in the United States are technically without housing.[22] In Chicago, the number of people without homes is approximately 5,657, and 1,561 of those people are "unsheltered," or physically living outdoors.[23] For Chicago public housing residents, the possibility of homelessness is ever present. The demolitions of high-rise public housing developments and CHA's failure to find housing for many displaced residents make that point ever clearer.[24] At Altgeld Gardens, some long-term residents were moved out of apartments they had previously lived in for decades.[25] Given these policy and spatial realities, this chapter is informed by the narratives told by respondents who were attempting to go about everyday life amid all this uncertainty.

When activist Max Shaw (a respondent whose narrative is featured in this chapter) reported that entire voting blocks were destroyed by the Plan, she meant that multiple social networks connected through their multigenerational residence within Chicago public housing developments were separated from the places they identified as home.[26] In essence, this policy of displacement led to an erosion of sociopolitical community, creating large networks of residents who subsequently experienced a sense of disconnection from their residential neighborhoods. Networks who may have formerly been invested in making sure their communities evolved for the better were later consumed with escaping to the next place. As postdemolition networks appeared in Altgeld, older residents observed the shift in values separating the residents of formerly cohesive blocks from the new tenants. Unlike the older residents, many of whom had chosen to reside in Altgeld decades before, many new residents were placed in Altgeld through no choice of their own.

A sense of belonging is a critical proxy required to understand the individual PPS. To what extent does the individual feel they belong to their neighborhood? To their city? And to their nation? Because of the stigma, surveillance, and lack of access to public resources that came with living in the Altgeld Gardens public housing development, many respondents understood the geography they belonged to as being limited to a few neighborhood blocks.[27] As scholarly literature and ethnographic studies can confirm, the activism in public housing is often limited to these few blocks, not simply because residents have limited time and resources but because it is where they feel safest.[28]

Political scientists Cathy Cohen and Michael Dawson examined the extent to which impoverished neighborhoods shaped the political identity and engagement of Black residents.[29] They found that increased levels of poverty can shape the politics of Black Americans:

> Neighborhood poverty has a devastating effect on politically important indicators of social isolation, even after controlling for individual characteristics, including individual poverty. . . . The neighborhoods with the very highest concentration of poverty (above 30%) are particularly effective in restricting the social and networking opportunities of African Americans living in them. . . . Data indicate that the effects of contextual poverty on political participation are evidenced when the threshold of severe neighborhood poverty (over 21%) has been crossed.[30]

Critically, Cohen and Dawson found the higher "the concentration of poverty within a neighborhood, the more pessimistic community citizens become regarding any hope that a solution can be found for their problems."[31] In short, the spatial qualities of a residential space can have immeasurable effects on the development of an individual's sociopolitical tools and PPS.[32] As Cohen and Dawson note, these findings have critical implications for the full functioning of democracy. If people are limited in their ability to access institutions, let alone in their ability to shape and lobby those institutions, then the system has gone tragically awry. Therefore, studying the forces contributing to the sociopolitical development of Black communities living in poverty is critical important.[33]

The Power of Belonging within a Sociopolitical Community

When I interviewed Maxine "Max" Shaw, she was approaching her fiftieth year of living in Altgeld Gardens. As a younger woman, she had left the development for a handful of years after taking a job, but she returned once she began having children. When I asked her why she chose to return to Altgeld Gardens, she cited the support she had there. After growing up in Altgeld, Max had access to babysitters, her mother, her friends, and other family members who were able to help a young mother as she struggled to get on her feet. Max's mother was responsible for the founding of a local organization that did tremendous work around environmental justice. As a result, Max had the opportunity to travel around the country with her mother. Max also visited the White House, and over time she met three sitting presidents. Accordingly, it should be no surprise that Max was incredibly politically active. Max continued her mother's work after Ms. Shaw died and even after Max's children grew up and left the development. She conducted voter registration drives every year, she was responsible for organizing multiple protests on the development, and she also consistently raised enough grant money to pay everyone who worked in her organization's office, although she was unable to pay herself. As a result of Max's commitment to sociopolitical activism, she lived in poverty for most of her life.

Despite living in poverty, Max was and continues to be exceptionally active in both the public and the private spheres. In addition to running her organization, she also politicized, and in some ways radicalized, multiple women throughout the development. Many of Max's neighbors, who later became respondents, told me that she dragged them to meetings, protests, and other activities throughout the development. In this way, not only did Max's sociopolitical community remain active both publicly and privately but Max also single-handedly helped many adult women living in Altgeld Gardens become active members within various sociopolitical communities. Because of her political engagement, Max seems like a good place to start when thinking about how women living in public housing understand their own power and the power of others.

Since Max lived in the Altgeld development for most of her life, she understandably had close relationships with many of the maintenance people, as well as the managers who oversaw the bureaucracy within the development. In stark contrast to many of the respondent cases I've already discussed, whenever Max needed something fixed in her home, she was able to get the repair taken care of relatively quickly. On the other hand, some of the respondents I interviewed sometimes waited weeks, if not months, for things as simple as new light bulbs or as critical as new locks. Interpersonal relationships were everything when it came to psychoemotional well-being and personal safety on the development. Because of her many personal relationships with the privately owned management team, Max was able to keep a cute little dog she took with her everywhere (around the development, there was quite a bit of debate about whether dogs are actually allowed in Altgeld apartments). Max also took great pride in her apartment: the walls were painted, and her kitchen was quite clean. It is not an overstatement to say that Max had a strong sense of her own personal power. If she needed something from management, she was able to get it, and if it required bending the rules ever so slightly, Max knew how to make it happen.

A: [I've] heard different things, that management doesn't let people plant flowers. . . .

M: Yes, they do. They used to give them to you, back in the day. Back in the day, they used to give you flowers to plant. But you can do whatever you want to do now. That's not true. If I want to decorate my yard, I can go decorate it. If I need the tools to be able to decorate my yard, they'll give it to you. You just have to leave your state ID or something like that. And then you bring the tools; you get your state ID back. So that's not true. Now, what might be true, they might not have the tools; somebody stole them from the inside. It may not be available 'cuz they don't have it no more. But no, you can fix up your own yard. So that's not true. People just don't fix them. Maybe 'cuz I used to do that stuff so much when I was a kid, I would not plant a flower.

A: Yeah, I feel the same way after working in my mom's garden.

M: You see, no, no, no. Vegetable garden, raised bed . . . I will not garden, period, or take care of a yard. I will pay [somebody] to mow . . .

A: I feel the same way.

M: . . . to mow my yard, or something like that. But I know if I had to put flowers, I mean I got to water and maintain, I'm not doing that. I'm not with that, so I just keep my yard. I sweep in front . . . my neighbor real good; we'll sweep stuff up, but I'm not into that because I hated it when I was doing it when I was a kid, I guess, unconsciously.

When Max was a child growing up in Altgeld Gardens, her mother made her work in the garden every weekend. As a result, in her adult life, she had no desire to garden, maintain vegetables, or plant flowers. However, unlike a number of other respondents in the development, Max was well aware of the CHA gardening and yard maintenance rules, as well as how to access tools and other resources should she decide she was interested in gardening. Despite her lack of interest in yard upkeep, in stark contrast to Sofia from Chapter 4, Max had the resources to ensure her lawn was well cared for. Notably, she also had enough credibility with the local neighborhood kids to keep them from running across her lawn. Max frequently employed young men from around the neighborhood—many of whom she mentored—to do tasks around the house for her, like mowing the lawn, fixing a window, and doing other errands that would keep them out of trouble for the day. Max was able to build relationships within the neighborhood and create a home space where she felt comfortable and safe. She also had a tremendous sense of pride in the environment she created for herself. Altogether, Max had a sense of personal power, which fueled her daily participation within the local sociopolitical community.

In this way, a sense of belonging to a neighborhood community seemed to play a large role in shaping an individual's sense of power, agency, and authority throughout their life. When an individual felt they did not have power over their place of residence, it became even more challenging to create a sense of power, and by extension, sociopolitical confidence, in the same individual.

A: Yeah. Are people treated equally in this society?

M: Hell, no, you know that.

A: Who isn't treated equally?

M: The poor. The poor is not treated fairly, because if the poor don't know their power and understand the relationship of the power that they do have, you know . . . power's not defined by wealth. You know what I mean?

A: Absolutely.

M: And power is something . . . power is something that you want to make change or make it better and it gives you that dedication to make that change, you know. So what we don't understand is our power is among the people, but a lot of people think power is associated with how much money you got.

A: Right. Is that a power that you think you have?

M: I don't know . . . no . . . I have an influence power. I can influence people better than trying to acquire people to be on my side. I can influence you. And I can motivate you so my powers is in motivation too because I can motivate you and I can present a picture in a way that you can understand it.

Max's point about influence being a form of power is significant. She had the power to influence others, to go wherever she wanted in the development, and to do as she pleased with her apartment. It is a "power-to" that built her confidence as a member of the sociopolitical community, in large part because of the love that sociopolitical community had for her.[34] Max's friends, political comrades, and neighbors loved her deeply. It was not simply control; it was Max's ability to shape things according to the political imaginings she cocreated with other members of their sociopolitical community. Power, from this vantage point, lay entirely within Max's sense of her own ability to act, as well as to influence others to act. Max could not control how any woman on the development would act on their newfound political sensibility. After all, part of the political education she provided to residents involved convincing them they were also free. Max had a power of influence that facilitated her capacity to provide education in political skills and community building.

As a child, Max was fortunate enough to have a mother who taught her how to navigate government bureaucracies of all shapes and sizes. As a result, Max's personal sense of power was birthed in her ability to advocate for herself from an early age. This personal sense of power was further cultivated by always living in a home where either she or a member of her family felt, and behaved, as though they were fully in control of their home. What is often left out of conversations about public housing residents is the role the home plays in the individual life. As Howard Mansfield makes clear, the home is where we begin the process of cocreating who we want to become:

> All houses are mysteries. In all houses we are struggling to live the life we should; we are confined cluttered, slothful, or ambitious, planning, rebuilding, self-improving. In all houses we are hiding out, from the neighbors, from the world out there, from the world in here, from each other, from ourselves.[35]

In this way, residents of public housing are similar to everyone else. The individual spaces and places we live in shape the sociopolitical possibilities we can imagine for ourselves.[36] As one example, my mother has lived in the same house in Detroit for almost forty years. She remodeled it with her father and my father right before she had her first child (me). Over the years, she has built relationships with neighbors and local businesses, all of which played a core role in helping her care for her children, as well as her father before he died. Needless to say, the neighborhood and the house she has spent most of her adult life in carry a lot of meaning for her. As she approaches her midseventies, she has no intention of ever leaving her home. She has spent years making her house and her neighborhood beautiful in a way that speaks to her as an individual. Her community provides a source of support and refuge that could not possibly be replicated anywhere else.

In numerous studies of neighborhoods, one social scientist after another notes that people tend to not leave their neighborhoods, mostly for the same reasons as my mother.[37] Puzzlingly though, despite the generally common experience of becoming attached to home and its surrounding community, critics of public housing policy don't seem to think about the same experience among the poor. Perhaps one of the biggest problems in media and academic analysis of Black populations living below the poverty line is the propensity to treat groups on the margins as though they are alien. It seems fairly obvious that every community, including marginalized Black communities, seeks the safety and stability of home. Max was clear, she stayed in public housing for almost fifty years because Altgeld Gardens is where her mother raised her. Altgeld was where Max and her mother developed a community that sustained them politically, emotionally, and spiritually. Altgeld was Max's home and her legacy.

Practically, some of the respondents I interviewed may never make enough money to care for their families and pay for childcare during the day while they work. For many, staying in Altgeld meant they had a free (or nearly free) babysitter in one neighbor or another. Practically, emotionally, and spiritually (there are more than three churches within the Altgeld Gardens development and a countless number surrounding the development in other neighborhoods), the connections and attachments respondents developed within public housing left them just as deeply rooted to their communities as their wealthier American counterparts.[38] It is critical to consider these embedded relationships and attachments when thinking about how and why one's connection to home can be a source of sociopolitical empowerment, or alternately alienation.

In this way, the ability to call your place of residence "home" becomes political. In today's political climate, access to a home (regardless of whether it is rented, owned, or passed down) becomes a surprisingly classed thing, and women living below the poverty line are very much aware of this.[39] During and after the renovation at Altgeld, many women were moved from apartments they had lived in for decades. Along with the move, residents were required to get rid of laundry machines, ceiling fans, and other household items that were no longer allowed in the renovated development. While the CHA hailed these changes as improvements, many women interpreted them as a loss of agency within one of the few spaces they felt they had autonomy. In this way, housing decisions made by housing authority street-level bureaucrats, on both the local and federal levels, can chip away at the power residents feel they have over and within their households.

I asked every respondent whether she had heard of the Plan for Transformation, and many had no idea what I was talking about. Older residents did know, however; they had been required to get rid of several expensive household items and appliances during the renovation. While my mother has the power to go to a neighborhood board meeting and protest any major changes (a political power to act),[40] many, if not most, Chicago public housing residents were simply informed of the changes and asked to throw away certain belongings when they were moved. In my mother's neighborhood, board meetings are held during the evening after everyone is home from work. Most Chicago Public Housing Authority meetings started between 9:00 A.M. and 10:00 A.M., during the workday. For residents able to attend public housing meetings (a handful), the extent to which their influence was considered in final decisions was indiscernible.

These realities are critically important to remember when thinking about the way the politics of homemaking can add or detract from an individual's sense of belonging to their local sociopolitical community.[41] By slowly chipping away at resident sociopolitical agency, public housing authorities can also begin to chip away at their efficacy and, ultimately, their sense of belonging.[42] As cliché as it may now sound, as feminists have said many times before, the personal is political, or maybe it is better said that the private is as political as the public.[43]

Max's PPS fell approximately dead center within the liberatory domain (the far upper right corner of the PPS matrix). She received a thorough sociopolitical education from her mother from a very young age. Max also finished high school and college, earned a master's degree, and traveled nationally and internationally. As a result, her sociopolitical imagination was extensive, and it was appropriate to place her near the uppermost end of the political imagination spectrum. Because she had lived at Altgeld Gardens most of her life, Max had an extensive sociopolitical network throughout the development, Chicago public housing, and the city of Chicago. She was also generous, kind, and social. As a result, Max had a tremendous sense of belonging to her local sociopolitical community, and it was appropriate to place her near the uppermost limit of the belonging spectrum. Overall, Max's case is a fantastic example of how much can be learned about political identity and sociopolitical tools by paying close attention to the role belonging plays throughout the individual life.

Given Max's ability to negotiate the bureaucracy of the CHA, she was able to create a home space that maintained her own internal power. In addition, Max had interpersonal relationships that facilitated her safety throughout her lifetime. Her highly visible sociopolitical tools, among other skills, sustained her activism within the community organization whose leadership she inherited after her mother's death. Max's mother taught her how to be a political activist and how to work the system. Her upbringing gave Max a sense of personal capacity that facilitated her work across the country. As I mentioned briefly, she also had a community of friends and family who looked out for her and provided her with emotional and financial support. Throughout her interview, she talked about both of her children (now young adults in their twenties and thirties) and the ways they ensured she could take care of herself. More than anyone else, she talked about the women at the development with whom she shared most of her life.

A: Are there any other kinds of activities you participate in at Altgeld? Besides your work with your organization?

M: Well, I network with a lot of organizations on a local or national level. That's what we do. I'm focusing more on engaging the community. I'm starting a group called [organization name redacted] . . . well, I'm part of a membership that got started bringing communities on the southeast side together. And we call ourselves [organization name redacted]. We fight these developments that's coming in, the fire range the city trying to propose.

[I] want to put these manufacturing companies in there, but they're using tires as their means of burning, which would be hazardous to people health. The quality of life is already diminished because of poor air quality now. We not against economic development. It's just that we want safe, healthy, clean development for this area. Why we always get this polluting stuff? So that's why [organization name redacted] can help, and we work real well together. . . . Also, I'm the one who [helped] Regine Hunter [become a] community politician; golly, she flying with it! You know! I inspired her to get that talk together. So it's inspiring and training that you do, that I'm trying to do, that's a level of empowerment because long as somebody else doing it, you're depending on something. It's all about being independent or voicing your concern. . . .

A: Anything social? Any social activities?

M: My social thing . . . my girlfriends, we hang out, or we may come over here and go over there. I might go out and party some, but you know, I did that at a very young age, and my mama told me when you get old enough to do it, you ain't going to want to do it. And she didn't lie. So it's all about, if it's not stimulating me or teaching me or educating me or collaborating with each other, all that other stuff is not important for me. That's my social stuff too. I like going to listen to somebody being socially conscious about something. I do take trips, go visit friends. My daughter took me to the Bahamas last year though . . .

A: Oh, that's nice.

M: . . . for my fiftieth birthday. They tried to give me a party; I was like, nah. You know, they trying to give me a party this year. My birthday March 11, so they trying to give me a party this year. My niece is really geared up with this party, and I'm like, I'm not feeling this party, you know.

For Max, one of the most important aspects of her life was empowering other women to take on their own political projects. Two of the respondents in my sample were Max's neighbors. They were new residents who moved in a year or so before I began visiting Altgeld Gardens. Both women were politically educated via their relationship with Max. It began by Max teaching them how to get maintenance to address their concerns quickly, and from there, she was able to motivate them to become more active throughout the Altgeld sociopolitical community. Max also mentored Regine Hunter, another woman who lived in the development. Initially,

Regine had little to no interest in anything remotely political. By the time I met Regine years later, she was leading a protest against a local grocery store, serving on the LAC executive board, and working as a neighborhood block captain (an elected position).* When Max called her a "community politician," she wasn't joking. Ultimately, Max's case taught me that it was the everyday pieces of their lives that developed their sense of connection, commitment, and belonging to their local sociopolitical community.

Does Policy Shape Political Identity?

Given how central the social networks and interpersonal relationships were to the respondents I interviewed at Altgeld Gardens, it is particularly important to think about how public policy can encourage or thwart the development of local social networks and local sociopolitical communities. Because people living in poverty are more vulnerable to changes within public policy, this is particularly important when studying the politics of marginalized populations, such as Black women living in public housing.[44] Political scientist Traci Burch argues that although "the obvious goal of government policy is to affect people, usually by encouraging or enabling them to do things that they might not otherwise do," governments "may also restructure future politics in unexpected ways" when they bestow benefits.[45] Along the same lines, Joe Soss argues that welfare policy influences behavior through specific program designs and that welfare clients develop program-specific beliefs about the wisdom and efficacy of asserting themselves. He writes, "Because clients associate the agency with government as a whole, these program-specific beliefs, in turn, become the basis for broader orientation toward government and action."[46] Soss found that recipients of Aid to Families with Dependent Children (AFDC) are less politically active (here, he defines political action using traditional measures) than recipients of Social Security Disability (SSDI) and attributes the difference to the designs of these two programs.[47]

While SSDI recipients did not feel they were stigmatized or berated by program officers, AFDC clients viewed the agency as a "pervasive threat in their life, as a potent force whose limits were unclear."[48] According to Soss AFDC clients determined that engaging with the bureaucracy was almost futile.[49] This, in turn, led them to believe that engaging with government more generally (using traditional measures) was also futile. This finding is critical when considering if living in public housing can shape the politics of residents, as Lerman and Weaver make clear:

---

* For Regine Hunter's story, see Chapters 1 and 2.

Welfare positions recipients as "undeserving" through stigmatizing rules and requirements for receiving aid. In some places, for instance, individuals receiving benefits must submit to home searches and drug tests, toil in prisonlike garb along highways, and take any job given them.[50]

Lerman and Weaver note that when welfare recipients' experiences with government bureaucracies—be it a housing authority, a welfare office, or a job placement agency—are mostly negative, the likelihood they will develop a sense of hopelessness about their political agency becomes exponentially higher.

> The design of political institutions is politically consequential because it provides a direct view of how government works, what role individuals are expected to play and their worth vis-a-vis other citizens and the state. Through social programs, citizens garner important material resources, but also receive a blueprint of the character, capabilities and commitments of the state. These lessons feed back into citizen participation and engagement.[51]

This is why the study of spatial contexts and local sociopolitical communities is critically important. As I pointed out at the beginning of this chapter, CHA street-level bureaucrats can control everything from which friends resident children are allowed to play with to whether the leaseholders are allowed to have a reunion barbecue for former residents. It is astonishing to think that government bureaucracy has such complete control over the friendships, families, and communities of everyone participating in public housing. For Black people living in poverty, freedom of association simply does not exist. If a formerly incarcerated child comes to visit his mother briefly, she can be immediately evicted and permanently banned from public housing. Every day, bureaucrats who implement government policies can have a profound impact on the politics residents adopt.[52]

But the impact of housing on individual political identity is not limited to policy; the shape, form, and condition of neighborhoods matter as well. In her work, Clarissa Rile Hayward echoes Pierre Bourdieu in her push to think more deeply about space, context and citizenship.[53]

> As people engage in practical activities in such physical spaces, his [Bourdieu] claim is (as they sow and reap in the fields, as they buy and sell at market, as they cook and care for the sick and dying in

the house), they learn and relearn implicitly the meanings built into material forms.[54]

Residents learn politics (and their political value to the public sphere) via the material form of public housing itself.[55] Neighborhood placement and design have a profound impact on everyone's political development.[56] Each neighborhood teaches distinctive lessons about what a citizen could and should look like, as well as what residents can reasonably expect from the state over their lifetime. Like Eliasoph, I am arguing that people learn what politics look like via their experience within neighborhoods.[57]

Vesla Weaver, Gwen Prowse, and Spencer Pison show that many citizens are not limited to learning politics from friends and coworkers, or even from formal civics education classes and organizations.[58] Instead, marginalized populations, in this case Black people living below the poverty line, frequently learn about the state via personal experiences and their surroundings.[59] These conclusions are consistent with my own research. This knowledge becomes part of a community knowledge network operating within the Black enclave public sphere(s) of public housing developments, welfare offices, and the street.[60] Respondents like Max, Toni, Shug, and Khadijah were deeply plugged into this community knowledge network. They took this knowledge and used it to educate their friends and neighbors throughout Altgeld's local sociopolitical community.

For respondents who felt they belonged to the local sociopolitical communities within Altgeld, this informal information dissemination often kept them safe. Even if a respondent didn't personally experience a violent interaction with the state, when it came to the police, they almost always knew somebody in their community who did. As you'll remember from Chapter 2, the local police screamed at Toni and ransacked her apartment. Later she watched them do the same thing to her neighbor. Significantly, by witnessing what happened to her neighbor, Toni learned a new strategy for managing this unique gendered form of police brutality experienced by Black women behind closed doors. Often, discussions with neighbors and other members of their local sociopolitical community helped respondents put their personal experiences into context and gain a deeper understanding of their political implications.[61]

Relationships, Safety, and Belonging

Respondents who had relationships within their community—that is, women who felt they belonged to their local sociopolitical community—

were able to establish networks that helped them develop sociopolitical tools. Building local sociopolitical community could include making friends with neighbors or classmates and also collecting resources and systems of support that facilitated an internal feeling of safety and security. Take Sinclair James, for example. She moved to Altgeld Gardens in 1987 after testifying at a trial against a resident in the Robert Taylor Homes. Not only was she active in the Altgeld community (in terms of going to local community organization meetings and participating in other forms of politics) but Sinclair also knew how to access CHA resources. When Sinclair needed an emergency transfer from CHA because her life was being threatened, she was successful in her self-advocacy. Because Sinclair had a deep foundation of belonging to her local sociopolitical community and significant experience navigating CHA bureaucracy, she was able to advocate for herself and get what she needed.

During her time at Altgeld, Sinclair became well connected and knew most of the community organizations and resources available to seniors within the development. This knowledge about the community and the inner workings of the development itself allowed for a PPS that provided Sinclair with enough confidence to care for herself and her community.

> A: So have you ever had any problems with robbery or being stuck up?
>
> S: My son.
>
> A: So he was robbed [while] walking around [Altgeld]?
>
> S: Going over here to the garbage. Yeah. A boy walked up to him and his friend and stuck them up. He didn't have but ten dollars on him, and I always told my kids if you got some, let it go because your life is more important. You can always get that money again.
>
> A: They had a gun . . . ?
>
> S: The two boys, my son and the other boy, said they didn't know if he had a gun or not, but he was in his coat with his—they don't know if it was finger or gun. You know, you can't take a chance 'cuz you don't know. So he gave it to them. But they've been doing a follow-up with me, you know. The police. And the boy, we contact him, and I came and talked to him, and he told me, "OK, I'm going to give your son his money back 'cuz I was wrong."
>
> A: Oh, so you went and talked to him.
>
> S: Mm-hmm. I had seen him walking to the Rosebud Farm, and I had asked him, "Why did you take my son's money? Why did

you do that?" He was like, "I'm sorry, we didn't have no food," this, that, and the other. And I was like, "Well, you shouldn't do stuff like that 'cuz you could of easily got yourself killed." But now he waves at me and everything.

A: And you weren't afraid to go talk to him?

S: No, because I had heard this kid had been sticking up other people out here.

A: So that was pretty brave of you to go talk to him!

S: Yeah, yeah. [*Laughter.*] I used to do security work back in the day and stuff, so I try to be a little cautious. You don't come to a kid in a rough tone of voice and everything; sometime you get a little information out of them, you know. And the problem really what's going on and the reason he's doing it.

Instead of being paralyzed by fear when her son was robbed at gunpoint, Sinclair used her knowledge of the community to find a solution. She was able to find out who the child was and what he had been up to through various social networks within Altgeld. Knowing who the child was and where he was from transformed him from some anonymous "violent predator" to a kid from the neighborhood who was obviously having some problems. This allowed Sinclair to feel safe and secure enough to go find the child and find out why he was behaving that way. As the transcript makes clear, it turns out that the child didn't have enough food to eat at home. Critically, Sinclair did not experience this incident as an emotional violation; instead, she experienced it as a problem that she had the wherewithal to solve. Sinclair's lifelong experience in public housing taught her how to intervene in the space in a way that protected and benefited herself and her family.

What is crucial here is to think through what it means to experience violence. Often, violence causes an individual to feel that they have lost control of their lives and their bodies in some fundamental way.[62] First when Sinclair was under threat of violence in the Robert Taylor Homes and then when her son was robbed, she was able to assert a level of political capacity over what that violence could do to her life. It is the experience of not feeling fully violated by Altgeld Gardens that allows Sinclair a fuller expression of her sociopolitical tools.

A: What are your interactions with the police like? What is your opinion of them?

S: I'm cool with them. I go to some of the CAPS meeting. . . . And I used to go to them. They have them at the end of the month all the time. Sometime it used to be on a Wednesday or Thursday, and that is Beat 005, I think they gave me.

A: What are those meetings like?

S: They tell you what places that they, when people call in, senior citizens, they tell you what places that they done shut down, drug houses, places that was abandon people was calling and saying they were seeing people going in and out. They tell you about when the next meeting. Sometime they give little trinket gifts, things like that, door prizes, but they mainly try to keep the community together. If people not together, it's going to fall apart.

A: So you find them useful.

S: Mm-hmm, I go every now and then. Yeah, and they tell you about the next places that they looking at, because they say somebody called in and say it's a vacant lot here but they notice it's an abandoned car there and people been sleeping in it, and they go check it out and everything. It's been pretty reasonable though.

By going to the CAPS meetings held every month at the local police station, Sinclair was able to stay informed about what was going on in her neighborhood. Her participation allowed her full knowledge of whatever crime or violence was reported to the police in Altgeld Gardens. This is significant because, again, it moved physical violence and crime from some unknown specter that could attack at any time to a spatial reality that had certain logics and targets. By continually gathering information, from both the police and local community organizations, Sinclair was able to create a more balanced view of what was happening within her local sociopolitical community. In this sense, knowledge really is power. Critically, Sinclair's engagement with the local CAPS meetings also helped her build the institutional relationships that could assist her during her time of need. As I noted earlier, it was Sinclair's institutional relationships at the Robert Taylor Homes that facilitated her emergency transfer when her life was in danger. In the same vein, Sinclair built similar institutional relationships with the local police, CHA employees, and local activists at Altgeld Gardens.

By gathering information, building institutional relationships, and interacting regularly with their neighbors, Black women living below the poverty line in neighborhoods with high rates of violence can develop a PPS with room for them to express visible sociopolitical tools. Sociopolitical tools are not limited to singular (traditional) political actions. Instead, they are a set of behaviors that happen in collaboration with other people to shift the reality of things within a given sociopolitical community. Community-based collaborative efforts are central to the BFDC of *politics*:

The acts, ideas, or set of behaviors named as "politics" are rooted in the effort of two or more people attempting to use power to create (or limit) possibilities via acts or behaviors in service of a political goal. Specifically, this is the set of behaviors people engage in together to have possibilities created (or limited) by (or for) their targets.

This belief in the possibility of a future, including a cleaner neighborhood, access to jobs, and a safe, daily lived experience, allowed respondents like Sinclair to fully participate in their own lives, publicly and visibly. To put it simply, respondents who believed that the material reality of their world could change had sociopolitical tools that reflected that core belief. In this sense, Sinclair's PPS leaned toward the more efficacious end of the political spectrum.

A: When you interact with people who live here, what do you typically talk about?

S: Most the time I be talking about going out of town, talking about the kids, because I was just telling some people just two weeks ago I notice, you know I don't mind the kids playing basketball behind my house and everything, but when they leave they papers, cups, and trash back there, that's what bothers me. Even though I tie a bag on that bench right there, they still throw it on the ground. So I have gotten so now I don't too much even say nothing. I just tie the bag and a lot of times come in here. The reason I don't say nothing 'cuz my son play basketball with them too. . . .

A: Do you feel like a member of this community?

S: Yeah, somewhat, because I know a lot of people and I don't know a lot of people, which really with the new peoples that have moved out here, I don't know hardly, just some of them. Like they's some that they moved from Robert Taylor. There's two of the ladies I know that moved from Robert Taylor out here. She was saying, "Oh, I hate it over in this block." They talk about Block 10, that they hate it over here. They be like, "Oh, I wish they'd have moved me over where you at because you got it peaceful and quiet and y'all keep it clean right along here." I say the reason we keep it clean too because a lot of times when people go to the liquor store and the store up here, they come through here. 'Cuz we get good compliments a lot of times in the summer. People be like, why is y'all stuff so clean through here! When you get to the other part, they be like, what happened over there!

I be like, no, it's not like that; it's that we all on this row, we try
to keep it a little decent, you know.

In this vignette, Sinclair described her block's commitment to keeping their
part of the development clean. Even though there was a lot of foot traffic
through their block because of their proximity to the local liquor store and
the basketball courts, they managed to keep their space clean from debris.
While it may seem like a relatively trivial and politically benign behavior,
in fact, this could not be further from the truth.

In a Black enclave public sphere like Chicago public housing, a refusal
to give in to presumptions about the development or to the benign neglect
forced upon residents by CHA became a means through which residents
could assert political self-determination.[63] In short, neighborhood cleanup became another signal of Sinclair's belief in the political possibilities
for her future.* Respondents I interviewed who were not only depressed
but totally politically disengaged from the local community had no desire
to leave their homes, let alone participate in activities with their neighbors. Sinclair's desire to clean up stemmed from a deep desire to improve
and provide support to her block and the larger Altgeld community.

A: Do you think you could make a difference by participating in
politics?
S: Yes, I believe maybe so, 'cuz at one time I had wanted to work
for Carol Moseley Braun. We have did literature work for her
[passing out flyers]. We have had kids go out and do literature
work for her, but they didn't want to go back. I don't know why.
But we did it one time. I think we went down Seventy-Ninth
Street. Passing out the literature in the door. We took some of
our kids and did it for her. But I don't judge nobody because I
say maybe one day I might be out there.
A: So you think you could be a politician one day?
S: Maybe, yeah, maybe.
A: But you definitely feel you have the ability to.
S: Yes.

---

* This is not meant in any way to perpetuate broken windows theory, which has been widely
debunked by scholars (Harcourt, *Illusion of Order*; Michener, *Fragmented Democracy*). Instead, I am trying to make clear that the respondents in this study had a diverse set of sociopolitical tools. For some women, it included running for block captain; for Sinclair, it included
cleaning up her block. The point is that as political scientists we have to provide room for
respondents to articulate their sociopolitical tools, in whatever form they may take.

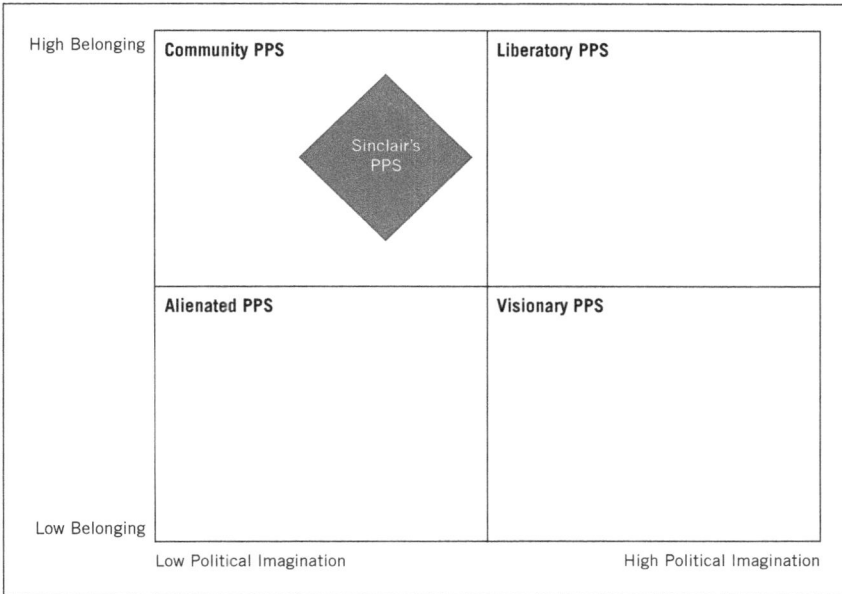

Figure 5.2 Sinclair's Political Possible-Self

In this vignette, Sinclair clearly articulated her commitment to politics in a more traditional sense. She had a PPS that was coherent and acted upon. Throughout the interview, she mentioned her participation in get-out-the-vote activities for various Chicago politicians like Harold Washington, Carol Moseley Braun, and her district alderman. Not only did she participate in these activities but she also brought along neighborhood kids from her former residence, the Robert Taylor Homes, and her current residence, Altgeld Gardens. In this way, Sinclair acted as a political bridge maker, linking younger people with political activities that they otherwise may not have been able to access.[64]

Sinclair's PPS fell approximately right of center within the community domain (the upper far left corner of the PPS matrix). When I interviewed Sinclair, she had lived in Chicago public housing for most of her life. In October 2011, she had been leasing an apartment at Altgeld Gardens for seventeen years. Before that, she had lived in the (now-demolished) Robert Taylor Homes. Like most respondents with ten or more years of lived experience within Chicago public housing, Sinclair was knowledgeable about and adept at navigating CHA and welfare bureaucracies. As a result, her sense of belonging within Altgeld and the larger Chicago public housing Black enclave public sphere was extensive. Most of her political imagination was focused on creating an environment within Altgeld's local sociopolitical community that could provide comfort, aid, and solace to the people who lived there. Sinclair spoke extensively about how much she had learned via her relationships with Khadijah James, Max Shaw, and other friends and family who lived in Altgeld, as well as in other public housing developments. Sinclair's PPS is an important example of how critical local community-based networks can be to the political development of individuals and communities.[65]

Because of her sense of belonging to the wider CHA Black enclave public sphere, in contrast to other respondents, Sinclair was relatively fearless in her willingness to pass out leaflets in a variety of neighborhoods. For Carol Moseley Braun's campaign, Sinclair took the children down Seventy-Ninth Street from east to west. Sinclair also regularly passed out flyers throughout Altgeld for several different community organizations. This activity required self-confidence and a relatively impenetrable sense of safety. As ethnographers have noted, many people living in low-income neighborhoods do not venture farther than the major streets that enclose their community.[66] In Chicago, this was especially the case as the danger of crossing various gang lines throughout the city was always present.[67] In Altgeld, as more and more new residents moved in from across the city, the rates of violence continued to rise. This was due in no small part to the arrival of people with opposing gang affiliations who used to live in other public housing developments demolished by the Plan for Transformation. Many continued to be placed in Altgeld Gardens throughout my year interviewing and observing the local sociopolitical community. Yet, in the face of this, Sinclair did not allow her mobility to be limited; her sense of security and safety provided her with the opportunity to do political work.

Conclusion

It's not enough to say that poor people and individuals with less formal education have lower levels of political participation.[68] Social scientists have established that individuals living in poverty have unique and nontraditional means of expressing their membership in the political community.[69] This chapter illustrates the need for more refined analyses of the social networks within friendship groups and local residential neighborhoods. Scholars of political networks have done an excellent job of measuring the connections between individual sociopolitical tools and their social networks.[70] However, places like Altgeld, where there are spatial characteristics like high levels of residential isolation and high rates of violence, could potentially complicate those studies.[71]

Marginalized populations, particularly those living below the poverty line, require an analysis that accounts for spatial obstacles to an active and fully developed political identity.[72] The cases presented here illustrate that the spatial conditions of neighborhoods, beyond the level of income, need closer consideration. The violence an individual has experienced and the level of interconnectedness they feel within a community are critical factors in understanding political behavior. Whether an individual is living in poverty or not, if they are surrounded by daily violence and believe that they have no meaningful way to protect themselves or their family, they are unlikely to connect with their local sociopolitical communities, politically or otherwise.[73] It is meaningful that many of the respondents who felt threatened by the violence within the community placed their children in schools outside the Altgeld Gardens development complex when they had the resources to do so (car, time, etc.). When interviewing individuals who live in urban environments with high rates of crime and violence, political practitioners benefit from asking respondents about how they perceive and manage crime and violence (and whether the respondent perceives violence, crime, or other spatial realities as an impediment to their sociopolitical engagement).[74] Political practitioners benefit from considering how violence, neighborhoods, and friendship networks function in relationship to the sociopolitical development of U.S. citizens.[75] Given the disproportional impact public policy has on the lives of people who live in poverty, we must also continue to pay close attention to the relationships between housing and welfare policies and the sociopolitical development of the people affected by those policies.[76]

6

CONCLUSION

Introduction

In *Redefining the Political*, I am continuing the Black feminist project toward a more expansive vision of *politics* and the *political*[1]—a vision that considers the unique and stigmatized intersections of the marginalized in addition to race and gender.[2] This framework of sociopolitical community provide a framework for understanding how people with multiple intersecting high-stigma identities when cocreating community based political power. As Joy James points out, any set of intellectual ideas grounded in Black feminism must make central the practice of community building.[3]

> Not unique to, but nevertheless a strong characteristic of, black feminisms are expressions of responsibility and accountability that place community as a cornerstone in the lives and works of black females. Community in fact is understood as requiring and sustaining intergenerational responsibilities that foster the well-being of family, individuals and as people, male and female. Even if the idea is discredited by the dominant culture, the knowledge that individual hope, sanity and the development come through relationship in community resonates in black politics.[4]

As several Black feminist political theorists have argued, a commitment to community has been and continues to be a foundational aspect of Black sociopolitical life.[5] The function of the Black feminist definitional criterion (BFDC) of *politics* and the *political* is to recognize the PPS and sociopolitical tools of Black diasporic people globally, as they occur in the world. This capacity is rooted in the BFDC's capacity to recognize and document the real political work of building intentional local sociopolitical community. An expanded BFDC of *politics* and the *political* must also consider the way an individual's socioeconomic status and culture in the United States can often overdetermine how they are treated by the government and other political practitioners, according to the *identity politics* of their communities.[6] Additional definitional criteria of *politics* and the *political* should also consider the intersectional stigma of gender identity, nationality, first language, disability/ability, neurodiversity, ambulation, and sexual orientation, to name a few.[7]

Political scientist Zenzele Isoke (2013) argued that the key terms used to describe Black lived experiences and Black politics frequently fail to accurately depict Black marginalized communities writ large and Black marginalized women living below the poverty line specifically.[8] Because of this language dilemma, scholars like Michael Dawson, Cathy J. Cohen, Zenzele Isoke, Michele Berger, Rhonda Y. Williams, Melissa Harris-Perry, Lester Spence, and Michael Hanchard, among many others, continue to develop theoretical frameworks and conceptual tools meant to facilitate the accurate documentation of nontraditional (extrasystemic) political engagement within marginalized Black communities.[9]

Throughout the book, I have focused on a central question: What sociopolitical concepts and frameworks are capable of recognizing and documenting the styles of political engagement, political rebellion, and political identity creation used by marginalized Black women within the United States? Black feminist and Black politics scholars have worked hard to develop and publish a clear understanding of the Black sociopolitical world.[10] The goal of this project was to continue the work of these scholars via a focus on marginalized Black women living below the poverty line. Through the use of Black feminist political theory, Black politics scholarship, existing conceptions of extrasystemic politics, and original ethnographic data, I developed two theoretical frameworks: (1) a BFDC of politics and the political and (2) the PPS. Both theoretical frameworks are a reconsideration of the holistic political identity of individuals within marginalized Black populations.

I argued that to fully understand the sociopolitical power of Black women living below the poverty line, studies must build upon the existing scholarship.[11] Developing additional theoretical and conceptual tools capable of fully seeing, analyzing, and describing the vast nontraditional, and extrasystemic, political expression of the Black sociopolitical world provides a deeper look at the multiple Black publics—in particular, the enclave public sphere of marginalized Black populations within the United States.[12]

Both frameworks feature (1) the flexibility to recognize the theories and concepts developed by scholars whose work precedes mine and (2) the capacity to facilitate the recognition of traditional, extrasystemic, and subversive sociopolitical tools in the field, to support continued theory generation specific to marginalized Black folks throughout the United States. It is critical to develop clear conceptual categories and theoretical frameworks capable of seeing a politics that often goes unseen.[13] I argue that the PPS can help develop a fuller understanding of the sociopolitical tools and political identities of marginalized Black women in the United States who live below the poverty line. The PPS framework facilitates additional clarity through its rejection of rigidness and its flexibility in embracing differing spatial realities, as well as a variety of socio-political-cultural contexts. However, it is also analytically precise enough to be useful to academics and other political practitioners.

There is a need for more culturally relevant and flexible understandings of political identity. Additionally, there is a necessity for a theoretical framework capable of continuing the process of bringing the many expanded understandings of *politics* and the *political* in conversation with one another across disciplines and diverse creative forms. I developed the BFDC to facilitate this interdisciplinary process, as well as to assist in the recognition of extrasystemic politics (or political engagement) when in the field.

The PPS is made up of two concepts: (1) a sense of belonging to a sociopolitical community and (2) political imagination. In *Redefining the Political*, I delved into several respondent case studies to demonstrate why studying respondent sociopolitical belonging to a residential local community is deeply important. It also matters whether an individual respondent articulates a sense of political imagination. A clear and holistic understanding of the politics of marginalized Black populations cannot be achieved without first understanding spatial context, sociopolitical community, and the public spheres the populations of interest have access to.

Ultimately, the book argues, belonging and political imagination are two key factors in accurately recognizing and documenting individual political identity within marginalized Black communities. Through the study of Black feminist scholarship within the social sciences, Black politics scholarship, and an original ethnography of thirty-one Black women who live (or used to live) in Chicago public housing, I found Black women living below the poverty line in the United States who developed a subversive and extrasystemic politics. Their politics were facilitated via informal information dissemination within their local sociopolitical community, as well as intercommunity political education. Through community-based political education, respondents enabled the cocreation of individual political identity and the capacity to move from one PPS domain to another.

In the two empirical chapters (Chapters 4 and 5), I discussed what the PPS looked like in the context of the Altgeld Gardens sociopolitical community. I used each case as a study illustrating the theoretical frameworks I developed in this book. Chapter 4 focused on the axis of political imagination and the role pleasure, intellect, and alienation play in understanding the individual PPS. I argued that political imagination absent interpersonal relationships connecting the individual to their residential sociopolitical community seemed to result in an individual politics disassociated from the public sphere and the local sociopolitical community.

In Chapter 5, I considered the role of public housing as a Black enclave public sphere. Altgeld Gardens functioned as a sociopolitical community where some respondents felt they could belong. Specifically, this chapter focused on the *y* axis of the PPS matrix, the PPS representation of individual sociopolitical belonging. Throughout my research on the politics of marginalized Black communities, one truth consistently came to the forefront in discussions about political identity: it begins in the local residential community. To be invested in national or even city politics, respondents needed to feel they belonged to a residential neighborhood or a group of people living in their local community.

In this concluding chapter, I walk through what this work of Black feminist political theory adds to the study of U.S. politics and its understanding of the sociopolitical lives of marginalized Black women living below the poverty line. From there, I discuss the eight key findings of my research. Finally, I briefly discuss whether this work ultimately matters and what work I am leaving for future scholars to accomplish.

The Contributions This Project Has Made to U.S. Politics Research

Redefining the Political has contributed to theories of political identity formation by developing theoretical frameworks capable of helping scholars recognize and document the sociopolitical identities of people within marginalized Black communities. The first theoretical framework, the PPS, illustrates a more expansive context through which to understand dynamics between local sociopolitical communities and individual political imagination. When thinking about political behavior as a matrix instead of a static binary, political researchers have room to consider a wider range of activities and behaviors as political. As was demonstrated in this project, the PPS allows us to understand what traditional political behavior studies could not initially see: politics is just as much about cultural forms of engagement in the public sphere as it is about out how we have traditionally understood the formal work of democracies.[14]

Key to my findings is how critical it is to develop a sense of belonging to a local sociopolitical residential community and to actively cultivate political imagination. Belonging could function as a stand-in for membership in a sociopolitical community, as it indicates a level of investment and commitment to entities beyond the self—a quality that is key to the relational nature of politics and the political. While a respondent may not be able to respond to traditional politics questions like "Who is your congressional representative?" many of the respondents I interviewed in Chicago knew and had even engaged previously with their local alderman or their neighborhood block captain. These neighborhood-level expressions of politics are important to measure when studies continue to demonstrate how pressed for time and energy individuals living in poverty are.[15] If we want to understand the politics of marginalized Black communities, we must understand to whom and to what they are committed. Ultimately, I found that respondents who had experienced multiple forms of violence and also lacked interpersonal support seemed to develop an isolated PPS almost entirely focused on their individual future outcomes.

Membership within a local sociopolitical community can and should be understood as a type of political power. I suggest that the sociopolitical membership of Black women living in poverty helped respondents develop a politics of self and community governance. The sociopolitical education of the respondents I interviewed placed a high value on developing the ability to navigate government institutions and to navigate their communities safely. Even those who felt most victimized by their surroundings expressed a politics of self-governance that dictated how they chose to show up in the world. For respondents who faced simultaneous oppression in the public and private spheres, their perceived ability to self-govern was a critical source of power and efficacy building that shaped the personal and political arc of their lives.

Last but not least, this research meaningfully contributes to a greater understanding of key concepts like *extrasystemic politics* and *sociopoliti-*

cal community. In the previous chapters, I outlined the connection between sociopolitical communities and *power.* That is, you cannot have one without the other. To have power is to have the capacity to act on your own volition and to compel others to act. Being a member of a sociopolitical community allows an individual to act politically and to compel others to act within a sociopolitical framework. In short, within a democratic context, membership within a sociopolitical community can be a form of power, assuming you have the political imagination to make it so.

The theoretical development of these two conceptual categories (belonging and political imagination) is crucial when considering power and oppression.[16] While it would be easy to say the respondents in this study had no power, politically or otherwise, that would be disingenuous at best. The better question to ask is what kind of power, if any, these women have. By assessing whether they have power and then defining power through their own words and perspectives, I was able to gather a more nuanced set of political criteria, sensitive to the context of their lived reality and subsequently their everyday politics. The respondents described their power as the ability to direct their daily lives. It is an autonomy that allowed them to decide how they raised their children, whom they spent time with, and what they ate, even within a sociopolitical context that frequently demanded otherwise.[17] With this in mind, next I consider the eight central takeaways from my research in the field, the archives and past scholarship.

Key Findings

First, I found that spatial characteristics like violence, isolation, interpersonal relationships, and an individual sense of power and self-governance over residential space can have a significant impact on the look and feel of an individual's sociopolitical tools and political identity.

Second, in the BFDC of politics and the political, I argue that politics and the political must be defined in relationship to power. But, as Iris Marion Young persuasively argued, politics and the political must also be understood as relational.[18] My ethnographic data confirmed that the relationality of politics and the political requires that they happen within a community context.

Third, Black women continue to resist sociopolitical oppression at every opportunity, in spite of, and sometimes because of, their many sites of intersectional stigma. Political scientist Zenzele Isoke explains this dynamic via an exploration of the inner character of Black women's sociopolitical tools, a set of behaviors and political experiences that she calls resistance politics:[19]

> Resistance politics are deeply spatialized and rooted in the politics of collective memory. They are realized through the intentional creation of social space in which activists revise and reformulate narratives of black political resistance. . . . Through testimony, truth-telling and spontaneous communal storytelling, black women imbue the ailing physical and political infrastructure of the city with meaning and instigate counter-hegemonic forms of social action. They actively create geographies of resistance by mobilizing disparate pockets of the black communities (i.e., black queers, hip hop heads, anti-violence activists, and antipoverty activists) to mitigate the interlocking effects of black heteropatriarchy and white economic hegemony.[20]

Black feminist scholars regularly point to the work of storytelling, institutional memory, guardianship of ancestral history, recordkeeping, community creation, volunteering, and community education as central sociopolitical tools to and for Black women and their communities throughout the Afro-diaspora.[21] Many ethnographic and qualitative projects point to the political and social role Black women play within their communities all over the world.[22] So much so, Keisha-Khan Perry noted in her study of Brazilian social movements that "Black women shape the everyday and structural conditions of those living 'below the asphalt.'"[23] In other words, Black women across the Afro-diaspora serve as a key and binding tie, holding their communities together via political work made invisible by the mainstream public sphere. Isoke's description of resistance politics serves as a poignant reminder of the way Black women have historically and contemporaneously engaged in sociopolitical tools that elude traditional definitions of politics and the political.[24]

While I was in the field, I regularly found Black women engaged in sociopolitical tactics like storytelling, informal information dissemination, and a "politics of homemaking." This politics of homemaking prioritized the creation of sociopolitical power via self-governance and the reclamation of Black women's right to make their homes a site of beauty, comfort, sociopolitical consciousness-raising, community building, and mutual aid.*[25] Similarly, my experience interviewing respondents in the field rei-

---

* In "The Politics of Homemaking," Zenzele Isoke argues that "homemaking is a central mode of Black women's political resistance in Newark. It stretches beyond individual women's work in households and the sphere of domesticity. Instead, homemaking involves creating

fied Terrion L. Williamson's assertion that storytelling is a methodology of Black life.[26] Thus, the Black feminist theoretical foundations of this project require that I acknowledge the unique intersectional position of poor Black women living in Chicago public housing and the way those identities can, have, and likely will continue to shape their sociopolitical tools.

Fourth, mainstream feminists, Black feminists, and Black politics scholars have argued for the last few decades that there is a need to continue the work of expanding the definitions, and indeed our entire conceptualization, of what constitutes politics and the political.[27] In *Grassroots Warriors: Activist Mothering, Community Work, and the War on Poverty*, Nancy Naples argues that contemporary definitions of politics in the U.S. political mainstream only serve to obscure, and indeed erase, the politics of women, and women of color in particular.

> When we adopt a definition of politics that is limited to voting behavior, membership in political clubs or parties, and running for public office, we obscure the political practice of community workers, the grassroots warriors. Since much of the community workers' activity occurred outside the formal political establishment, traditional measures underestimate the extent of their political participation. Many of the resident community workers I interviewed rarely engaged in electoral politics, especially through established political parties, although many participated in voter-registration drives. Few expressed an interest in running for public office. Rather, they challenged the authority of city and state agencies, landowners and developers, and police and public-school officials. They maintained a close watch over the actions of elected officials to ensure that the interests of their communities were served. Furthermore, they were vocal participants in community-based protests against racism and other forms of discrimination in their neighborhoods.[28]

The erasure of the politics of women of color is not simply about the everyday acts that make up individual sociopolitical tools, although they are a part of it. It is also about a consistent theme that shows up time and time again in some of the research done about communities of poor women of color and women of color writ large; in short, there is a belief that poor Black people do not participate in mainstream politics.[29] However, as political

---

homeplaces to affirm African American life, history, culture, and politics. Homeplaces are political spaces that Black women create to express care for each other and their communities, and to re-member, revise, and revive scripts of Black political resistance" (Isoke 117).

scientist Michele Berger argues, "commonsense" models of politics do not represent the politics of all U.S. citizens accurately:

> The idea that all participation comes from general self-interest is a model that does not resonate with women's forms of participation and reasons for participation (Acklesberg 1988). Women's involvement in charitable organizations to community groups has been an important part of women's political landscape (Cottonmouths 1987; Naples 1984).[30]

Still, electoral idioms that say "you vote with your feet" or "you vote with your pocketbook" are all based on the same premise; as Spence argues, the U.S. neoliberal political framework only values how much money the individual can produce via their "human capital."[31] But scholars like Naples show that "women community workers . . . view citizenship as something achieved in community and for the benefit of the collectivity rather than as an individual possession."[32] Similarly, Berger argues that "community work captures a more-comprehensive spectrum of American women, and it potentially provides an in-depth mapping of informal political participation."[33] Whether Black feminist scholars are studying the sociopolitical impact of Black women in Chicago, Newark, or Brazil, the conclusion remains the same: the political work of Black women is rooted in a community context beginning in the local residential neighborhood.[34]

Black and gender studies professor Terrion L. Williamson argues that the central terms of U.S. mainstream political culture fundamentally fail to accurately depict marginalized communities writ large, especially Black women living below the poverty line.

> *Scandalize My Name* is thus an inquiry into the representability of black social life primarily by way of poor and working-class black women and the narratives that have come to define them in public culture. . . . I consider how the logics of representation, coded by terms such as "value," "visibility," "citizenship," "morality," "respectability," and "responsibility," necessarily fail to account for the reality of black lived experience.[35]

What is particularly important about Williamson's intervention is that it lays bare how the language of U.S. political culture writ large, words like "citizenship," "responsibility," and "respectability," fails to adequately map onto the sociopolitical everyday lives of Black women. *Redefining the Political* continues the legacy of Black politics and Black feminist scholarships, in their work to continue correcting the colonialist impulses underlying the urge to apply a one-size-fits-all set of political descriptors and theories to a diverse set of groups regardless of their socio-political-cultural histories and contexts.[36] It seeks to create an opportunity for political practitioners to stop and ask themselves if their political language choices are truly representative of the political languages used by the communities they are embedded in or doing outreach to.

The colonialism embedded within mainstream U.S. political and academic cultures becomes ever more important when taking into consideration arguments made by Michael Hanchard.[37] He contends that the nontraditional aspects of Black sociopolitical tools, and the sociopolitical tools of most marginalized groups, are in no small part a direct result of oppressive structures and institutions built within the United States to create obstacles for Black people who wanted to participate in any public, let alone an explicitly political, sphere.

> The condition of spatial and formal exclusion from a polity has been a hallmark of most of African descended and aboriginal populations of the Americas, Australia, and New Zealand from the moment of conquest and enslavement up until the granting of formal legal rights and spatial reserves (reservations and land grants).[38]

Therefore, Hanchard argues, Black people throughout the diaspora, as well as Indigenous and Latinx communities, have had to adopt at least some nontraditional sociopolitical tools to access the power needed to shift and change their communities in the way they desire.[39]

> Exclusion from the polis and polity in several societies led black political actors to pursue politics and the political in spaces deemed "extra-political" or "apolitical." One of the commonalities of the inception of black politics across the Americas, Europe, as well as in nationalist struggle in Africa was the utilization for political purposes of spaces designed and classified as "social" or "cultural" in the spheres of the dominant. Lunchroom sit-ins, for example, brought together members of a state recognized political community (whites with individual voting rights who managed and serviced those lunch counters) with members of a political community not sanctioned by the state (civil rights activists, some of whom were officially sanctioned by the state to fully participate in formal politics). Those lunch counters (and for Brazil and South Africa, the streets of São Paulo and Sharpeville) became sites for disputation over the right to con-

sume in specific public spaces, which in itself was premised upon prior political and social exclusion. Yet neither lunch counters nor the retail stores housing them were intended for political disputation.[40]

In the same vein as Hanchard, Keisha-Khan Perry notes that in Brazil, "Black women are celebrated for their role in maintaining Afro-Brazilian culture and religious traditions."[41] But as a result, there is an assumption that Black woman who live in poor neighborhoods "lack the political sophistication needed to organize social movements."[42] Throughout the diaspora, Afro-descended people have had to contend with a complicated set of assumptions around their ability to entertain and create cultural and religious artifacts, while also believing that they do not have the political wherewithal to engage in traditional or mainstream political engagement.

However, the Black sociopolitical world does engage in politics and the political; it is a political practice that understands, as Michael Dawson argues, that their sociopolitical fate is intrinsically linked with Black people throughout their country, and sometimes Afro-descended people globally.[43] Black feminist political scientist Evelyn Simien astutely notes, "The bottom line is this: the conceptualization of black political behavior must be determined, in part, by an appreciation of the lived experience and the political objectives of both African American women and men."[44] Ultimately, definitional criteria of politics and the political flexible enough to fit a diverse set of socio-cultural-economic-ethnic-sexual-gendered experiences help political practitioners to accurately assess the political practices of marginalized communities. Theorists interested in quotidian politics have done important work that recognizes the extrasystemic political practices of Black folks living in poverty.[45] As political scientist Michael Hanchard notes, the "explication of quotidian politics serves as a corrective to political and cultural analysis that reduces all politics to the state or macroeconomic factors"; in other words, politics is about more than direct engagement with state institutions.[46]

Fifth, the study of quotidian politics has played a significant role in the development of my work.[47] However, my capacity to create research centered on extrasystemic definitions of politics and the political is also due to history and anthropology scholars who made significant contributions to the study of nontraditional politics[48]—in particular, the ways the extrasystemic has shaped and been shaped via the intersections of race, gender, sexual orientation, and class.[49] As Dietlind Stolle, Marc Hooghe, and Michele Micheletti note, the emergence of nontraditional political practices has been well documented in other disciplines (e.g., James C. Scott's and

Robin D. G. Kelley's individual work around infrapolitics).[50] Thus, political practitioners cannot exclude nontraditional, infrapolitic, hidden transcript, quotidian politics from close study and analysis.[51] But more than that, as Hanchard, Kelley, and Isoke clarify, the Black diasporic sociopolitical experience has been so specific, political practitioners are unable to limit sociopolitical interactions with the Black sociopolitical world to elections and cultural engagement.[52] Kelley argues that, while both are needed, they do not make up the totality of the Black American political experience:

> We need to break away from traditional notions of politics. We must not only redefine what is "political" but question a lot of common ideas about what "authentic" movements and strategies of resistance are. . . . Such an approach not only disregards diversity and conflict within groups, but it presumes that the only struggles that count take place through institutions.[53]

In the preceding paragraph, Kelley makes clear the central problem with exclusively framing politics and the political within a traditional electoral framework: the sole use of that framework will almost always implicitly erase the experiences of marginalized groups.[54]

In the tradition of Robin D. G. Kelley and his push to move mainstream U.S. political culture beyond traditional political frameworks, in *Urban Black Women and the Politics of Resistance*, Zenzele Isoke astutely focuses in on the political experience of poor Black women.[55] Isoke argues that the "conventional approaches to the study of politics often depict low-income black women as apolitical, and worse as lacking in respectable claims to citizenship and belonging. When judged in accordance with accepted categories of political participation, many black women fare poorly."[56] In large part, this is because conventional approaches to politics research neglect to consider the interiority of respondent political identity. Instead, as numerous Black feminist political science scholars have pointed out, the impulse of the group consciousness literature is to compare all groups using the same set of variable measures.[57] While at first this may seem like a good idea for the sake of "objectivity," it ultimately only serves to erase the political engagement of groups existing on the margins, and in particular the sociopolitical tools of Black women living below the poverty line.[58] This is especially problematic given that, as Nikol Alexander-Floyd and Julia S. Jordan-Zachery note, "in political science, where Political Man (Lipset 1960) and Political Woman (Kilpatrick 1974) are still seen as White, and in the study of Black politics where the focus is often on Black men," there are few statistical measures designed with the political experiences of Black women more generally—and for the sake of this conversation, poor Black American women specifically—in mind.[59]

Sixth, given how much my project owes to the scholarship that precedes my own, in *Redefining the Political*, I work to ensure that this research adds to Black feminist political theory by developing a theoretical framework that helps scholars assess and recognize the sociopolitical tools of marginalized groups.[60] The political identity framework, which I named the political possible-self (PPS), provides a broader and more expansive context with which to understand how communities and individuals understand and participate in politics. When thinking about political behavior as a matrix, instead of a static binary, political practitioners have room to consider a wider range of activities and behaviors as political. As is demonstrated in this project, the PPS allows us to appreciate what traditional "commonsense" understandings of politics could not initially see: politics is just as much about cultural forms of engagement in the public sphere as it is about electoral democracies.[61]

Seventh, many within the world of traditional electoral politics mistakenly believe that poor Black people do not engage politically and lack political sophistication.[62] Typically, these lower numbers of engagement have been attributed to time and education constraints or alienation from state-sanctioned bureaucracies and other forms of state power.[63] However, anthropologists, policy feedback scholars, Black feminists, and sociologists have argued that not only do people living in poverty have a high level of political knowledge but, in fact, they have their own unique forms of politics.[64] My work extends the work of policy feedback scholars more generally and in particular takes Jamila Michener's contextual feedback framework of political participation as a site of departure.[65] The contextual feedback framework combined with the PPS framework can capture extrasystemic sociopolitical tools that occur beyond the reach of government institutions and bureaucracies. This extends the work of policy feedback by illustrating how contextual and spatial features of public housing shape a largely extrasystemic set of sociopolitical tools within CHA local sociopolitical communities.

In *The Politics of Public Housing: Black Women's Struggles against Urban Inequality*, Rhonda Williams wrote a careful and thoroughly researched analysis of the progressive politics of poor Black women living in Baltimore public housing. Williams points to the spaces and places responsible for shaping the sociopolitical tools of those poor Black women. Williams's insistence that we take seriously the need for "activism at the point of consumption—that is, around housing, food, clothing, and daily life in community spaces"—is a prescient reminder that politics exists beyond electoral fights for power.[66] For Black women living below the poverty line, politics are a fight for basic survival. Although Black women living in poverty, as public assistance recipients, must contend with onerous and intrusive regulations, numerous Black women do receive a sociopolitical education through their engagement with the welfare system. The federal government's subsidy of low-rent housing implies a right to decent living conditions for U.S. citizens.[67] From the beginning, this implied right has highlighted poor people's low citizenship status and politicized groups of tenants. For poor Black women, subsidized public housing has created a sense that the previously private sphere of home has become public sociopolitical space.[68]

Like the respondents in this research, the Black women Williams chronicled illustrated how the spatial context of state-sponsored public housing (e.g., the infrastructure, local sociopolitical communities, and street-level bureaucrats) functioned as part of resident sociopolitical education. Lisa Levenstein argued that there was "a mass movement of African American women to claim the benefits and use the services of public institutions."[69] Similarly, Williams noted that "in their own way, poor black women, who increasingly relied on public assistance, placed pressure on the welfare state to make good on its promise of provision and social rights, especially for some of its most marginalized citizens."[70] Ultimately, both authors used their work to illustrate how the determined sociopolitical effort of Black marginalized women led to a sociopolitical breakthrough: the understanding that "the government's subsidy of low-rent housing implied a right to decent living conditions for U.S. citizens."[71] Both authors clarify that engagement with the welfare state is not simply a legitimate sociopolitical action but a meaningful one.[72] By grounding my project within their work, I was able to continue the work of pointing to the urgency of this political moment. Scholars, activists, policymakers, and political practitioners of all sorts must take seriously the importance of constantly expanding our understanding of politics and the political. By using the work of Black feminist political scientists, political theorists, historians, anthropologists, sociologists, and humanities scholars, I can clarify the power and significance of the Black feminist politics of the everyday.

In Altgeld Gardens, housing policy seemed to create additional spatial features that shaped the sociopolitical identity development of CHA residents. In Chapters 4 and 5, I demonstrated that violence and the quality of interpersonal relationships within a neighborhood can shape the form and function of membership within a political community. Whether an individual is living in poverty or not, if they are surrounded by daily residential violence and believe they have no meaningful way of protecting themselves or their family, they are unlikely to participate within their communities, politically or otherwise. Key to my findings was discovering how critical a sense of belonging to a residential neighborhood and broader political community is to an engaged PPS. Belonging could function as a stand-in for membership in a sociopolitical community because it indicated a level of investment and commitment to entities beyond the self.[73] While a respondent may not be able to respond to traditional politics questions like "Who is your congressional representative?" many know and have even engaged with their local alderman or neighborhood block captain.* These neighborhood-level expressions of politics are important to measure when studies have continued to demonstrate how pressed for time and energy individuals living in poverty are.[74] Ultimately, I found that residents who have experienced multiple forms of violence and also lack interpersonal support tend to develop a PPS that is isolated and almost entirely focused on their own individual future outcomes. Spatial realities like interpersonal relationships, violence, aesthetics, and communication with representatives of the state can all potentially alienate or empower individuals in terms of their relationships to government and political participation more broadly.[75]

Like Williamson and Isoke, I demonstrate that public housing aesthetics helped to shape the sociopolitical tools and PPSs of low-income Black women I interviewed.[76] Aesthetics also played a fundamental role in structuring how marginalized Black women understood power in the U.S. context. I argue that we can understand Black women's politics as a form of power—a power shaping the institutions governing U.S. sociopolitical life. I suggest that, via the experience of belonging to their local sociopolitical residential communities, respondents learned a politics of self- and community governance. Belonging to local sociopolitical residential communities taught the respondents I interviewed how to navigate welfare institutions safely and efficiently. Belonging to local communities also helped respondents to navigate their neighborhoods safely.

Eighth, the CHA also played a significant role in the cocreation of the political identity and sociopolitical tools of individual respondents. The CHA sponsored several meetings between residents and CHA street-level bureaucrats throughout the month. These meetings provided residents with the opportunity to express concerns about public housing development infrastructure, CHA employees, and services provided by local and state government via the CHA. Meetings created a public sphere unique to the life experience of CHA residents. Many residents were limited in their ability

---

* At Altgeld Gardens, the neighborhood block captain is an elected official.

to access larger, citywide public spheres because of severe constraints on their access to public transportation, as well as the sociopolitical restrictions placed on them due to the intersections of their race, gender, and class identities.[77] On the other hand, CHA meetings provided a space residents could access regularly, given its proximity to their homes, as well as a particular set of rules and logics they were taught to engage and manipulate by past and present public housing residents.[78] These public spheres facilitated the development of political imagination among residents that created some unique and innovative sociopolitical tools.

The PPS considers sociopolitical tools to be a broad matrix of thoughts and behaviors.[79] In essence, context is what connects the theoretical work of the PPS to the empirical work of the case bracing this project. Michener rightly argues that "accounting for context sheds a different light" on the political behaviors of marginalized people.[80] She points out that for Black people living below the poverty line, their political story is "not just about political apathy, as traditional participation theories might have us believe; it is also about how local constraints, state policies and individual factors work in distinct ways to structure political life and shape a range of political actions."[81] I extend this argument by clarifying how public housing policy creates a context shaping the extrasystemic sociopolitical tools of residents, beyond traditional political participation and engagement with street-level bureaucrats.[82]

The PPS, broadly speaking, is a framework linking the relationship between a sense of belonging to local sociopolitical community and political imagination within an individual's "sociopolitical DNA." My research clarifies the importance of data collection on respondent spatial context, sociopolitical-friendship networks, and the individual's relationship to their local residential context. It is not enough to collect respondent location data and their personal residential timeline. Instead, *Redefining the Political* clarifies the importance of asking respondents how they feel about where they live, whether they feel they belong, and what relationship they have to their space. These questions matter when attempting to discern how, when, and where individuals think and act on the political.

Over the course of this project, I have learned that neighborhoods shape the type of sociopolitical community members we become.[83] If one person is fortunate enough to grow up in a neighborhood facilitating engaged sociopolitical membership, and another community of people are being relegated to neighborhoods depressing sociopolitical membership, this is a democratic crisis warranting attention. When marginalized populations have large numbers of people with depressed sociopolitical memberships and they typically live in neighborhoods constructed by the state (e.g., public housing, income-based housing, and multi-income housing), it follows that the circumstances creating those lived sociopolitical realities require urgent attention.

Does Any of This Matter?

From the outset of this project, my goal was to write a book accessible to the broadest segments of the population. I wanted to write a book useful to a variety of political practitioners. The limitations embedded within traditional "commonsense" definitions of politics constitute an important issue for everyone to take on. After all, if activists cannot reach out to a diverse set of communities because they do not know how marginalized communities engage with or define power, their campaigns will fail to achieve success. If policymakers do not understand the high-salience political issues within marginalized sociopolitical communities, they will fail to correct ongoing problems among groups made up of folks with stigmatized intersectional identities. If academics limit themselves to a narrow understanding of the political, they will experience failure within their statistical data, not only in polling but in major studies as well.[84] As political practitioners, we have reached a nadir in our understanding and outreach to nonwhite populations. If we hope to ever create a truly egalitarian democracy, then we must become serious about creating broader and more flexible political definitions.

In the years following empirical interventions like Cohen's *Democracy Remixed*, we now know that young Black people (and potentially a number of other minority groups) are engaged in a politics that eludes traditional political research measures.[85] In *Black Visions*, Michael Dawson made clear that Black Americans have a varied spectrum of sociopolitical identities demanding a closer look into the sociopolitical motivations of Black folks living in the United States (beyond an assessment of political alienation from government more generally).[86] In turn, my project contributes to this growing literature around traditional and extrasystemic sociopolitical tools among Black Americans by identifying the conceptual categories and mechanisms facilitating extrasystemic politics within Black marginalized communities.[87]

Conclusion

By developing the PPS theoretical framework and a BFDC of politics and the political, I have created a set of theoretical frameworks with the capacity to help scholars fully interrogate political behavior in relationship to belonging and political imagination. I have also developed theoretically rooted conceptual categories capable of traveling the world. Last, I have provided frameworks that could help political practitioners to better understand political behavior and engagement across marginalized populations. Beyond the PPS, I have also identified mechanisms that connect concepts like power, political membership, and belonging to the everyday sociopolitical experiences of Black women living in poverty.

It is critical that future scholars interested in continuing the theoretical work necessary to fully parse out the politics of marginalized Black communities understand how oppression shapes the individual relationship to politically important conceptual categories. This project began by focusing tightly on the shape of socioeconomic status and the sociopolitical experience of Black women living in public housing. Future scholars should explore a more thorough analysis of the intersections of race, gender, sexuality, orientation, disability, neurodivergence, and class and the ways those identities shape the individual relationship to the PPS and their position within the public sphere. It is my hope that future scholars will think through the theoretical relationship between liberation and membership in the sociopolitical community, particularly when it comes to the intersections of race, gender, and class. As many a Black feminist has said before, free Black people create more free Black people.

By thinking through how individuals understand their own liberation, or lack thereof, political practitioners can come closer to understanding what marginalized populations want from politics. In a sense, this question is one about desire, a concept only rarely considered.[88] What exactly do Black women desire from their sociopolitical lives? What does it mean when Black feminists and activists of all sorts make requests for a fully liberated political membership within civil society? Is this desire simply relegated to those Black women who work within political public spheres? Or is a political desire for liberation and freedom widely held by all? To use the framework of this project, is there a language of political desire and liberation among Black American women living below the poverty line? If so, what does that language look like, and what does it mean for the shape and form of their PPSs? Going forward, if scholars of the Black sociopolitical world begin to think broadly about conceptual categories like liberation, joy, and desire, we will have a fuller and more nuanced understanding of who engages sociopolitical life.

NOTES

CHAPTER 1

1. Verba, Schlozman, and Brady, *Voice and Equality*.

2. Iton, *In Search of the Black Fantastic*; Kelley, *Race Rebels*; Collins, *From Black Power to Hip Hop*; N. Brown and Young, "Ratchet Politics."

3. Kelley, *Race Rebels*; Spence, *Knocking the Hustle*; Dawson, *Black Visions*; Hanchard, *Party/Politics*; Cohen, "Deviance as Resistance"; Isoke, *Urban Black Women*; Berger, *Workable Sisterhood*.

4. Collins, *From Black Power to Hip Hop*; Iton, *In Search of the Black Fantastic*; Kelley, *Race Rebels*; Feimster, *Southern Horrors*; Mitchell-Walthour, *Politics of Survival*; K. Mitchell, *From Slave Cabins to the White House*; Jordan-Zachery, "Beyond the Side Eye."

5. Collins, *From Black Power to Hip Hop*; *Chicago Talks*, "Occupy the Hood Strikes Back."

6. Hanchard, *Party/Politics*; Kelley, *Race Rebels*; Cohen, "Deviance as Resistance"; Isoke, *Urban Black Women*; Berger, *Workable Sisterhood*; T. Williamson, *Scandalize My Name*.

7. Amy Allen, *The Power of Feminist Theory: Domination, Resistance, Solidarity* (London, United Kingdom: Routledge, 2018), https://doi.org/10.4324/9780429495939; Cudd, *Analyzing Oppression*; Clarissa Rile Hayward, *De-Facing Power* (Cambridge, United Kingdom: Cambridge University Press, 2010), https://doi.org/10.2307/3235365; Iris Marion Young, *Justice and the Politics of Difference* (Princeton, NJ: Princeton University Press, 1990).

8. Young, *Justice and the Politics of Difference*.

9. Hanchard, *Party/Politics*; Mouffe, *On the Political*; Eliasoph, *Avoiding Politics*; Young, *Justice and the Politics of Difference*.

10. Prestage, "In Quest of African American Political Woman"; Simien, *Black Feminist Voices in Politics*; Cohen, "Punks, Bulldaggers and Welfare Queens"; Hancock, *Politics of Disgust*; Richie, *Arrested Justice*.

11. Prestage, "In Quest of African American Political Woman"; Simien, *Black Feminist Voices in Politics*; Alexander-Floyd, "Why Political Scientists"; Jordan-Zachery, "I Ain't Your Darn Help"; Hancock, *Politics of Disgust*; Cohen, "Punks, Bulldaggers and Welfare Queens"; hooks, *Where We Stand*; Simien, *Black Feminist Voices in Politics*; Alexander-Floyd, "Why Political Scientists," 3–17; Jordan-Zachery, "I Ain't Your Darn Help," 19–30.

12. Davis, *Women, Race and Class*; K. Mitchell, *From Slave Cabins to the White House*; K. Mitchell, *Living with Lynching*; K. Williams, *They Left Great Marks*; Carter and Willoughby-Herard, "What Kind of Mother Is She?"

13. Moffett-Bateau, "Strategies of Resistance"; Moffett-Bateau, "I Can't Vote."

14. Cohen and Dawson, "Neighborhood Poverty"; Cohen, *Boundaries of Blackness*; Berger, *Workable Sisterhood*; Watkins-Hayes, *Remaking a Life*; Isoke, *Urban Black Women*.

15. Coffey et al., "Poisonous Homes"; Gay, "Putting Race in Context," 547–62; Cutter, Boruff, and Shirley, "Social Vulnerability to Environmental Hazards"; Brinson, "Altgeld Gardens Lawsuit Settlement"; White and Hall, "Perceptions of Environmental Health Risks."

16. Simien, *Black Feminist Voices in Politics*; D. Harris, *Black Feminist Politics*; Prestage, "In Quest of African American Political Woman"; Harris-Perry, *Sister Citizen*; Alexander-Floyd, "Why Political Scientists"; Jordan-Zachery, "Resistance and Redemption Narratives."

17. Lerman and Weaver, *Arresting Citizenship*.

18. Simien, *Black Feminist Voices in Politics*; Isoke, *Urban Black Women*; Berger, *Workable Sisterhood*.

19. Dawson, *Behind the Mule*; Cohen, "Deviance as Resistance"; Simien, *Black Feminist Voices in Politics*; Berger, *Workable Sisterhood*; Isoke, *Urban Black Women*; Spence, *Knocking the Hustle*.

20. Schmidt, *Interpreting Racial Politics*; G. King et al., "Enhancing the Validity"; Junn, "Participation in Liberal Democracy."

21. Junn, "Participation in Liberal Democracy"; Simien, *Black Feminist Voices in Politics*; Alexander-Floyd, "Why Political Scientists"; Jordan-Zachery, "I Ain't Your Darn Help."

22. Simien, *Black Feminist Voices in Politics*; Junn, "Participation in Liberal Democracy."

23. Naples, *Grassroots Warriors*; Feldman and Stall, *Dignity of Resistance*; R. Williams, *Politics of Public Housing*; Soss, *Unwanted Claims*.

24. Cohen, *Boundaries of Blackness*.

25. Mitchell-Walthour, *Politics of Survival*.

26. Hanchard, *Party/Politics*; Dawson, *Black Visions*; Cohen and Dawson, "Neighborhood Poverty"; Kelley, *Race Rebels*; Carter and Willoughby-Herard, "What Kind

of Mother Is She?"; Cohen, "Deviance as Resistance"; Cohen, "Punks, Bulldaggers and Welfare Queens"; Hancock, *Politics of Disgust*.

27. Berger, *Workable Sisterhood*; Watkins-Hayes, *Remaking a Life*; Perry, *Black Women*; Harris-Perry, *Sister Citizen*; Richie, *Arrested Justice*; Mitchell-Walthour, *Politics of Survival*; Isoke, *Urban Black Women*.

28. Robnett, *How Long?*; R. Williams, *Politics of Public Housing*; Feldman and Stall, *Dignity of Resistance*; Roth, *Separate Roads to Feminism*; Harris-Perry, *Sister Citizen*.

29. Feldman and Stall, *Dignity of Resistance*; Naples, *Grassroots Warriors*; Gold, *When Tenants Claimed the City*; Levenstein, *Movement without Marches*; Richie, *Arrested Justice*; Gurusami, "Working for Redemption"; P. J. Harris, "Gatekeeping and Remaking."

30. Weaver, Prowse, and Piston, "Too Much Knowledge"; Simien, *Black Feminist Voices in Politics*.

31. Friedrich, "Income, Poverty"; N. Jones et al., "Improved Race and Ethnicity Measures."

32. National Partnership for Women and Families, *Black Women and the Wage Gap*.

33. Haider, Frye, and Khattar, "Census Data Show Historic Investments."

34. Soss, *Unwanted Claims*; Fording, Soss, and Schram, "Race and the Local Politics"; Richie, *Arrested Justice*; Ritchie, *Invisible No More*; INCITE!, *Color of Violence*.

35. Roberts, *Shattered Bonds*; Hancock, *Politics of Disgust*; Fording, Soss, and Schram, "Race and the Local Politics"; H. Hansen, Bourgois, and Drucker, "Pathologizing Poverty."

36. Soss, *Unwanted Claims*; Fording, Soss, and Schram, "Race and the Local Politics"; Hancock, *Politics of Disgust*; H. Hansen, Bourgois, and Drucker, "Pathologizing Poverty"; Roberts, *Shattered Bonds*.

37. Hancock, *Politics of Disgust*; Berger, *Workable Sisterhood*; Fording, Soss, and Schram, "Race and the Local Politics."

38. "The Combahee River Collective Statement"; hooks, *Ain't I a Woman: Black Women and Feminism*; Hull, Bell Scott, and Smith, *But Some of Us Are Brave*; Guy-Sheftall, *Words of Fire*; James, *Shadowboxing: Representations of Black Feminist Politics*.

39. Evans-Winters, *Black Feminism in Qualitative Inquiry*.

40. Mitchell-Walthour, *Politics of Survival*.

41. Mouffe, *On the Political*; Soss, *Unwanted Claims*; Soss, "Lessons of Welfare"; Mettler and Soss, "Consequences of Public Policy"; Popkin, *No Simple Solutions*; Hanchard, *Party/Politics*; Kelley, *Race Rebels*; Cohen, "Deviance as Resistance"; Perry, *Black Women*; Isoke, *Urban Black Women*; Berger, *Workable Sisterhood*; Naples, *Grassroots Warriors*.

42. Mitchell-Walthour, *Politics of Survival*.

43. T. Williamson, *Scandalize My Name*.

44. Williamson, 7–8.

45. Isoke, *Urban Black Women*; T. Williamson, *Scandalize My Name*.

46. D. Harris, *Black Feminist Politics*.

47. Mitchell-Walthour, *Politics of Survival*; Moffett-Bateau, "Feminist Erasures."

48. Simien, *Black Feminist Voices in Politics*; D. Harris, *Black Feminist Politics*; Mitchell-Walthour, *Politics of Survival*; Isoke, *Urban Black Women*; Berger, *Workable Sisterhood*.

49. Moffett-Bateau, "Feminist Erasures"; Dillard, *Learning to (Re)Member*; Evans-Winters, *Black Feminism in Qualitative Inquiry*.

50. Mitchell-Walthour, *Politics of Survival*.

51. Coffey et al., "Poisonous Homes"; Cutter, Boruff, and Shirley, "Social Vulnerability to Environmental Hazards"; White and Hall, "Perceptions of Environmental Health Risks"; Chase, "Public Housing Residents"; Gay, "Putting Race in Context"; Holifield, "Defining Environmental Justice"; McKittrick, *Demonic Grounds*; Brinson, "Altgeld Gardens Lawsuit Settlement."

52. CHA, "Plan for Transformation"; Fuerst and Hunt, *When Public Housing Was Paradise*; Hunt, *Blueprint for Disaster*; Feldman and Stall, *Dignity of Resistance*; Popkin, *No Simple Solutions*.

53. CHA, "Plan for Transformation"; CHA, "Altgeld Gardens and Phillip Murray Homes"; Moore, "Residents Question Chicago Housing Authority"; D. Williams, "Altgeld Gardens"; Polikoff, *Waiting for Gautreaux*; Baron, *What Is Gautreaux?*; Feldman and Stall, *Dignity of Resistance*.

54. CHA, "Altgeld Gardens and Phillip Murray Homes."

55. D. King, "Multiple Jeopardy, Multiple Consciousness." "The Combahee River Collective Statement"; James and Guy-Sheftall, *Seeking the Beloved Community*; James, *Shadowboxing: Representations of Black Feminist Politics*.

56. Roth, "Making of the Vanguard Center"; Roth, *Separate Roads to Feminism*; Collins, *Black Feminist Thought*.

57. Roth, *Separate Roads to Feminism*; Weaver, Prowse, and Piston, "Too Much Knowledge"; Prowse, Weaver, and Meares, "State from Below"; Soss and Weaver, "Police Are Our Government."

58. Roth, "Making of the Vanguard Center."

59. C. Jones, "End to the Neglect"; D. King, "Multiple Jeopardy, Multiple Consciousness"; Crenshaw, "Mapping the Margins"; "The Combahee River Collective Statement." Collins, *Intersectionality as Critical Social Theory*.

60. Roth, *Separate Roads to Feminism*, 76–77.

61. Berger, *Workable Sisterhood*; Perry, *Black Women*; Mitchell-Walthour, *Politics of Survival*; Cohen, "Punks, Bulldaggers and Welfare Queens?"; Hancock, *Politics of Disgust*.

62. Soss, *Unwanted Claims*; Soss, "Lessons of Welfare"; Moffett-Bateau, "Strategies of Resistance"; Naples, *Grassroots Warriors*; Feldman and Stall, *Dignity of Resistance*; R. Williams, *Politics of Public Housing*; K. Mitchell, *From Slave Cabins to the White House*.

63. "Combahee River Collective Statement"; Roth, "Making of the Vanguard Center"; Guy-Sheftall, *Words of Fire*; Alexander-Floyd, "Radical Black Feminism"; hooks, *Ain't I a Woman*.

64. Mitchell-Walthour, *Politics of Survival*.

65. hooks, *Outlaw Culture*; Collins, *From Black Power to Hip Hop*; Collins, *Black Feminist Thought*; Guy-Sheftall, *Words of Fire*; Hurston, *Dust Tracks on a Road*; "Combahee River Collective Statement"; James, *Shadowboxing*; Mitchell-Walthour, *Politics of Survival*.

66. Moffett-Bateau, "Feminist Erasures"; Evans-Winters, *Black Feminism in Qualitative Inquiry*; Burack, *Healing Identities*.

67. Mitchell-Walthour, *Politics of Survival*; Isoke, *Urban Black Women*; Berger, *Workable Sisterhood*; Watkins-Hayes, *Remaking a Life*.

68. "Combahee River Collective Statement."

69. "Combahee River Collective Statement"; Cohen, "Deviance as Resistance"; Harris-Lacewell, *Barbershops, Bibles, and BET*.

70. Kelley, *Race Rebels*; Cohen, *Boundaries of Blackness*; Cohen, "Deviance as Resistance"; Cohen, "Punks, Bulldaggers and Welfare Queens"; Cohen, *Democracy Remixed*; Dawson, *Behind the Mule*; Dawson, *Black Visions*; Hanchard, "Acts of Misrecognition"; Hanchard, *Party/Politics*; Hanchard, "Contours of Black Political Thought"; Perry, *Black Women*; Isoke, *Urban Black Women*; Berger, *Workable Sisterhood*; Watkins-Hayes, *Remaking a Life*; Spence, *Knocking the Hustle*.

71. Spence, *Knocking the Hustle*, 25.

72. hooks, *Outlaw Culture*.

73. Cohen, *Boundaries of Blackness*; Hancock, *Politics of Disgust*; Rios, *Punished*; Watkins-Hayes, *Remaking a Life*; Berger, *Workable Sisterhood*; Isoke, *Urban Black Women*; R. Williams, *Politics of Public Housing*; Perry, *Black Women*; Mitchell-Walthour, *Politics of Survival*.

74. C. Jones, "End to the Neglect"; D. King, "Multiple Jeopardy, Multiple Consciousness"; hooks, *Ain't I a Woman*; Collins, *Black Feminist Thought*; Roth, "Making of the Vanguard Center"; James, *Shadowboxing*.

75. Moore, "Residents Question Chicago Housing Authority"; Moore, "Chicago Housing Authority Residents."

76. "Isabel Wilkerson."

77. *Chicago Talks*, "Occupy the Hood Strikes Back."

78. G. King and Wand, "Comparing Incomparable Survey Responses"; G. King et al., "Enhancing the Validity"; Hopkins, Daniel and King, "Improving Anchoring Vignettes"; Junn, "Participation in Liberal Democracy"; Simien, *Black Feminist Voices in Politics*.

79. G. King et al., "Enhancing the Validity"; Junn, "Participation in Liberal Democracy"; G. King and Wand, "Comparing Incomparable Survey Responses"; Simien, *Black Feminist Voices in Politics*; Berger, *Workable Sisterhood*; Isoke, *Urban Black Women*.

80. Prestage, "In Quest of African American Political Woman"; D. Harris, *Black Feminist Politics*; Simien, *Black Feminist Voices in Politics*; Cohen, "Deviance as Resistance"; Jordan-Zachery, "I Ain't Your Darn Help"; Alexander-Floyd, "Why Political Scientists"; Isoke, *Urban Black Women*.

81. Prestage, "In Quest of African American Political Woman"; Simien, *Black Feminist Voices in Politics*; Isoke, *Urban Black Women*; Berger, *Workable Sisterhood*; Cohen, *Boundaries of Blackness*; Hanchard, *Party/Politics*.

82. G. King and Wand, "Comparing Incomparable Survey Responses."

83. Junn, "Participation in Liberal Democracy"; Simien, *Black Feminist Voices in Politics*; Isoke, *Urban Black Women*; T. Williamson, *Scandalize My Name*; Naples, *Grassroots Warriors*.

84. Acheson, *Abolishing State Violence*; Jeffrey and Sargrad, "Strengthening Democracy"; Love, *We Want to Do More*; hooks, *Teaching to Transgress*; hooks, *Teaching Community*.

85. Acheson, *Abolishing State Violence*; hooks, *Teaching to Transgress*.

86. Healy, "Momentum Grows."

87. Healy.

88. Jeffrey and Sargrad, "Strengthening Democracy"; Maroni, "Americans' Civics Knowledge"; Healy, "Momentum Grows."

89. Acheson, *Abolishing State Violence*; Jeffrey and Sargrad, "Strengthening Democracy."

90. Acheson, *Abolishing State Violence*, loc. 149–211.

91. Acheson; Bruch and Soss, "Schooling as a Formative Political Experience"; Butler, "Quiltmaking among African-American Women"; hooks, *Teaching to Transgress*; Su, *Streetwise for Book Smarts*; Cramer and Toff, "Fact of Experience"; Weaver, Prowse, and Piston, "Too Much Knowledge"; Collins, *Black Feminist Thought*; Rios, *Punished*; Charron, *Freedom's Teacher*; Healy, "Momentum Grows."

92. Acheson, *Abolishing State Violence*.

93. Ferguson, "Why Does Political Science Hate American Indians?"; Acheson, *Abolishing State Violence*.

94. Davis, *Women, Race and Class*; Ferguson, "Why Does Political Science Hate American Indians?"; hooks, *Teaching to Transgress*; Acheson, *Abolishing State Violence*.

95. Acheson, *Abolishing State Violence*; hooks, *Teaching to Transgress*.

96. Healy, "Momentum Grows"; Jeffrey and Sargrad, "Strengthening Democracy"; Maroni, "Americans' Civics Knowledge"; Vasilogambros, "After Capitol Riot."

97. Spence, *Knocking the Hustle*, 16–17.

98. Acheson, *Abolishing State Violence*, loc. 149–215.

99. Spence, *Knocking the Hustle*, 36–38; Cohen, "Punks, Bulldaggers and Welfare Queens"; Hancock, *Politics of Disgust*; Fording, Soss, and Schram, "Race and the Local Politics."

100. Wilson Gilmore, "Organized Abandonment and Organized Violence."

101. D. Williams, "Altgeld Gardens."

102. Hudson, "Altgeld Gardens"; Le Mignot, "4 Dead, 2 Wounded"; Grotto, Cohen, and Olkon, "Public Housing's Island."

103. D. Williams, "Altgeld Gardens."

104. Richie, *Arrested Justice*; Ritchie, *Invisible No More*; Cohen, *Boundaries of Blackness*; Berger, *Workable Sisterhood*; Watkins-Hayes, *Remaking a Life*; Isoke, *Urban Black Women*; R. Williams, *Politics of Public Housing*; Feldman and Stall, *Dignity of Resistance*.

105. D. Williams, "Altgeld Gardens"; Coffey et al., "Poisonous Homes"; Gay, "Putting Race in Context"; White and Hall, "Perceptions of Environmental Health Risks";

Cutter, Boruff, and Shirley, "Social Vulnerability to Environmental Hazards"; Brinson, "Altgeld Gardens Lawsuit Settlement"; Hudson, "Altgeld Gardens"; Grotto, Cohen, and Olkon, "Public Housing's Island"; Chase, "Public Housing Residents"; Kasakove, "Major Chicago Public-Housing Lawsuit"; Feldman and Stall, *Dignity of Resistance*; Polikoff, *Waiting for Gautreaux*.

106. Grotto, Cohen, and Olkon, "Public Housing's Island"; Hudson, "Altgeld Gardens."

107. D. Williams, "Altgeld Gardens"; Coalition to Protect Public Housing, "Written Submission"; Moore, "Residents Question Chicago Housing Authority"; D. Williams, "Altgeld Gardens"; Hudson, "Altgeld Gardens."

108. Feldman and Stall, *Dignity of Resistance*; Naples, *Grassroots Warriors*; T. Williamson, *Scandalize My Name*; Levenstein, *Movement without Marches*; Gold, *When Tenants Claimed the City*; Gotham and Brumley, "Using Space"; Desmond, Papachristos, and Kirk, "Police Violence."

109. Weaver, Prowse, and Piston, "Too Much Knowledge"; Prowse, Weaver, and Meares, "State from Below"; Soss, *Unwanted Claims*; Michener, "Policy Feedback in a Racialized Polity"; Mettler and Soss, "Consequences of Public Policy"; Popkin, *No Simple Solutions*; A. L. Campbell, *How Policies Make Citizens*.

110. Weaver, Prowse, and Piston, "Too Much Knowledge"; Cramer and Toff, "Fact of Experience"; Prowse, Weaver, and Meares, "State from Below"; Lerman and Weaver, *Arresting Citizenship*.

111. Acheson, *Abolishing State Violence*; Moffett-Bateau, "Strategies of Resistance"; Hanchard, *Party/Politics*; Kelley, *Race Rebels*; Iton, *In Search of the Black Fantastic*.

112. Hanchard, "Contours of Black Political Thought."

113. Scott, *Domination and the Arts of Resistance*; Kelley, *Race Rebels*; Hanchard, "Acts of Misrecognition"; Hanchard, *Party/Politics*; Hanchard, "Contours of Black Political Thought"; Perry, *Black Women*; Iton, *In Search of the Black Fantastic*; Cohen, "Deviance as Resistance"; Cohen, "Punks, Bulldaggers and Welfare Queens."

114. Hanchard, "Acts of Misrecognition."

115. Schmidt, *Interpreting Racial Politics*; Junn, "Participation in Liberal Democracy"; Simien, *Black Feminist Voices in Politics*; Cohen, "Deviance as Resistance."

116. For further work on cultural incomparability, see Junn, "Participation in Liberal Democracy"; G. King and Wand, "Comparing Incomparable Survey Responses."

117. Schmidt, *Interpreting Racial Politics*; Collins, *From Black Power to Hip Hop*.

118. Moffett-Bateau, "Strategies of Resistance."

119. Acheson, *Abolishing State Violence*; Davis, *Women, Race and Class*; Gilmore, "Fatal Couplings of Power and Difference"; Wilson Gilmore, "Organized Abandonment and Organized Violence"; Wilson Gilmore, *Golden Gulag*; Kaba, *Against Punishment*; Richie, *Arrested Justice*; Ritchie, *Invisible No More*.

120. Scott, *Domination and the Arts of Resistance*; Kelley, *Race Rebels*; Cohen, "Deviance as Resistance"; Cohen, "Punks, Bulldaggers and Welfare Queens"; Cohen, *Democracy Remixed*; Dawson, *Black Visions*; Hanchard, "Acts of Misrecognition"; Hanchard, *Party/Politics*; Hanchard, "Contours of Black Political Thought"; Berger, *Workable Sisterhood*; R. Williams, *Politics of Public Housing*; Isoke, *Urban Black*

Women; Perry, *Black Women*; Mouffe, *On the Political*; Simien, *Black Feminist Voices in Politics*.

121. Lipsky, *Street-Level Bureaucracy*.

122. Isoke, "Politics of Homemaking"; Berger, *Workable Sisterhood*; Perry, *Black Women*; Michener, "Neighborhood Disorder and Local Participation"; Lerman and Weaver, *Arresting Citizenship*; Naples, *Grassroots Warriors*; R. Williams, *Politics of Public Housing*; V. Williamson, Trump, and Einstein, "Black Lives Matter"; K. Williams, *They Left Great Marks*; Cohen, *Democracy Remixed*.

123. Scholz, "Empowering Resistance."

124. R. Williams, *Politics of Public Housing*; Berger, *Workable Sisterhood*; Isoke, *Urban Black Women*; Watkins-Hayes, *Remaking a Life*; Naples, *Grassroots Warriors*; Weaver, Prowse, and Piston, "Too Much Knowledge"; Michener, "Power from the Margins"; Perry, *Black Women*.

125. Hanchard, *Party/Politics*, 29.

126. Hanchard, 30.

127. Hanchard.

128. Hanchard, 28.

129. Scott, *Domination and the Arts of Resistance*; Hanchard, *Party/Politics*; Kelley, *Race Rebels*.

130. Berger, *Workable Sisterhood*, 11.

131. Scott, *Domination and the Arts of Resistance*; Kelley, *Race Rebels*; Hanchard, "Acts of Misrecognition"; Dawson, *Black Visions*; Cohen, "Deviance as Resistance"; Jordan-Zachery and Alexander-Floyd, *Black Women in Politics*; Alexander-Floyd, "Why Political Scientists"; Jordan-Zachery, "Beyond the Side Eye."

132. Scott, *Domination and the Arts of Resistance*; Kelley, *Race Rebels*; Kelley, *Yo' Mama's Disfunktional!*; Dawson, *Black Visions*; Iton, *In Search of the Black Fantastic*; Hanchard, *Party/Politics*; Hanchard, "Acts of Misrecognition"; Schneider, *Police Power and Race Riots*; Collins, *From Black Power to Hip Hop*; Butler, "Quiltmaking among African-American Women"; Isoke, *Urban Black Women*; Berger, *Workable Sisterhood*; Perry, *Black Women*; Jordan-Zachery, "Resistance and Redemption Narratives"; Jordan-Zachery and Alexander-Floyd, *Black Women in Politics*.

133. Moffett-Bateau, "Strategies of Resistance"; Jordan-Zachery, "Resistance and Redemption Narratives"; Cohen, "Deviance as Resistance."

134. Dion, "Political Ideology."

135. Butler, "Quiltmaking among African-American Women."

136. Mouffe, "Democratic Citizenship and the Political Community"; Hanchard, "Contours of Black Political Thought."

137. Harris-Perry, *Sister Citizen*; Berger, *Workable Sisterhood*; R. Williams, *Politics of Public Housing*; Young, *Justice and the Politics of Difference*.

138. Cohen, "Deviance as Resistance"; Cohen, "Punks, Bulldaggers and Welfare Queens"; Kelley, *Race Rebels*; Kelley, *Yo' Mama's Disfunktional!*; Iton, *In Search of the Black Fantastic*; Hanchard, *Party/Politics*; Berger, *Workable Sisterhood*; Isoke, "Politics of Homemaking."

139. Hanchard, "Acts of Misrecognition"; Kelley, *Race Rebels*; Isoke, "Politics of Homemaking"; R. Williams, *Politics of Public Housing*; T. Williamson, *Scandalize My Name*; Collins, *Black Feminist Thought*.

140. Hanchard, "Contours of Black Political Thought"; Dawson, *Behind the Mule*; Simien, "Race, Gender, and Linked Fate"; Dawson, *Black Visions*; D. King, "Multiple Jeopardy, Multiple Consciousness"; Jordan-Zachery, "Beyond the Side Eye"; Alexander-Floyd, "Why Political Scientists"; Naples, *Grassroots Warriors*; Gold, *When Tenants Claimed the City*; Mouffe, "Democratic Citizenship and the Political Community"; Mouffe, *Return of the Political*.

141. Huckfeldt, "Variable Responses"; Gilmore, "Fatal Couplings of Power and Difference"; McKittrick, *Demonic Grounds*; Hayward, *How Americans Make Race*; Cohen and Dawson, "Neighborhood Poverty"; R. Williams, *Politics of Public Housing*.

142. Hayward, *How Americans Make Race*; McKittrick, *Demonic Grounds*; Trounstine, *Segregation by Design*; Michener, "Neighborhood Disorder and Local Participation"; Gay, "Putting Race in Context"; Burch, "Neighborhood Effects of Incarceration"; Bolland and Moehle McCallum, "Neighboring and Community Mobilization"; Huckfeldt, "Variable Responses."

143. Huckfeldt, "Variable Responses"; Lipsky, *Street-Level Bureaucracy*; Bolland and Moehle McCallum, "Neighboring and Community Mobilization"; Ralph, *Renegade Dreams*.

144. Naples, *Grassroots Warriors*; Isoke, *Urban Black Women*; Watkins-Hayes, *Remaking a Life*; Feldman and Stall, *Dignity of Resistance*; Berger, *Workable Sisterhood*.

145. Masuoka and Junn, *Politics of Belonging*; hooks, *Belonging*; Harris-Perry, *Sister Citizen*; Bolland and Moehle McCallum, "Neighboring and Community Mobilization"; James, *Shadowboxing*.

146. Polikoff, *Waiting for Gautreaux*; Burch, *Trading Democracy for Justice*; Ralph, *Renegade Dreams*; Feldman and Stall, *Dignity of Resistance*; Venkatesh, *American Project*.

147. Polikoff, *Waiting for Gautreaux*; Burch, *Trading Democracy for Justice*; Ralph, *Renegade Dreams*; Feldman and Stall, *Dignity of Resistance*; Venkatesh, *American Project*.

148. Hanchard, "Contours of Black Political Thought"; Scott, *Domination and the Arts of Resistance*; Huckfeldt, "Variable Responses"; McKittrick, *Demonic Grounds*.

149. Hanchard, *Party/Politics*; Perry, *Black Women*.

150. Mouffe, *Return of the Political*.

151. Hanchard, "Contours of Black Political Thought."

152. Mouffe, "Democratic Citizenship and the Political Community"; Mouffe, *Return of the Political*; Cohen, *Boundaries of Blackness*; Dawson, *Behind the Mule*; Dawson, *Black Visions*.

153. Hanchard, "Contours of Black Political Thought."

154. Dawson, *Behind the Mule*.

155. Collins, *Black Feminist Thought*; hooks, *Ain't I a Woman*; hooks, *Outlaw Culture*; Ransby, *Ella Baker*; Robnett, *How Long?*; James, *Shadowboxing*.

156. Berger, *Workable Sisterhood*; Watkins-Hayes, *Remaking a Life*; Cohen, *Boundaries of Blackness*.

157. Polikoff, *Waiting for Gautreaux*; K. Mitchell, *From Slave Cabins to the White House*; Naples, *Grassroots Warriors*; Wilson Gilmore, "Organized Abandonment and Organized Violence"; Gold, *When Tenants Claimed the City*; Trounstine, *Segregation by Design*.

158. Levenstein, *Movement without Marches*; R. Williams, *Politics of Public Housing*; T. Williamson, *Scandalize My Name*; Isoke, *Urban Black Women*; Watkins-Hayes, *Remaking a Life*; Berger, *Workable Sisterhood*; K. Mitchell, *From Slave Cabins to the White House*; Isoke, "Politics of Homemaking"; Naples, *Grassroots Warriors*; Feldman and Stall, *Dignity of Resistance*.

159. Ransby, *Making All Black Lives Matter*; Carruthers, *Unapologetic*; Dawson, *Black Visions*.

160. Feldman and Stall, *Dignity of Resistance*; Gold, *When Tenants Claimed the City*; Naples, *Grassroots Warriors*; R. Williams, *Politics of Public Housing*; Isoke, *Urban Black Women*; K. Mitchell, *From Slave Cabins to the White House*.

161. Frazer, "Marry Wollstonecraft on Politics and Friendship."

162. Sinclair, *Social Citizen*; Verba, Schlozman, and Brady, *Voice and Equality*; Morenoff, Sampson, and Raudenbush, "Neighborhood Inequality."

163. Polikoff, *Waiting for Gautreaux*; Gay, "Moving to Opportunity"; Goetz, *New Deal Ruins*; Popkin, *No Simple Solutions*; Fuerst and Hunt, *When Public Housing Was Paradise*.

164. L. Bennett, Smith, and Wright, *Where Are Poor People to Live?*; Popkin, *No Simple Solutions*; Popkin, Levy, et al., "HOPE VI Program"; de Souza Briggs, Popkin, and Goering, *Moving to Opportunity*; Hunt, *Blueprint for Disaster*; Feldman and Stall, *Dignity of Resistance*.

165. Berger, *Workable Sisterhood*, 11.

166. R. Williams, *Politics of Public Housing*, 6.

167. Harris-Lacewell, *Barbershops, Bibles, and BET*; Watkins-Hayes, *Remaking a Life*; R. Williams, *Politics of Public Housing*; T. Williamson, *Scandalize My Name*; Isoke, "Politics of Homemaking"; Isoke, *Urban Black Women*.

168. Simien, *Black Feminist Voices in Politics*; D. Harris, *Black Feminist Politics*; Harris-Perry, *Sister Citizen*; Cohen, "Punks, Bulldaggers and Welfare Queens"; Hancock, *Politics of Disgust*; Berger, *Workable Sisterhood*; Watkins-Hayes, *Remaking a Life*; Isoke, *Urban Black Women*; Perry, *Black Women*; T. Williamson, *Scandalize My Name*; K. Mitchell, *From Slave Cabins to the White House*; Jordan-Zachery, "I Ain't Your Darn Help."

169. Young, *Justice and the Politics of Difference*.

170. Young, 234.

171. Hanchard, *Party/Politics*, 30.

172. R. Williams, *Politics of Public Housing*, 14; Naples, *Grassroots Warriors*; Feldman and Stall, *Dignity of Resistance*; Gallagher, *Black Women and Politics*; Soss, *Unwanted Claims*; Levenstein, *Movement without Marches*.

173. Berger, *Workable Sisterhood*, 18.

174. Harris-Perry, *Sister Citizen*.

175. Young, *Justice and the Politics of Difference*.

176. McAdam, *Political Process*.

177. Young, *Justice and the Politics of Difference*, 9.

178. Cohen, "Deviance as Resistance."

179. Cohen, 39.

180. Cohen, 39.

181. Schneider, *Police Power and Race Riots*; Osterweil, *In Defense of Looting*.

182. D. Harris, *Black Feminist Politics*.

183. Acheson, *Abolishing State Violence*.

184. Mouffe, *On the Political*.

185. M. Mitchell et al., *Black Women in Politics*; Jordan-Zachery, "I Ain't Your Darn Help"; Alexander-Floyd, "Why Political Scientists"; Simien, *Black Feminist Voices in Politics*; D. Harris, *Black Feminist Politics*; Berger, *Workable Sisterhood*; Isoke, *Urban Black Women*; T. Williamson, *Scandalize My Name*; Perry, *Black Women*; Collins, *Black Feminist Thought*.

186. Naples, *Grassroots Warriors*.

187. Cohen, "Deviance as Resistance."

188. Gotham and Brumley, "Using Space"; Huckfeldt, *Politics in Context*; Isoke, "Politics of Homemaking"; Berger, *Workable Sisterhood*; Massey and Kanaiapuni, "Public Housing"; Brison, *Aftermath*.

189. Kelley, *Race Rebels*, 10.

190. Hayward, *How Americans Make Race*.

191. R. Williams, *Politics of Public Housing*; Levenstein, *Movement without Marches*.

192. R. Williams, *Politics of Public Housing*.

193. Perry, *Black Women*; Naples, *Grassroots Warriors*; Berger, *Workable Sisterhood*; Watkins-Hayes, *Remaking a Life*; Isoke, *Urban Black Women*; R. Williams, *Politics of Public Housing*; Feldman and Stall, *Dignity of Resistance*; Gold, *When Tenants Claimed the City*.

194. Gotham and Brumley, "Using Space"; Huckfeldt, "Variable Responses"; Huckfeldt, *Politics in Context*; Kang and Kwak, "Multilevel Approach to Civic Participation"; Morenoff, Sampson, and Raudenbush, "Neighborhood Inequality"; Sampson, *Great American City*; Isoke, *Urban Black Women*; Isoke, "Politics of Homemaking"; Berger, *Workable Sisterhood*.

195. Oyserman and Fryberg, "Possible Selves of Diverse Adolescents"; Oyserman, Gant, and Ager, "Socially Contextualized Model"; Oyserman et al., "Possible Selves as Roadmaps."

196. McKittrick, *Demonic Grounds*; Berger, *Workable Sisterhood*; Naples, *Grassroots Warriors*; Watkins-Hayes, *Remaking a Life*; Rios, *Punished*; Hayward, *How Americans Make Race*; R. Williams, *Politics of Public Housing*; Feldman and Stall, *Dignity of Resistance*.

197. Simien, *Black Feminist Voices in Politics*; Isoke, *Urban Black Women*; Alex-Assensoh, "Race, Concentrated Poverty"; Desmond and Travis, "Political Consequences."

198. Masuoka and Junn, *Politics of Belonging*; C. Wong, *Boundaries of Obligation*.

199. hooks, *Ain't I a Woman*; Collins, *Black Feminist Thought*; Collins, *From Black Power to Hip Hop*; Roth, "Making of the Vanguard Center."

200. C. Jones, "End to the Neglect"; Guy-Sheftall, *Words of Fire*; "Combahee River Collective Statement"; Roth, "Making of the Vanguard Center."

201. "Buy-cott" is a word used to describe economic boycotts. As Cohen notes in *Democracy Remixed*, it is an increasingly popular mode of political protest, particularly within communities of color in the United States. Stolle, Hooghe, and Micheletti, "Politics in the Supermarket"; Micheletti, Follesdal, and Stolle, *Politics, Products, and Markets*; Cohen, *Democracy Remixed*.

202. Gainous and Wagner, *Tweeting to Power*; McGregor, Mourão, and Molyneux, "Twitter as a Tool"; Gil de Zúñiga, Molyneux, and Zheng, "Social Media, Political Expression"; Gil de Zúñiga, "Social Media Use"; W. L. Bennett, "Personalization of Politics."

203. Scott, *Domination and the Arts of Resistance*; Hanchard, *Party/Politics*; Kelley, *Yo' Mama's Disfunktional!*; Harris-Lacewell, *Barbershops, Bibles, and BET*.

204. D. Wong, "Shop Talk," 137; Harris-Lacewell, *Barbershops, Bibles, and BET*.

205. Harris-Lacewell, *Barbershops, Bibles, and BET*; D. Wong, "Shop Talk"; Isoke, *Urban Black Women*.

206. D. Wong, "Shop Talk"; Harris-Lacewell, *Barbershops, Bibles, and BET*.

207. Spence, "Ella Baker and the Challenge of Black Rule"; Davies, *Left of Karl Marx*; Roth, "Making of the Vanguard Center"; James, *Shadowboxing*.

208. Isoke, *Urban Black Women*; Isoke, "Politics of Homemaking."

CHAPTER 2

1. Roth, "Making of the Vanguard Center."

2. Lipsky, *Street-Level Bureaucracy*; Soss, *Unwanted Claims*; Michener, *Fragmented Democracy*; Weaver, Prowse, and Piston, "Too Much Knowledge"; R. Williams, *Politics of Public Housing*; T. Williamson, *Scandalize My Name*.

3. Kelley, *Race Rebels*; Kelley, *Yo' Mama's Disfunktional!*

4. Michael Hawthorne and Darnell Little, "Our Toxic Air," *Chicago Tribune*, December 29, 2008, https://www.chicagotribune.com/news/ct-xpm-2008-09-29-0809290162-story.html.

5. Baron, *What Is Gautreaux?*; Polikoff, *Waiting for Gautreaux*.

6. Baron, *What Is Gautreaux?*, 3.

7. Robnett, *How Long?*; Francis, *Civil Rights*.

8. Isoke, "Politics of Homemaking"; Isoke, *Urban Black Women*; T. Williamson, *Scandalize My Name*; Kelley, *Race Rebels*; Shingles, "Black Consciousness and Political Participation."

9. Feldman and Stall, *Dignity of Resistance*; Baron, *What Is Gautreaux?*; Polikoff, *Waiting for Gautreaux*.

10. Baron, *What Is Gautreaux?*, 3.

11. Feldman and Stall, *The Dignity of Resistance*; Fuerst and Hunt, *When Public Housing Was Paradise*; Williams, *The Politics of Public Housing*; Gold, *When Tenants Claimed the City*; Levenstein, *A Movement Without Marches*.

12. Shingles, "Black Consciousness and Political Participation."

13. A. Campbell et al., *American Voter*; Alex-Assensoh, "Race, Concentrated Poverty"; Brady, Verba, and Schlozman, "Beyond SES."

14. Brady, Verba, and Schlozman, "Beyond SES."

15. Eliasoph, *Avoiding Politics*; Isoke, *Urban Black Women*; Perry, *Black Women*; Berger, *Workable Sisterhood*.

16. T. Williamson, *Scandalize My Name*.

17. Hanchard, *Party/Politics*.

18. Naples, *Grassroots Warriors*; Isoke, "Politics of Homemaking"; Isoke, *Urban Black Women*; T. Williamson, *Scandalize My Name*; Cohen and Dawson, "Neighborhood Poverty"; Berger, *Workable Sisterhood*; Perry, *Black Women*.

19. Hackworth, *Neoliberal City*; Spence, *Knocking the Hustle*.

20. Masuoka and Junn, *Politics of Belonging*; C. Wong, *Boundaries of Obligation*; D. Wong, "Shop Talk"; Naples, *Grassroots Warriors*; Berger, *Workable Sisterhood*; Isoke, *Urban Black Women*; Perry, *Black Women*.

21. Desmond and Travis, "Political Consequences."

22. Gay, "Moving to Opportunity."

23. Dawson, *Behind the Mule*; Gay, "Moving to Opportunity"; Dumke et al., "Daley's CHA Plan Jolted Region."

24. Spence, *Knocking the Hustle*; Hackworth, *Neoliberal City*.

25. Tim Novak et al., "Chicago Public Housing Authority Places Families in Crime Plagued Neighborhoods," *Better Government Association: Illinois' Non-partisan Full-Service Watchdog*, September 10, 2016, https://www.bettergov.org/news/chicago-housing-authority-places-families-in-crime-plagued-neighborhoods.

26. Naples, *Grassroots Warriors*; Isoke, *Urban Black Women*; Berger, *Workable Sisterhood*; R. Williams, *Politics of Public Housing*; Feldman and Stall, *Dignity of Resistance*; Gold, *When Tenants Claimed the City*.

27. Masuoka and Junn, *Politics of Belonging*; C. Wong, *Boundaries of Obligation*; D. Wong, "Shop Talk"; Perry, *Black Women*; Naples, *Grassroots Warriors*; Berger, *Workable Sisterhood*.

28. Hancock, *Politics of Disgust*; Watkins-Hayes, *Remaking a Life*; Berger, *Workable Sisterhood*; R. Williams, *Politics of Public Housing*; Feldman and Stall, *Dignity of Resistance*; Levenstein, *Movement without Marches*.

29. Feldman and Stall, *Dignity of Resistance*; R. Williams, *Politics of Public Housing*.

30. Shingles, "Black Consciousness and Political Participation"; Eliasoph, *Avoiding Politics*; Bruch and Soss, "Schooling as a Formative Political Experience"; Soss and Weaver, "Police Are Our Government"; Isoke, "Politics of Homemaking"; Naples, *Grassroots Warriors*; R. Williams, *Politics of Public Housing*; Feldman and Stall, *Dignity of Resistance*; Perry, *Black Women*.

31. Eliasoph, *Avoiding Politics*, 11.

32. Gay, "Moving to Opportunity."

33. Fuerst and Hunt, *When Public Housing Was Paradise: Building Community in Chicago*.

34. Gay, "Putting Race in Context"; Gay, "Moving to Opportunity"; Hackworth, *Neoliberal City*; Spence, *Knocking the Hustle*.

35. Simien, *Black Feminist Voices in Politics*, 5.

36. Berger, *Workable Sisterhood*.

37. Richie, *Arrested Justice*; Berger, *Workable Sisterhood*, 131–32.

38. Simien, *Black Feminist Voices in Politics*.

39. Dawson, *Behind the Mule*.

40. Collins, *Black Feminist Thought*; Roth, "Making of the Vanguard Center."

41. "Combahee River Collective Statement"; Berger, *Workable Sisterhood*; Isoke, "Politics of Homemaking"; Isoke, *Urban Black Women*; T. Williamson, *Scandalize My Name*; Alexander-Floyd, "Why Political Scientists"; Jordan-Zachery, "I Ain't Your Darn Help"; Simien, *Black Feminist Voices in Politics*; D. Harris, *Black Feminist Politics*; Collins, *Black Feminist Thought*; Richie, *Arrested Justice*; Cohen, *Boundaries of Blackness*; Dawson, *Black Visions*; Hanchard, *Party/Politics*; Perry, *Black Women*.

42. Mitchell et al.; Simien, *Black Feminist Voices in Politics*; Collins, *Black Feminist Thought*.

43. M. Mitchell et al., *Black Women in Politics*.

44. Naples, *Grassroots Warriors*; Isoke, *Urban Black Women*; Berger, *Workable Sisterhood*.

45. Lerman and Weaver, *Arresting Citizenship*, 14–15.

46. Moffett-Bateau, "I Can't Vote"; Brison, *Aftermath*; Peterson, Krivo, and Hagan, *Divergent Social Worlds*.

47. Soss and Weaver, "Police Are Our Government."

48. McGuire, *At the Dark End of the Street*; Feimster, *Southern Horrors*; Ritchie, *Invisible No More*; Ritchie, *Shrouded in Silence*; Richie, *Arrested Justice*; Cohen, "Punks, Bulldaggers and Welfare Queens."

49. Soss and Weaver, "Police Are Our Government."

50. Weaver, Prowse, and Piston, "Too Much Knowledge."

51. Baron, *What Is Gautreaux?*

52. Alexander Polikoff, *Waiting for Gautreaux: A Story of Segregation, Housing, and the Black Ghetto* (Evanston: Northwestern University Press, 2006).

53. Baron, 3.

54. Baron, 3.

55. Hearsey, "Sabbath Time!"

56. Isoke, *Urban Black Women*.

57. Isoke, 34–36.

58. Dreier, Mollenkopf, and Swanstrom, *Place Matters*.

59. Naples, *Grassroots Warriors*; Berger, *Workable Sisterhood*; Perry, *Black Women*; Watkins-Hayes, *Remaking a Life*; R. Williams, *Politics of Public Housing*; Feldman and Stall, *Dignity of Resistance*; Gold, *When Tenants Claimed the City*.

60. Brison, *Aftermath*; Richie, *Arrested Justice*; Ritchie, *Invisible No More*.

61. McKittrick, *Demonic Grounds*, xviii.

62. Sinclair, *Social Citizen*.

63. Eliasoph, *Avoiding Politics*.

64. Eliasoph.

65. Eliasoph.

66. Cohen, "Deviance as Resistance"; Simien, *Black Feminist Voices in Politics*; D. Harris, *Black Feminist Politics*; Berger, *Workable Sisterhood*; Naples, *Grassroots Warriors*; Watkins-Hayes, *Remaking a Life*; Isoke, *Urban Black Women*; Perry, *Black Women*; T. Williamson, *Scandalize My Name*; Hanchard, *Party/Politics*; Dawson, *Black Visions*.

CHAPTER 3

1. Baron, *What Is Gautreaux?*; Polikoff, *Waiting for Gautreaux*; Feldman and Stall, *Dignity of Resistance*; Brinson, "Altgeld Gardens Lawsuit Settlement."

2. Eliasoph, *Avoiding Politics*.

3. Eliasoph.

4. Eliasoph, 11.

5. Eliasoph, 11.

6. Eliasoph, 11.

7. Wright Mills, *Sociological Imagination*; Eliasoph, *Avoiding Politics*.

8. Wright Mills, *Sociological Imagination*; Eliasoph, *Avoiding Politics*; Eliasoph, "Evaporation of Politics."

9. Eliasoph, *Avoiding Politics*.

10. Eliasoph, 15.

11. Black Public Sphere Collective, *Black Public Sphere*; Squires, "Rethinking the Black Public Sphere"; Cohen, *Boundaries of Blackness*; Cohen, *Democracy Remixed*; Hanchard, *Party/Politics*; Hanchard, "Acts of Misrecognition."

12. Squires, "Rethinking the Black Public Sphere," 448–49.

13. Burch, *Trading Democracy for Justice*; *New York Times* Editorial, "Opinion"; Western, *Punishment and Inequality in America*.

14. *New York Times* Editorial, "Opinion"; Burch, *Trading Democracy for Justice*.

15. Nunnally, *Trust in Black America*; Cohen, *Democracy Remixed*; Lyons, "Political Socialization of Ghetto Children"; Rios, *Punished*.

16. Cohen, *Democracy Remixed*; Hanchard, *Party/Politics*; Dawson, *Black Visions*; Hancock, *Politics of Disgust*; Roberts, *Killing the Black Body*.

17. Squires, "Rethinking the Black Public Sphere"; Robnett, *How Long?*; McAdam, *Political Process*; Desmond and Travis, "Political Consequences"; Francis, "Strange Fruit of American Political Development."

18. Black Public Sphere Collective, *Black Public Sphere*; Squires, "Rethinking the Black Public Sphere."

19. Squires, "Rethinking the Black Public Sphere," 454.

20. Squires, 448.

21. Cohen, *Boundaries of Blackness*; Cohen, *Democracy Remixed*; F. Harris, "Rise of Respectability Politics."

22. Levenstein, *Movement without Marches*; Bakshi, Meares, and Weaver, "Portals to Politics"; Desmond and Travis, "Political Consequences"; Moffett-Bateau, "Strategies

of Resistance"; Feldman and Stall, *Dignity of Resistance*; Naples, *Grassroots Warriors*; Berger, *Workable Sisterhood*; Isoke, *Urban Black Women*; Watkins-Hayes, *Remaking a Life*; Hanchard, *Party/Politics*; Perry, *Black Women*; D. Wong, "Shop Talk."

23. Black Public Sphere Collective, *Black Public Sphere*; Squires, "Rethinking the Black Public Sphere."

24. Squires, "Rethinking the Black Public Sphere"; Black Public Sphere Collective, *Black Public Sphere*.

25. Squires, "Rethinking the Black Public Sphere," 456.

26. Moffett-Bateau, "I Can't Vote"; Gotham and Brumley, "Using Space"; R. Williams, *Politics of Public Housing*; T. Williamson, *Scandalize My Name*; K. Mitchell, *From Slave Cabins to the White House*.

27. Squires, "Rethinking the Black Public Sphere," 448.

28. Squires; Scott, *Domination and the Arts of Resistance*; Kelley, *Race Rebels*; Cohen, *Democracy Remixed*; Cohen, "Deviance as Resistance"; Cohen, "Punks, Bulldaggers and Welfare Queens"; Moffett-Bateau, "Strategies of Resistance"; Levenstein, *Movement without Marches*; Soss, *Unwanted Claims*; Roberts, *Killing the Black Body*.

29. Soss, *Unwanted Claims*; Weaver, Prowse, and Piston, "Too Much Knowledge"; Kelley, *Race Rebels*; Hanchard, *Party/Politics*; Perry, *Black Women*; Isoke, *Urban Black Women*; Berger, *Workable Sisterhood*. For more on "street-level bureaucrats," see Michael Lipsky, *Street-Level Bureaucracy*.

30. Squires, "Rethinking the Black Public Sphere," 454.

31. Collins, *Black Feminist Thought*; Collins, *From Black Power to Hip Hop*; "Combahee River Collective Statement"; Alexander-Floyd, "Radical Black Feminism"; Jordan-Zachery, "Resistance and Redemption Narratives"; Simien, *Black Feminist Voices in Politics*; D. Harris, *Black Feminist Politics*.

32. Isoke, *Urban Black Women*; Isoke, "Politics of Homemaking"; T. Williamson, *Scandalize My Name*; R. Williams, *Politics of Public Housing*; Naples, *Grassroots Warriors*; Berger, *Workable Sisterhood*; Watkins-Hayes, *Remaking a Life*; Perry, *Black Women*.

33. Squires, "Rethinking the Black Public Sphere," 456 (emphasis mine).

34. Isoke, *Urban Black Women*; Berger, *Workable Sisterhood*; Perry, *Black Women*.

35. Isoke, *Urban Black Women*; Isoke, "Politics of Homemaking"; Berger, *Workable Sisterhood*; Naples, *Grassroots Warriors*; Perry, *Black Women*; Black Public Sphere Collective, *Black Public Sphere*; Squires, "Rethinking the Black Public Sphere"; Gotham and Brumley, "Using Space"; Eliasoph, *Avoiding Politics*.

36. Berger, *Workable Sisterhood*; Naples, *Grassroots Warriors*; Watkins-Hayes, *Remaking a Life*; Isoke, *Urban Black Women*.

37. Berger, *Workable Sisterhood*; Watkins-Hayes, *Remaking a Life*; Naples, *Grassroots Warriors*; R. Williams, *Politics of Public Housing*; Feldman and Stall, *Dignity of Resistance*; Soss, *Unwanted Claims*; Michener, *Fragmented Democracy*.

38. Eliasoph, *Avoiding Politics*.

39. Eliasoph.

40. Eliasoph; Squires, "Rethinking the Black Public Sphere."

41. Young, *Justice and the Politics of Difference*.

42. Steve Bogira, "Separate, Unequal and Ignored," *Chicago Reader*, February 10, 2011, https://www.chicagoreader.com/chicago/chicago-politics-segregation-african-american-black-white-hispanic-latino-population-census-community/Content?oid=3221712; Venkatesh, *American Project*.

43. Sisson, Freund, and Koziarz, "How Mayor Rahm Emanuel Changed the Look of Chicago."

44. Venkatesh, *American Project*.

45. Venkatesh.

46. Venkatesh. IX.

47. Trounstine, *Segregation by Design*, 3.

48. Trounstine, 3.

49. Trounstine.

50. Goetz, *New Deal Ruins*.

51. Goetz, 36.

52. Fuerst and Hunt, *When Public Housing Was Paradise*, 2.

53. Goetz, *New Deal Ruins*, 37.

54. Chicago Public Housing, *Chicago Housing Authority Quarterly Report 3rd Quarter 2017*, Chicago: Chicago Housing Authority, 2017, http://www.thecha.org/assets/1/6/CHA_Q3_2017_Quarterly_Report.pdf.

55. Goetz, *New Deal Ruins*, 40.

56. Cohen, *Boundaries of Blackness*; Hancock, *Politics of Disgust*; Berger, *Workable Sisterhood*; Watkins-Hayes, *Remaking a Life*.

57. Levenstein, *Movement without Marches*; Venkatesh, *American Project*; Trounstine, *Segregation by Design*; Feldman and Stall, *Dignity of Resistance*; Massey and Kanaiapuni, "Public Housing"; Gay, "Moving to Opportunity"; Kirk and Wakefield, "Collateral Consequences of Punishment"; Goetz, *New Deal Ruins*.

58. Fuerst and Hunt, *When Public Housing Was Paradise*; Hunt, *Blueprint for Disaster*; Feldman and Stall, *Dignity of Resistance*; Polikoff, *Waiting for Gautreaux*; Venkatesh, *American Project*.

59. Chan, "40-Year Fight"; Chase, "Public Housing Residents."

60. McAvoy, "Lost in the Shuffle."

61. Coffey et al., "Poisonous Homes."

62. McAvoy, "Lost in the Shuffle."

63. McAvoy.

64. Grotto, Cohen, and Olkon, "Public Housing's Island."

65. Housing Authority Risk Retention Group v. Chicago Housing Authority, 378 F.3d 596 (7th Cir. 2004), https://caselaw.findlaw.com/us-7th-circuit/1380122.html.

66. Coffey et al., "Poisonous Homes"; Chase, "Public Housing Residents"; Brinson, "Altgeld Gardens Lawsuit Settlement"; White and Hall, "Perceptions of Environmental Health Risks"; Chan, "40-Year Fight."

67. Johnson, "Altgeld Gardens Moved."

68. Brinson, "Altgeld Gardens Lawsuit Settlement."

69. Grotto, Cohen, and Olkon, "Public Housing's Island."

70. Hudson, "Altgeld Gardens."

71. Susan J. Popkin, "Hard Lessons from Chicago's Public Housing Reform," *City Lab*, February 7, 2017, https://www.citylab.com/equity/2017/02/hard-lessons-from-chicagos-public-housing-reform/515934/.

72. Kristine Berg, "Implementing Chicago's Plan to Transform Public Housing," (Changing Face of Metropolitan Chicago Conference on Chicago Research and Public Policy, May 12, 2004).

73. Berg.

74. Popkin and Cunningham.

75. Popkin and Cunningham.

76. Natalie Moore, "Why the Chicago Housing Authority Failed to Meet Its Mixed Income Ambitions," WBEZ, March 23, 2017, http://interactive.wbez.org/cha/.

77. Robert Chaskin, "Transformed: 16,000 Families Moved out of Traditional Public Housing in Chicago," *SSA Magazine* 21, no. 1 (Winter 2014), http://ssa.uchicago.edu/ssa_magazine/transformed.

78. Natalie Moore, "Public Housing Residents Learn the Rules for Mixed Income," WBEZ 91.5 Chicago, June 3, 2008, https://www.wbez.org/shows/wbez-news/public-housing-residents-learn-the-rules-for-mixed-income/1b440f45-6b5f-4895-a1a0-d8e328d62017.

79. Hackworth, *Neoliberal City*.

80. David C. Ranney and Patricia A. "Wright, Race, Class, and The Abuse of State Power: The Case of Public Housing in Chicago," Nathalie P. Voorhees Center for Neighborhood and Community Improvement (March 2000). www.uic.edu/cuppa/voorhesctr/racepaper.htm.

81. Hackworth, *Neoliberal City*. Location 1077–1085.

82. Wilson Gilmore, "Organized Abandonment and Organized Violence."

83. Cohen, *Boundaries of Blackness*; Cohen, "Deviance as Resistance"; Hancock, *Politics of Disgust*; Berger, *Workable Sisterhood*.

84. Cohen, *Boundaries of Blackness*, 64.

85. Jason Hackworth, *The Neoliberal City: Governance, Ideology, and Development in American Urbanism* (Ithaca, NY: Cornell University Press, 2014), 51. https://doi.org/10.7591/9780801461590.

86. Davenport, "Public Accountability and Political Participation"; Gay, "Moving to Opportunity"; Coalition to Protect Public Housing, "Written Submission."

87. Susan J. Popkin, Megan Gallagher, et al., "CHA Residents and the Plan for Transformation," *Urban Institute*, January 2013, https://www.urban.org/sites/default/files/publication/23376/412761-CHA-Residents-and-the-Plan-for-Transformation.PDF.

88. Hackworth, *Neoliberal City*.

89. Massey and Kanaiapuni, "Public Housing"; Sampson, *Great American City*; Popkin, *No Simple Solutions*; Popkin, Levy, et al., "HOPE VI Program."

90. McKittrick, *Demonic Grounds*; Perry, *Black Women*; Isoke, *Urban Black Women*.

91. Hayward, *How Americans Make Race*; McKittrick, *Demonic Grounds*; Naples, *Grassroots Warriors*; Gold, *When Tenants Claimed the City*; Gallagher, *Black Women and Politics*; Feldman and Stall, *Dignity of Resistance*; R. Williams, *Politics of Public*

Housing; Isoke, *Urban Black Women*; Watkins-Hayes, *Remaking a Life*; Berger, *Workable Sisterhood*.

92. A. L. Campbell, *How Policies Make Citizens*; Mettler, *Soldiers to Citizens*; Skocpol, *Protecting Soldiers and Mothers*; Soss, *Unwanted Claims*.

93. Mettler, *Soldiers to Citizens*; A. L. Campbell, *How Policies Make Citizens*; Skocpol, *Protecting Soldiers and Mothers*.

94. Lerman and Weaver, *Arresting Citizenship*; Roberts, *Killing the Black Body*.

95. Fording, Soss, and Schram, "Race and the Local Politics"; A. L. Campbell, *How Policies Make Citizens*; Watkins-Hayes, *New Welfare Bureaucrats*; Watkins-Hayes, *Remaking a Life*; Berger, *Workable Sisterhood*.

96. Levenstein, *Movement without Marches*; Venkatesh, *American Project*; Trounstine, *Segregation by Design*; Goetz, *New Deal Ruins*.

97. Wilson Gilmore, "Organized Abandonment and Organized Violence"; Gilmore, "Fatal Couplings of Power and Difference."

98. Tanous and Eghbariah, "Organized Violence and Organized Abandonment," 2.

99. Wilson Gilmore, "Organized Abandonment and Organized Violence."

100. Hanchard, "Acts of Misrecognition"; Kelley, *Race Rebels*; Perry, *Black Women*.

101. Eliasoph, *Avoiding Politics*; R. Williams, *Politics of Public Housing*; Levenstein, *Movement without Marches*; Gold, *When Tenants Claimed the City*; Gallagher, *Black Women and Politics*; Naples, *Grassroots Warriors*; Isoke, *Urban Black Women*; T. Williamson, *Scandalize My Name*.

102. Weaver, Prowse, and Piston, "Too Much Knowledge"; Rios, *Punished*; Bruch and Soss, "Schooling as a Formative Political Experience"; Cramer and Toff, "Fact of Experience."

103. Levenstein, *Movement without Marches*; R. Williams, *Politics of Public Housing*; Feldman and Stall, *Dignity of Resistance*; Gold, *When Tenants Claimed the City*.

104. Hackworth, *Neoliberal City*; Hunt, *Blueprint for Disaster*; Harcourt, *Illusion of Order*.

105. Hackworth, *Neoliberal City*. Location 2853.

106. Hackworth, *Neoliberal City*; Hunt, *Blueprint for Disaster*.

107. Washington, "Narrowing the Digital Divide."

108. Young, *Justice and the Politics of Difference*, 75.

109. Hackworth, *Neoliberal City*; Spence, *Knocking the Hustle*.

110. Young, *Justice and the Politics of Difference*.

111. Young, 75.

112. Young, 75.

113. Isoke, "Politics of Homemaking."

114. Spence, *Knocking the Hustle*; Cohen, *Boundaries of Blackness*; Dawson, *Black Visions*; Lipsky, *Street-Level Bureaucracy*.

115. Soss, *Unwanted Claims*.

116. Soss; Soss, "Lessons of Welfare"; Levenstein, *Movement without Marches*; R. Williams, *Politics of Public Housing*.

117. Soss, *Unwanted Claims*.

118. R. Williams, *Politics of Public Housing*; Naples, *Grassroots Warriors*; Gallagher, *Black Women and Politics*; Feldman and Stall, *Dignity of Resistance*; Levenstein, *Movement without Marches*.

119. Levenstein, *Movement without Marches*.

120. Levenstein.

121. R. Williams, *Politics of Public Housing*.

122. Levenstein, *Movement without Marches*; R. Williams, *Politics of Public Housing*.

123. R. Williams, *Politics of Public Housing*; Naples, *Grassroots Warriors*; Feldman and Stall, *Dignity of Resistance*; Gold, *When Tenants Claimed the City*; Isoke, *Urban Black Women*; Berger, *Workable Sisterhood*; Watkins-Hayes, *New Welfare Bureaucrats*; Venkatesh, *American Project*; Levenstein, *Movement without Marches*; Watkins-Hayes, *Remaking a Life*.

124. R. Williams, *Politics of Public Housing*.

125. R. Williams.

126. Lipsky, *Street-Level Bureaucracy*; Gold, *When Tenants Claimed the City*; Roberts, *Killing the Black Body*; Katznelson, *City Trenches*; R. Williams, *Politics of Public Housing*.

127. R. Williams, *Politics of Public Housing*.

128. Gay, "Moving to Opportunity."

129. Sinclair, *Social Citizen*.

130. Prowse, Weaver, and Meares, "State from Below"; Weaver, Prowse, and Piston, "Too Much Knowledge"; Soss and Weaver, "Police Are Our Government."

131. Huckfeldt, *Politics in Context*.

132. Huckfeldt, "Variable Responses."

133. Soss and Weaver, "Police Are Our Government"; Prowse, Weaver, and Meares, "State from Below"; Naples, *Grassroots Warriors*; Isoke, *Urban Black Women*; T. Williamson, *Scandalize My Name*; Berger, *Workable Sisterhood*; Watkins-Hayes, *Remaking a Life*; Feldman and Stall, *Dignity of Resistance*; Gold, *When Tenants Claimed the City*; Levenstein, *Movement without Marches*.

134. Perry, *Black Women*; R. Williams, *Politics of Public Housing*; Feldman and Stall, *Dignity of Resistance*.

135. Gallagher, *Black Women and Politics*; Naples, *Grassroots Warriors*; Feldman and Stall, *Dignity of Resistance*; Gold, *When Tenants Claimed the City*; Simien, *Black Feminist Voices in Politics*; D. Harris, *Black Feminist Politics*; M. Mitchell et al., *Black Women in Politics*; Jordan-Zachery and Alexander-Floyd, *Black Women in Politics*; Burack, *Healing Identities*; N. Brown, *Sisters in the Statehouse*; Berger, *Workable Sisterhood*; Watkins-Hayes, *Remaking a Life*; Foreman, *Activist Sentiments*; R. Williams, *Politics of Public Housing*; McGuire, *At the Dark End of the Street*.

136. N. Brown, *Sisters in the Statehouse*; Isoke, "Politics of Homemaking"; Isoke, "Black Ethnography"; Berger, *Workable Sisterhood*; Watkins-Hayes, *Remaking a Life*.

137. Junn, "Participation in Liberal Democracy"; G. King et al., "Enhancing the Validity"; Alexander-Floyd, "Why Political Scientists"; Jordan-Zachery, "Beyond the Side Eye"; Jordan-Zachery, "I Ain't Your Darn Help"; D. Harris, *Black Feminist Politics*; Simien, "Gender Differences"; Simien, *Black Feminist Voices in Politics*; Junn et al.,

"What Revolution?"; Junn, "Participation in Liberal Democracy"; Richie, *Arrested Justice*.

138. M. Mitchell et al., *Black Women in Politics*; Jordan-Zachery and Alexander-Floyd, *Black Women in Politics*; Jordan-Zachery, "I Ain't Your Darn Help"; Jordan-Zachery, "Beyond the Side Eye"; D. Harris, *Black Feminist Politics*; Simien, *Black Feminist Voices in Politics*; Harris-Perry, *Sister Citizen*; Simien, "Gender Differences"; Junn et al., "What Revolution?"; Junn, "Participation in Liberal Democracy"; Richie, *Arrested Justice*; Cohen, *Boundaries of Blackness*; Cohen, "Deviance as Resistance."

139. Weaver, Prowse, and Piston, "Too Much Knowledge"; Prowse, Weaver, and Meares, "State from Below"; Michener, "Policy Feedback in a Racialized Polity"; Michener, "People, Places, Power"; D. Wong, "Shop Talk"; Cohen, *Democracy Remixed*; Dawson, *Black Visions*; Simien, *Black Feminist Voices in Politics*; Jordan-Zachery and Alexander-Floyd, *Black Women in Politics*; M. Mitchell et al., *Black Women in Politics*; Alexander-Floyd, "Why Political Scientists"; Jordan-Zachery, "I Ain't Your Darn Help"; Prestage, "In Quest of African American Political Woman"; N. Brown, "Political Participation"; N. Brown and Young, "Ratchet Politics"; Roth, "Making of the Vanguard Center."

140. Hayward, *How Americans Make Race*.

141. Yin, *Case Study Research Design and Methods Fourth Edition*, 18.

142. Stake, *Art of Case Study Research*, xi.

143. Gotham and Brumley, "Using Space"; Feldman and Stall, *Dignity of Resistance*; R. Williams, *Politics of Public Housing*; T. Williamson, *Scandalize My Name*; Isoke, *Urban Black Women*.

144. Verba, Schlozman, and Brady, *Voice and Equality*.

145. Gotham and Brumley, "Using Space"; Gay, "Moving to Opportunity"; Gay, "Putting Race in Context"; Popkin, *No Simple Solutions*; Soss, *Unwanted Claims*.

146. Hackworth, *Neoliberal City*; Spence, *Knocking the Hustle*; Hunt, *Blueprint for Disaster*; Popkin, *No Simple Solutions*; Feldman and Stall, *Dignity of Resistance*.

147. Feldman and Stall, *Dignity of Resistance*; Levenstein, *Movement without Marches*; Naples, *Grassroots Warriors*; Gold, *When Tenants Claimed the City*; R. Williams, *Politics of Public Housing*; T. Williamson, *Scandalize My Name*; Isoke, *Urban Black Women*; Perry, *Black Women*; Berger, *Workable Sisterhood*; Watkins-Hayes, *Remaking a Life*.

CHAPTER 4

1. Harcourt, *Illusion of Order*.

2. Michener, "Neighborhood Disorder and Local Participation"; Harcourt, *Illusion of Order*.

3. Miller, *Getting Played*; Desmond and Travis, "Political Consequences"; Spence, *Knocking the Hustle*; Weaver, Prowse, and Piston, "Too Much Knowledge."

4. Michener, "Policy Feedback in a Racialized Polity"; Prowse, Weaver, and Meares, "State from Below"; Soss and Weaver, "Police Are Our Government." For more on "street-level bureaucrats," see Michael Lipsky, *Street-level Bureaucracy*.

5. McRoberts, "Beyond Mysterium Tremendum"; Isoke, "Politics of Homemaking"; Isoke, "Black Ethnography"; Isoke, *Urban Black Women*; Huckfeldt, "Variable Responses"; McKittrick, *Demonic Grounds*; T. Williamson, *Scandalize My Name*; K. Mitchell, *From Slave Cabins to the White House*; K. Mitchell, *Living with Lynching*.

6. McKittrick, *Demonic Grounds*, 6.

7. McKittrick.

8. Perry, *Black Women*; Hanchard, "Acts of Misrecognition"; Thurston, "Black Lives Matter"; Hunt, *Blueprint for Disaster*; Goetz, *New Deal Ruins*; Feldman and Stall, *Dignity of Resistance*; Gotham and Brumley, "Using Space"; Chaskin et al., "Public Housing Transformation."

9. McKittrick, *Demonic Grounds*, xiii.

10. Staples, "Death of the Black Utopia"; Pfeiffer, "Displacement through Discourse"; Hunt, *Blueprint for Disaster*; K. Mitchell, *From Slave Cabins to the White House*; K. Williams, *They Left Great Marks*.

11. Rios, *Punished*; Hayward, *How Americans Make Race*; Hanchard, "Contours of Black Political Thought."

12. hooks, *Sisters of the Yam*.

13. Alex-Assensoh, "Race, Concentrated Poverty"; Desmond and Travis, "Political Consequences."

14. Venkatesh, *American Project*; Ralph, *Renegade Dreams*; Garcia, Taylor, and Lawton, "Impacts of Violent Crime."

15. Hanchard, "Contours of Black Political Thought"; Hanchard, "Acts of Misrecognition."

16. Baron, *What Is Gautreaux?*; Polikoff, *Waiting for Gautreaux*.

17. Polikoff, *Waiting for Gautreaux*; Hunt, *Blueprint for Disaster*.

18. Brinson, "Altgeld Gardens Lawsuit Settlement"; White and Hall, "Perceptions of Environmental Health Risks"; Chase, "Public Housing Residents"; Feldman and Stall, *Dignity of Resistance*; Coffey et al., "Poisonous Homes."

19. Coffey et al., "Poisonous Homes"; Brinson, "Altgeld Gardens Lawsuit Settlement"; Grotto, Cohen, and Olkon, "Public Housing's Island."

20. Venkatesh, *American Project*; Rios, *Punished*; Ralph, *Renegade Dreams*.

21. Le Mignot, "4 Dead, 2 Wounded."

22. Ralph, *Renegade Dreams*.

23. Cohen, *Democracy Remixed*.

24. Kelley, *Race Rebels*; Iton, *In Search of the Black Fantastic*; Hanchard, *Party/Politics*.

25. Cohen, *Boundaries of Blackness*, 64.

26. Cohen.

27. Cohen, 64.

28. Cohen; Cohen, "Deviance as Resistance"; Cohen, "Punks, Bulldaggers and Welfare Queens"; Cohen, *Democracy Remixed*; Harris-Perry, *Sister Citizen*; F. Harris, "Rise of Respectability Politics"; Harris-Lacewell, *Barbershops, Bibles, and BET*; Weaver, Prowse, and Piston, "Too Much Knowledge"; Prowse, Weaver, and Meares, "State from Below."

29. Cohen, *Democracy Remixed*, 196.

30. Richie, *Arrested Justice*; Cohen and Dawson, "Neighborhood Poverty"; Cohen, *Boundaries of Blackness*; Cohen, "Punks, Bulldaggers and Welfare Queens"; Cohen, *Democracy Remixed*; Bunyasi and Smith, "Do All Black Lives Matter Equally?"; Hancock, *Politics of Disgust*; Gurusami, "Motherwork under the State"; Roberts, *Killing the Black Body*; Harris-Lacewell, *Barbershops, Bibles, and BET*; INCITE!, *Color of Violence*; Feimster, *Southern Horrors*; Collins, "On Violence, Intersectionality and Transversal Politics"; McGuire, *At the Dark End of the Street*.

31. Cohen, *Democracy Remixed*; Richie, *Arrested Justice*.

32. Harris-Perry, *Sister Citizen*; Young, *Justice and the Politics of Difference*; Cohen, *Democracy Remixed*.

33. Harris-Perry, *Sister Citizen*.

34. Harris-Perry; Young, *Justice and the Politics of Difference*; F. Harris, "Rise of Respectability Politics"; Cohen, *Boundaries of Blackness*; Cohen and Dawson, "Neighborhood Poverty"; Hanchard, *Party/Politics*; Iton, *In Search of the Black Fantastic*; Squires, "Rethinking the Black Public Sphere"; Black Public Sphere Collective, *Black Public Sphere*; "Combahee River Collective Statement"; Alexander-Floyd, "Radical Black Feminism."

35. Harris-Perry, *Sister Citizen*; Cohen, *Democracy Remixed*; Hanchard, *Party/Politics*; Black Public Sphere Collective, *Black Public Sphere*; F. Harris, "Rise of Respectability Politics."

36. F. Harris, "Rise of Respectability Politics"; P. J. Harris, "Gatekeeping and Remaking"; Harris-Lacewell, *Barbershops, Bibles, and BET*; Harris-Perry, *Sister Citizen*; Cohen and Dawson, "Neighborhood Poverty"; Cohen, *Boundaries of Blackness*; Dawson, *Behind the Mule*; Berger, *Workable Sisterhood*; Watkins-Hayes, *Remaking a Life*; Hancock, *Politics of Disgust*; Gurusami, "Motherwork under the State"; Roberts, *Killing the Black Body*; H. Hansen, Bourgois, and Drucker, "Pathologizing Poverty"; Cohen, "Punks, Bulldaggers and Welfare Queens"; Cohen, *Democracy Remixed*; Black Public Sphere Collective, *Black Public Sphere*; Squires, "Rethinking the Black Public Sphere."

37. Cohen, *Democracy Remixed*; Hancock, *Politics of Disgust*.

38. Cohen, *Democracy Remixed*.

39. *Chicago Talks*, "Occupy the Hood Strikes Back."

40. Gotham and Brumley, "Using Space."

41. Gotham and Brumley.

42. Gotham and Brumley.

43. Cudd, *Analyzing Oppression*; Scholz, "Empowering Resistance."

44. Gotham and Brumley, "Using Space."

45. Harris-Lacewell, *Barbershops, Bibles, and BET*; Collins, *From Black Power to Hip Hop*; Iton, *In Search of the Black Fantastic*; T. Williamson, *Scandalize My Name*; Kelley, *Yo' Mama's Disfunktional!*

46. McRoberts, "Beyond Mysterium Tremendum," 199.

47. McRoberts.

48. Isoke, "Politics of Homemaking."

49. Isoke, 119.

50. McRoberts, "Beyond Mysterium Tremendum," 199.

51. McRoberts.

52. Grotto, Cohen, and Olkon, "Public Housing's Island"; Hudson, "Altgeld Gardens"; White and Hall, "Perceptions of Environmental Health Risks."

53. Isoke, "Politics of Homemaking"; Isoke, *Urban Black Women*; Isoke, "Black Ethnography"; T. Williamson, *Scandalize My Name*; K. Mitchell, *From Slave Cabins to the White House*; Feldman and Stall, *Dignity of Resistance*; R. Williams, *Politics of Public Housing*.

54. Jackson, *Islam and the Blackamerican*.

55. Gay, "Moving to Opportunity."

56. Coffey et al., "Poisonous Homes"; White and Hall, "Perceptions of Environmental Health Risks."

57. De Souza Briggs, Popkin, and Goering, *Moving to Opportunity*; Popkin, Levy, et al., "HOPE VI Program"; Popkin, *No Simple Solutions*; L. Bennett, Smith, and Wright, *Where Are Poor People to Live?*

58. De Souza Briggs, Popkin, and Goering, *Moving to Opportunity*; Gay, "Moving to Opportunity"; Comey, Popkin, and Franks, "MTO."

59. L. Bennett, Smith, and Wright, *Where Are Poor People to Live?*; Popkin, Levy, et al., "HOPE VI Program."

60. Popkin, *No Simple Solutions*.

61. Feldman and Stall, *Dignity of Resistance*; Polikoff, *Waiting for Gautreaux*.

62. Weaver, Prowse, and Piston, "Too Much Knowledge"; Prowse, Weaver, and Meares, "State from Below"; Feldman and Stall, *Dignity of Resistance*; Levenstein, *Movement without Marches*; R. Williams, *Politics of Public Housing*.

63. Lipsky, *Street-Level Bureaucracy*, xix–xx.

64. McKittrick, *Demonic Grounds*; R. Williams, *Politics of Public Housing*; Levenstein, *Movement without Marches*; Trounstine, *Segregation by Design*; Cohen and Dawson, "Neighborhood Poverty"; Gotham and Brumley, "Using Space."

65. CHA, "Plan for Transformation"; Popkin, Rich, et al., "Public Housing Transformation and Crime"; Hunt, *Blueprint for Disaster*; Moffett-Bateau, "Strategies of Resistance."

66. Lipsky, *Street-Level Bureaucracy*; Watkins-Hayes, *New Welfare Bureaucrats*.

67. Lipsky, *Street-Level Bureaucracy*; Watkins-Hayes, *New Welfare Bureaucrats*; Feldman and Stall, *Dignity of Resistance*.

68. Popkin, *No Simple Solutions*; Loyd and Bonds, "Where Do Black Lives Matter?"; Roberts, *Killing the Black Body*; Gurusami, "Motherwork under the State"; Cohen, "Punks, Bulldaggers and Welfare Queens"; Hancock, *Politics of Disgust*.

69. Isoke, *Urban Black Women*; Isoke, "Politics of Homemaking."

70. Isoke, *Urban Black Women*; Isoke, "Politics of Homemaking"; T. Williamson, *Scandalize My Name*; Collins, *Black Feminist Thought*; Butler, "Quiltmaking among African-American Women."

71. R. Williams, *Politics of Public Housing*; Watkins-Hayes, *Remaking a Life*; Rios, *Punished*; Roberts, *Killing the Black Body*.

72. Hancock, *Politics of Disgust*; Cohen, "Punks, Bulldaggers and Welfare Queens"; Levenstein, *Movement without Marches*; Roberts, *Killing the Black Body*; Harris-Lace-

well, *Barbershops, Bibles, and BET*; H. Hansen, Bourgois, and Drucker, "Pathologizing Poverty."

73. Popkin, *No Simple Solutions*.

74. Popkin; Hunt, *Blueprint for Disaster*; Polikoff, *Waiting for Gautreaux*; Feldman and Stall, *Dignity of Resistance*; Coffey et al., "Poisonous Homes"; White and Hall, "Perceptions of Environmental Health Risks"; Hudson, "Altgeld Gardens."

75. Isoke, *Urban Black Women*; Isoke, review of *Suffering Will Not Be Televised* and *Behind the Mask*; Isoke, "Black Ethnography"; Isoke, "Politics of Homemaking"; T. Williamson, *Scandalize My Name*; Jordan-Zachery, "I Ain't Your Darn Help"; K. Mitchell, *From Slave Cabins to the White House*.

76. Moffett-Bateau, "I Can't Vote."

77. Wilson Gilmore, "Organized Abandonment and Organized Violence"; Tanous and Eghbariah, "Organized Violence and Organized Abandonment"; Ralph, *Renegade Dreams*; Spence, *Knocking the Hustle*; Weaver, Prowse, and Piston, "Too Much Knowledge"; Hackworth, *Neoliberal City*.

78. McKittrick, *Demonic Grounds*; Hanchard, "Acts of Misrecognition"; Hanchard, *Party/Politics*; Cohen, *Democracy Remixed*; Cohen, *Boundaries of Blackness*; Cohen and Dawson, "Neighborhood Poverty"; F. Harris, "Rise of Respectability Politics"; Hancock, *Politics of Disgust*; Cohen, "Punks, Bulldaggers and Welfare Queens"; Fording, Soss, and Schram, "Race and the Local Politics."

79. Hanchard, "Acts of Misrecognition."

80. Hanchard.

81. Gay, "Moving to Opportunity"; Gotham and Brumley, "Using Space"; Popkin, *No Simple Solutions*; L. Bennett, Smith, and Wright, *Where Are Poor People to Live?*; Cohen, *Democracy Remixed*; Cohen and Dawson, "Neighborhood Poverty."

82. McKittrick, *Demonic Grounds*, xiv.

83. McKittrick; Hanchard, *Party/Politics*; Perry, *Black Women*; Gotham and Brumley, "Using Space"; D. Wong, "Shop Talk"; Gilmore, "Fatal Couplings of Power and Difference"; Hayward, *How Americans Make Race*; Gay, "Putting Race in Context"; Trounstine, *Segregation by Design*.

84. Huckfeldt, *Politics in Context*; Gay, "Putting Race in Context"; Trounstine, *Segregation by Design*; Gilmore, "Fatal Couplings of Power and Difference"; Morenoff, Sampson, and Raudenbush, "Neighborhood Inequality"; Sampson, Raudenbush, and Earls, "Neighborhoods and Violent Crime"; Sampson, *Great American City*.

85. Huckfeldt, *Politics in Context*; Gay, "Moving to Opportunity"; Krivo, Peterson, and Kuhl, "Segregation, Racial Structure"; Trounstine, *Segregation by Design*; Massey and Kanaiapuni, "Public Housing"; Gotham and Brumley, "Using Space."

CHAPTER 5

1. D. Wong, "Shop Talk"; Feldman and Stall, *Dignity of Resistance*; Isoke, *Urban Black Women*; Watkins-Hayes, *Remaking a Life*; Berger, *Workable Sisterhood*; Perry, *Black Women*.

2. Gotham and Brumley, "Using Space"; Hayward, *How Americans Make Race*; Naples, *Grassroots Warriors*; Gay, "Putting Race in Context"; Sampson, *Great American City*.

3. Eliasoph, *Avoiding Politics*, 11.

4. Reingold, "Public Housing, Home Ownership"; Levenstein, *Movement without Marches*; Feldman and Stall, *Dignity of Resistance*; Gay, "Moving to Opportunity"; Popkin, *No Simple Solutions*; de Souza Briggs, Popkin, and Goering, *Moving to Opportunity*; Gotham and Brumley, "Using Space"; R. Williams, *Politics of Public Housing*.

5. Watkins-Hayes, *Remaking a Life*; Berger, *Workable Sisterhood*; Perry, *Black Women*; Kelley, *Race Rebels*; Hanchard, "Acts of Misrecognition"; INCITE!, *Color of Violence*; Ritchie, *Invisible No More*; Richie, *Arrested Justice*; Cohen, *Boundaries of Blackness*.

6. Fuerst and Hunt, *When Public Housing Was Paradise*; Polikoff, *Waiting for Gautreaux*; Goetz, *New Deal Ruins*; Hunt, *Blueprint for Disaster*.

7. Popkin, *No Simple Solutions*; Comey, Popkin, and Franks, "MTO"; Popkin, Levy, et al., "HOPE VI Program"; Gay, "Moving to Opportunity."

8. Moffett-Bateau, "I Can't Vote."

9. Moffett-Bateau; Feldman and Stall, *Dignity of Resistance*; Polikoff, *Waiting for Gautreaux*.

10. Frasure-Yokley, Masuoka, and Barreto, "Introduction to Dialogues"; Simien, "Race, Gender, and Linked Fate"; Gershon et al., "Intersectional Linked Fate"; Dawson, *Behind the Mule*.

11. Venkatesh, *American Project*; Rios, *Punished*; Cohen, *Democracy Remixed*; Prowse, Weaver, and Meares, "State from Below."

12. Huckfeldt, "Variable Responses"; Huckfeldt, *Politics in Context*; Cohen and Dawson, "Neighborhood Poverty"; Gay, "Putting Race in Context"; Gotham and Brumley, "Using Space"; Sampson, *Great American City*.

13. Sinclair, *Social Citizen*; Verba, Schlozman, and Brady, *Voice and Equality*; Morenoff, Sampson, and Raudenbush, "Neighborhood Inequality"; Soss, *Unwanted Claims*; Mettler and Soss, "Consequences of Public Policy"; Fording, Soss, and Schram, "Race and the Local Politics"; Soss, "Classes, Races, and Marginalized Places."

14. De Souza Briggs, Popkin, and Goering, *Moving to Opportunity*; Comey, Popkin, and Franks, "MTO"; Popkin, Rich, et al., "Public Housing Transformation and Crime."

15. Trounstine, *Segregation by Design*; Popkin, Levy, et al., "HOPE VI Program"; Hunt, *Blueprint for Disaster*; Hancock, *Politics of Disgust*; Roberts, *Killing the Black Body*; H. Hansen, Bourgois, and Drucker, "Pathologizing Poverty"; L. Bennett, Smith, and Wright, *Where Are Poor People to Live?*; Rios, *Punished*; Fording, Soss, and Schram, "Race and the Local Politics"; Western, *Punishment and Inequality in America*; Soss, "Lessons of Welfare."

16. Fuerst and Hunt, *When Public Housing Was Paradise*.

17. Lipsky, *Street-Level Bureaucracy*.

18. Isoke, "Politics of Homemaking"; Isoke, *Urban Black Women*; Hayward, *How Americans Make Race*; T. Williamson, *Scandalize My Name*; Trounstine, *Segregation*

by Design; L. Bennett, Smith, and Wright, *Where Are Poor People to Live?*; Hancock, *Politics of Disgust*; Cohen, "Punks, Bulldaggers and Welfare Queens."

19. Hayward, *How Americans Make Race*; hooks, *Belonging*; Isoke, "Politics of Homemaking"; K. Mitchell, *From Slave Cabins to the White House*; R. Williams, *Politics of Public Housing*; T. Williamson, *Scandalize My Name*; Mansfield, *Dwelling in Possibility*; Chen, Dulani, and Piepzna-Samarasinha, *Revolution Starts at Home*; Reingold, "Public Housing, Home Ownership"; Huckfeldt, *Politics in Context*.

20. Warren, "Voting with Your Feet"; Cohen and Dawson, "Neighborhood Poverty"; Huckfeldt, "Variable Responses"; Sampson, *Great American City*.

21. R. Williams, *Politics of Public Housing*; Feldman and Stall, *Dignity of Resistance*; Levenstein, *Movement without Marches*; Gold, *When Tenants Claimed the City*; T. Williamson, *Scandalize My Name*; Berger, *Workable Sisterhood*; Watkins-Hayes, *Remaking a Life*; Hancock, *Politics of Disgust*; Naples, *Grassroots Warriors*.

22. Eli Day, "The Number of Homeless People in America Increased for the First Time in 7 Years," *Mother Jones*, December 21, 2017, https://www.motherjones.com/politics/2017/12/the-number-of-homeless-people-in-america-increased-for-the-first-time-in-7-years/.

23. Chad Yoder and Jonathon Berlin, "Who Are the Homeless Being Displaced from Lower Wacker? Annual Census Gives an Idea," *Chicago Tribune*, June 15, 2018, http://www.chicagotribune.com/ct-chicago-homeless-count-charts-htmlstory.html.

24. Popkin, *No Simple Solutions*.

25. CHA, *Plan for Transformation, Year 3*.

26. Feldman and Stall, *Dignity of Resistance*; Goetz, *New Deal Ruins*; de Souza Briggs, Popkin, and Goering, *Moving to Opportunity*; Gay, "Moving to Opportunity"; Comey, Popkin, and Franks, "MTO"; Hunt, *Blueprint for Disaster*; Fuerst and Hunt, *When Public Housing Was Paradise*.

27. Polikoff, *Waiting for Gautreaux*; White and Hall, "Perceptions of Environmental Health Risks"; Hudson, "Altgeld Gardens."

28. Feldman and Stall, *Dignity of Resistance*; R. Williams, *Politics of Public Housing*.

29. Cohen and Dawson, "Neighborhood Poverty."

30. Cohen and Dawson, 290, 297.

31. Cohen and Dawson, 293.

32. Cohen and Dawson; Huckfeldt, *Politics in Context*; Sampson, *Great American City*; Isoke, *Urban Black Women*; Feldman and Stall, *Dignity of Resistance*; Levenstein, *Movement without Marches*; R. Williams, *Politics of Public Housing*.

33. Gotham and Brumley, "Using Space."

34. Cudd, *Analyzing Oppression*; Scholz, "Empowering Resistance."

35. Mansfield, *Dwelling in Possibility*. Location 99.

36. McKittrick, *Demonic Grounds*; Gilmore, "Fatal Couplings of Power and Difference"; Burch, *Trading Democracy for Justice*; Trounstine, *Segregation by Design*; Sampson, *Great American City*; Huckfeldt, *Politics in Context*; Isoke, *Urban Black Women*; Berger, *Workable Sisterhood*; Watkins-Hayes, *Remaking a Life*; Naples, *Grassroots Warriors*; Feldman and Stall, *Dignity of Resistance*; R. Williams, *Politics of Public Housing*; T. Williamson, *Scandalize My Name*; Cohen and Dawson, "Neighborhood

Poverty"; Bolland and Moehle McCallum, "Neighboring and Community Mobilization"; Levenstein, *Movement without Marches*; Gold, *When Tenants Claimed the City*; L. Bennett, Smith, and Wright, *Where Are Poor People to Live?*; Moffett-Bateau, "Strategies of Resistance"; Fuerst and Hunt, *When Public Housing Was Paradise*; Hayward, *How Americans Make Race*; Gotham and Brumley, "Using Space"; Gay, "Putting Race in Context"; D. Wong, "Shop Talk"; C. Wong, *Boundaries of Obligation*.

37. Sampson, *Great American City*.

38. Hayward, *How Americans Make Race*; Hayward; Huckfeldt, *Politics in Context*.

39. Berger, *Workable Sisterhood*; Watkins-Hayes, *Remaking a Life*; R. Williams, *Politics of Public Housing*; Trounstine, *Segregation by Design*.

40. Cudd, *Analyzing Oppression*; Scholz, "Empowering Resistance."

41. For more on the "politics of homemaking," see Zenzele Isoke, *Urban Black Women*.

42. Mettler and Soss, "Consequences of Public Policy"; Michener, "Policy Feedback in a Racialized Polity"; Michener, "Medicaid and the Policy Feedback Foundations."

43. C. Jones, "End to the Neglect"; Guy-Sheftall, *Words of Fire*; Roth, "Making of the Vanguard Center"; Roth, *Separate Roads to Feminism*; James and Guy-Sheftall, *Seeking the Beloved Community*; Isoke, "Politics of Homemaking"; T. Williamson, *Scandalize My Name*; Simien, *Black Feminist Voices in Politics*; Collins, *Black Feminist Thought*; hooks, *Feminist Theory*; James, *Shadowboxing*; D. Harris, *Black Feminist Politics*; Carruthers, *Unapologetic*; D. King, "Multiple Jeopardy, Multiple Consciousness"; Burack, *Healing Identities*; Pateman, "Feminist Critiques of the Public/Private Dichotomy"; Moraga and Anzaldúa, *This Bridge Called My Back*; Hull, Bell Scott, and Smith, *But Some of Us Are Brave*.

44. L. Bennett, Smith, and Wright, *Where Are Poor People to Live?*; Michener and Brower, "What's Policy Got to Do with It?"; Soss, "Classes, Races, and Marginalized Places"; Gay, "Moving to Opportunity"; Sampson, *Great American City*.

45. Burch, "Neighborhood Effects of Incarceration."

46. Soss, "Lessons of Welfare," 364.

47. Soss, *Unwanted Claims*.

48. Soss, "Lessons of Welfare," 366.

49. Soss, *Unwanted Claims*.

50. Lerman and Weaver, *Arresting Citizenship*, 12.

51. Lerman and Weaver, 13.

52. Lipsky, *Street-Level Bureaucracy*.

53. Hayward, *How Americans Make Race*. Pierre Bourdieu, *Outline of a Theory of Practice*, trans. Richard Nice, 1st ed., Cambridge Studies in Social and Cultural Anthropology 16 (Cambridge, United Kingdom: Cambridge University Press, 1977), https://doi.org/10.1017/CBO9780511812507.

54. Hayward, 38; Bourdieu, *Outline of a Theory of Practice*.

55. Hayward; Gotham and Brumley, "Using Space"; Venkatesh, *American Project*; Hunt, *Blueprint for Disaster*; R. Williams, *Politics of Public Housing*; Feldman and Stall, *Dignity of Resistance*; Huckfeldt, *Politics in Context*; Sampson, *Great American City*; Gay, "Putting Race in Context."

56. Hayward, *How Americans Make Race*; McKittrick, *Demonic Grounds*; Naples, *Grassroots Warriors*; Gold, *When Tenants Claimed the City*; Gallagher, *Black Women and Politics*; Feldman and Stall, *Dignity of Resistance*; R. Williams, *Politics of Public Housing*; Isoke, *Urban Black Women*; Watkins-Hayes, *Remaking a Life*; Berger, *Workable Sisterhood*.

57. Eliasoph, *Avoiding Politics*; R. Williams, *Politics of Public Housing*; Levenstein, *Movement without Marches*; Gold, *When Tenants Claimed the City*; Gallagher, *Black Women and Politics*; Naples, *Grassroots Warriors*; Isoke, *Urban Black Women*; T. Williamson, *Scandalize My Name*.

58. Weaver, Prowse, and Piston, "Too Much Knowledge"; Sinclair, "Social Citizen"; Morenoff, Sampson, and Raudenbush, "Neighborhood Inequality"; Verba, Schlozman, and Brady, *Voice and Equality*.

59. Weaver, Prowse, and Piston, "Too Much Knowledge"; Prowse, Weaver, and Meares, "State from Below"; Rios, *Punished*; Gotham and Brumley, "Using Space"; Desmond and Travis, "Political Consequences."

60. Weaver, Prowse, and Piston, "Too Much Knowledge"; Prowse, Weaver, and Meares, "State from Below."

61. Eliasoph, *Avoiding Politics*; Isoke, *Urban Black Women*; Naples, *Grassroots Warriors*; R. Williams, *Politics of Public Housing*; T. Williamson, *Scandalize My Name*; Cohen, "Punks, Bulldaggers and Welfare Queens."

62. Brison, *Aftermath*.

63. Feldman and Stall, *Dignity of Resistance*; Hunt, *Blueprint for Disaster*; Fuerst and Hunt, *When Public Housing Was Paradise*.

64. Robnett, *How Long?*

65. Eliasoph, *Avoiding Politics*; Masuoka and Junn, *Politics of Belonging*; Hayward, *How Americans Make Race*; Junn, "Participation in Liberal Democracy"; Dawson, *Behind the Mule*; Gotham and Brumley, "Using Space"; Perry, *Black Women*; Isoke, *Urban Black Women*; Berger, *Workable Sisterhood*; Watkins-Hayes, *Remaking a Life*; Feldman and Stall, *Dignity of Resistance*; R. Williams, *Politics of Public Housing*.

66. Pattillo, *Black on the Block*.

67. Josh Eidelson and Sarah Jaffe, "*Belabored* Podcast, Episode 1: 'We Will Shut Down Your City," *Dissent Magazine*, April 12, 2013.

68. Verba, Schlozman, and Brady, *Voice and Equality*.

69. Scott, *Domination and the Arts of Resistance*; Kelley, *Race Rebels*; Naples, *Grassroots Warriors*; Berger, *Workable Sisterhood*; Watkins-Hayes, *Remaking a Life*; Isoke, *Urban Black Women*; T. Williamson, *Scandalize My Name*; R. Williams, *Politics of Public Housing*; Feldman and Stall, *Dignity of Resistance*; Gold, *When Tenants Claimed the City*.

70. Sinclair, *Social Citizen*.

71. Cohen and Dawson, "Neighborhood Poverty."

72. Cohen, *Boundaries of Blackness*.

73. Sampson, Wilson, and Katz, "Reassessing"; Krivo, Peterson, and Kuhl, "Segregation, Racial Structure"; Bolland and Moehle McCallum, "Neighboring and

Community Mobilization"; Tanous and Eghbariah, "Organized Violence and Organized Abandonment"; K. Brown and Weil, "Strangers in the Neighborhood."

74. Bateson, "Crime Victimization and Political Participation"; Stucky, "Local Politics and Violent Crime."

75. Frazer, "Marry Wollstonecraft on Politics and Friendship"; Naples, *Grassroots Warriors*; R. Williams, *Politics of Public Housing*; T. Williamson, *Scandalize My Name*; Isoke, *Urban Black Women*; Perry, *Black Women*; Berger, *Workable Sisterhood*.

76. Burch, *Trading Democracy for Justice*; Michener, *Fragmented Democracy*; Soss, *Unwanted Claims*; Fording, Soss, and Schram, "Race and the Local Politics"; Mettler and Soss, "Consequences of Public Policy"; Popkin, Rich, et al., "Public Housing Transformation and Crime"; Popkin, *No Simple Solutions*; Gay, "Putting Race in Context"; Gay, "Moving to Opportunity."

CHAPTER 6

1. Moraga and Anzaldúa, *This Bridge Called My Back*; Hull, Bell Scott, and Smith, *But Some of Us Are Brave*; Guy-Sheftall, *Words of Fire*; Collins, *Black Feminist Thought*; Collins, *From Black Power to Hip Hop*; Collins, "Truth-Telling and Intellectual Activism"; Roth, "Making of the Vanguard Center"; D. King, "Multiple Jeopardy, Multiple Consciousness"; T. Williamson, *Scandalize My Name*; James, *Shadowboxing*; Burack, *Healing Identities*.

2. Crenshaw, "Mapping the Margins"; Collins, "On Violence, Intersectionality and Transversal Politics"; Junn et al., "What Revolution?"; Collins, *Intersectionality as Critical Social Theory*; Jordan-Zachery, "I Ain't Your Darn Help"; Alexander-Floyd, "Why Political Scientists"; Davis, *Women, Race and Class*; Berger, *Workable Sisterhood*.

3. James, *Shadowboxing*; James and Guy-Sheftall, *Seeking the Beloved Community*.

4. James, *Shadowboxing*, 30.

5. James; D. Harris, *Black Feminist Politics*; Isoke, *Urban Black Women*; T. Williamson, *Scandalize My Name*.

6. Cohen, *Boundaries of Blackness*; Berger, *Workable Sisterhood*; Watkins-Hayes, *Remaking a Life*.

7. Cohen, *Boundaries of Blackness*; F. Harris, "Rise of Respectability Politics"; Bunyasi and Smith, "Do All Black Lives Matter Equally?"; P. J. Harris, "Gatekeeping and Remaking"; Berger, *Workable Sisterhood*; T. Williamson, *Scandalize My Name*; R. Williams, *Politics of Public Housing*. For more on intersectional stigma, see Berger, *Workable Sisterhood*.

8. Isoke, *Urban Black Women*; T. Williamson, *Scandalize My Name*.

9. Dawson, *Behind the Mule*; Cohen, *Boundaries of Blackness*; Isoke, *Urban Black Women*; Berger, *Workable Sisterhood*; R. Williams, *Politics of Public Housing*; Harris-Perry, *Sister Citizen*; Spence, *Knocking the Hustle*; Hanchard, *Party/Politics*.

10. Davis, *Women, Race and Class*; D. King, "Multiple Jeopardy, Multiple Consciousness"; Crenshaw, "Mapping the Margins"; Prestage, "In Quest of African American Political Woman"; Cohen and Dawson, "Neighborhood Poverty"; Dawson, *Behind the Mule*; Dawson, *Black Visions*; Cohen, *Boundaries of Blackness*; Cohen, "Deviance

as Resistance"; Cohen, "Punks, Bulldaggers and Welfare Queens"; Cohen, *Democracy Remixed*; Bobo and Hutchings, "Perceptions of Racial Group Competition"; Gay and Tate, "Doubly Bound"; Haynie and Tate, "From Protest to Politics"; Guy-Sheftall, *Words of Fire*; Hancock, *Politics of Disgust*; Simien, *Black Feminist Voices in Politics*; D. Harris, *Black Feminist Politics*; Spence, *Knocking the Hustle*; Alexander-Floyd, "Radical Black Feminism"; Jordan-Zachery and Alexander-Floyd, *Black Women in Politics*; Berger, *Workable Sisterhood*; Watkins-Hayes, *Remaking a Life*; Isoke, *Urban Black Women*; Perry, *Black Women*; Lerman and Weaver, *Arresting Citizenship*; Michener, *Fragmented Democracy*; Francis, *Civil Rights*; Greer, *Black Ethnics*; N. Brown, *Sisters in the Statehouse*; Carter and Willoughby-Herard, "What Kind of Mother Is She?"; Collins, *Black Feminist Thought*; Collins, *Intersectionality as Critical Social Theory*; James and Guy-Sheftall, *Seeking the Beloved Community*; James, *Shadowboxing*.

11. R. Williams, *Politics of Public Housing*; Feldman and Stall, *Dignity of Resistance*; Reingold, "Public Housing, Home Ownership"; Pfeiffer, "Displacement through Discourse"; Gotham and Brumley, "Using Space"; Fuerst and Hunt, *When Public Housing Was Paradise*; L. Bennett, Smith, and Wright, *Where Are Poor People to Live?*; Massey and Kanaiapuni, "Public Housing"; Popkin, *No Simple Solutions*; Goetz, *New Deal Ruins*; Hunt, *Blueprint for Disaster*; Davenport, "Public Accountability and Political Participation"; Gay, "Moving to Opportunity"; Michener, "Neighborhood Disorder and Local Participation"; Hancock, *Politics of Disgust*; Cohen, "Punks, Bulldaggers and Welfare Queens"; Cohen and Dawson, "Neighborhood Poverty"; Spence, *Knocking the Hustle*; Lerman and Weaver, *Arresting Citizenship*; Prowse, Weaver, and Meares, "State from Below"; Weaver, Prowse, and Piston, "Too Much Knowledge"; Soss and Weaver, "Police Are Our Government"; Naples, *Grassroots Warriors*; Levenstein, *Movement without Marches*; Gold, *When Tenants Claimed the City*; Venkatesh, *American Project*.

12. Black Public Sphere Collective, *Black Public Sphere*; Squires, "Rethinking the Black Public Sphere"; Eliasoph, "Evaporation of Politics."

13. Weaver, Prowse, and Piston, "Too Much Knowledge"; Soss and Weaver, "Police Are Our Government"; Prowse, Weaver, and Meares, "State from Below."

14. Hanchard, *Party/Politics*.

15. Soss, *Unwanted Claims*.

16. Cudd, *Analyzing Oppression*.

17. Roberts, *Killing the Black Body*; Roberts, *Shattered Bonds*.

18. Young, *Justice and the Politics of Difference*; Naples, *Grassroots Warriors*.

19. Isoke, "Politics of Homemaking"; Isoke, review of *Suffering Will Not Be Televised* and *Behind the Mask*; Isoke, *Urban Black Women*; Isoke, "Black Ethnography."

20. Isoke, *Urban Black Women*, 2.

21. Isoke; Isoke, "Politics of Homemaking"; Berger, *Workable Sisterhood*; Watkins-Hayes, *Remaking a Life*; T. Williamson, *Scandalize My Name*; R. Williams, *Politics of Public Housing*; Jordan-Zachery and Alexander-Floyd, *Black Women in Politics*; Jordan-Zachery, "Beyond the Side Eye."

22. Isoke, *Urban Black Women*; Isoke, "Politics of Homemaking"; Naples, *Grassroots Warriors*; R. Williams, *Politics of Public Housing*; Levenstein, *Movement with-*

out Marches; Robnett, *How Long?*; Kelley, *Race Rebels*; Kelley, *Yo' Mama's Disfunktional!*; Berger, *Workable Sisterhood*; Watkins-Hayes, *Remaking a Life*; Gallagher, *Black Women and Politics*; Feldman and Stall, *Dignity of Resistance*; Jordan-Zachery and Alexander-Floyd, *Black Women in Politics*.

23. Perry, *Black Women*, 20.

24. Isoke, *Urban Black Women*.

25. Isoke; Isoke, "Politics of Homemaking."

26. T. Williamson, *Scandalize My Name*.

27. Naples, *Grassroots Warriors*; Simien, *Black Feminist Voices in Politics*; Isoke, *Urban Black Women*; Berger, *Workable Sisterhood*.

28. Naples, *Grassroots Warriors*, 179.

29. Prestage, "In Quest of African American Political Woman"; Alexander-Floyd, "Why Political Scientists"; Jordan-Zachery, "I Ain't Your Darn Help."

30. Berger, *Workable Sisterhood*, 8.

31. Spence, *Knocking the Hustle*; Hackworth, *Neoliberal City*. For more on the concept of "human capital," see Spence, *Knocking the Hustle*.

32. Naples, *Grassroots Warriors*, 3.

33. Berger, *Workable Sisterhood*, 12.

34. Perry, *Black Women*; Harris-Lacewell, *Barbershops, Bibles, and BET*; Isoke, *Urban Black Women*; Berger, *Workable Sisterhood*; R. Williams, *Politics of Public Housing*.

35. T. Williamson, *Scandalize My Name*, 16–17.

36. Simien, *Black Feminist Voices in Politics*; Jordan-Zachery and Alexander-Floyd, *Black Women in Politics*; Alexander-Floyd, "Why Political Scientists"; Jordan-Zachery, "I Ain't Your Darn Help."

37. Hanchard, "Contours of Black Political Thought."

38. Hanchard, 523.

39. Hanchard.

40. Hanchard, 519.

41. Perry, *Black Women*, 15–16.

42. Perry, 15–16.

43. Dawson, *Behind the Mule*; Dawson, *Black Visions*.

44. Simien, *Black Feminist Voices in Politics*, 134.

45. Scott, *Domination and the Arts of Resistance*; Hanchard, *Party/Politics*; Kelley, *Yo' Mama's Disfunktional!*

46. Hanchard, *Party/Politics*; Kelley, *Race Rebels*, 29.

47. Hanchard, *Party/Politics*; Hanchard, "Acts of Misrecognition"; Hanchard, "Contours of Black Political Thought"; Black Public Sphere Collective, *Black Public Sphere*; Cohen, "Deviance as Resistance"; Dawson, *Black Visions*; Berger, *Workable Sisterhood*; Watkins-Hayes, *Remaking a Life*; Isoke, *Urban Black Women*; Perry, *Black Women*; D. Wong, "Shop Talk"; Eliasoph, *Avoiding Politics*; Iton, *In Search of the Black Fantastic*.

48. Scott, *Domination and the Arts of Resistance*; Kelley, *Race Rebels*; Kelley, *Yo' Mama's Disfunktional!*; Naples, *Grassroots Warriors*; R. Williams, *Politics of Public*

Housing; T. Williamson, *Scandalize My Name*; Feldman and Stall, *Dignity of Resistance*; Levenstein, *Movement without Marches*; Gold, *When Tenants Claimed the City*; McGuire, *At the Dark End of the Street*; Theoharris, *Rebellious Life of Mrs. Rosa Parks*; Feimster, *Southern Horrors*; Su, *Streetwise for Book Smarts*; Rios, *Punished*; Venkatesh, *American Project*; Ralph, *Renegade Dreams*; Desmond and Travis, "Political Consequences."

49. Kelley, *Race Rebels*; Scott, *Domination and the Arts of Resistance*; Iton, *In Search of the Black Fantastic*; Schneider, *Police Power and Race Riots*; Rios, *Punished*; Ralph, *Renegade Dreams*; Feldman and Stall, *Dignity of Resistance*; R. Williams, *Politics of Public Housing*; Naples, *Grassroots Warriors*; Watkins-Hayes, *Remaking a Life*; Eliasoph, *Avoiding Politics*; Guy-Sheftall, *Words of Fire*; Lorde, "Keynote Address."

50. Stolle, Hooghe, and Micheletti, "Politics in the Supermarket"; Kelley, *Race Rebels*; Scott, *Domination and the Arts of Resistance*.

51. Micheletti, Follesdal, and Stolle, *Politics, Products, and Markets*; Hanchard, "Contours of Black Political Thought"; Scott, *Domination and the Arts of Resistance*; Kelley, *Race Rebels*.

52. Cohen, "Deviance as Resistance"; Hanchard, "Contours of Black Political Thought"; Kelley, *Race Rebels*; Isoke, *Urban Black Women*.

53. Kelley, *Race Rebels*, 4.

54. Kelley; Junn, "Participation in Liberal Democracy"; Naples, *Grassroots Warriors*; Simien, *Black Feminist Voices in Politics*; Jordan-Zachery and Alexander-Floyd, *Black Women in Politics*.

55. Kelley, *Race Rebels*; Kelley, *Yo' Mama's Disfunktional!*; Isoke, *Urban Black Women*.

56. Isoke, *Urban Black Women*, 1.

57. Simien, *Black Feminist Voices in Politics*; Alexander-Floyd, "Why Political Scientists"; Jordan-Zachery, "I Ain't Your Darn Help"; Jordan-Zachery and Alexander-Floyd, *Black Women in Politics*; D. Harris, *Black Feminist Politics*; Prestage, "In Quest of African American Political Woman"; N. Brown and Young, "Ratchet Politics"; Berger, *Workable Sisterhood*; Isoke, *Urban Black Women*.

58. Simien, *Black Feminist Voices in Politics*; Jordan-Zachery and Alexander-Floyd, *Black Women in Politics*; Alexander-Floyd, "Why Political Scientists"; Jordan-Zachery, "I Ain't Your Darn Help."

59. Julia S. Jordan-Zachery and Nikol G. Alexander-Floyd, "Black Women's Political Labor: An Introduction," in *Black Women in Politics: Demanding Citizenship, Challenging Power, and Seeking Justice*, ed. Julia S. Jordan-Zachery and Nikol G. Alexander-Floyd, SUNY Series in African American Studies, SUNY Series in New Political Science (Albany: SUNY Press, 2018), https://sunypress.edu/Books/B/Black-Women-in-Politics2.

60. Kelley, *Race Rebels*; Hanchard, *Party/Politics*.

61. Hanchard, *Party/Politics*.

62. J. Hansen, "Mobilization, Participation, and Political Change."

63. Wolfinger and Rosenstone, *Who Votes?*

64. Scott, *Domination and the Arts of Resistance*; Kelley, *Race Rebels*; Kelley, *Yo' Mama's Disfunktional!*; Naples, *Grassroots Warriors*; Berger, *Workable Sisterhood*; Watkins-Hayes, *Remaking a Life*; Isoke, *Urban Black Women*; R. Williams, *Politics of Public Housing*; T. Williamson, *Scandalize My Name*; Feldman and Stall, *Dignity of Resistance*; Perry, *Black Women*.

65. Michener, *Fragmented Democracy*.

66. R. Williams, *Politics of Public Housing*, 14.

67. Feldman and Stall, *Dignity of Resistance*; Naples, *Grassroots Warriors*; Hancock, *Politics of Disgust*; Cohen, "Punks, Bulldaggers and Welfare Queens"; Soss, *Unwanted Claims*; Soss, "Lessons of Welfare"; A. L. Campbell, *How Policies Make Citizens*; Burch, *Trading Democracy for Justice*; R. Williams, *Politics of Public Housing*.

68. R. Williams, *Politics of Public Housing*.

69. Levenstein, *Movement without Marches*.

70. R. Williams, *Politics of Public Housing*, 14.

71. Williams, 6.

72. Levenstein, *Movement without Marches*; R. Williams, *Politics of Public Housing*.

73. Masuoka and Junn, *Politics of Belonging*.

74. Soss, *Unwanted Claims*.

75. Soss and Weaver, "Police Are Our Government"; Weaver, Prowse, and Piston, "Too Much Knowledge"; Lerman and Weaver, *Arresting Citizenship*; Prowse, Weaver, and Meares, "State from Below."

76. T. Williamson, *Scandalize My Name*; Isoke, *Urban Black Women*.

77. Davis, *Women, Race and Class*; Collins, *Black Feminist Thought*; Berger, *Workable Sisterhood*; Watkins-Hayes, *Remaking a Life*.

78. Naples, *Grassroots Warriors*; Berger, *Workable Sisterhood*; Watkins-Hayes, *Remaking a Life*; Feldman and Stall, *Dignity of Resistance*; Perry, *Black Women*.

79. J. Hansen, "Mobilization, Participation, and Political Change."

80. Michener, *Fragmented Democracy*, 32.

81. Michener, 32.

82. Michener; Lipsky, *Street-Level Bureaucracy*; Watkins-Hayes, *New Welfare Bureaucrats*; Soss, *Unwanted Claims*.

83. Huckfeldt, *Politics in Context*; Gay, "Putting Race in Context"; Alex-Assensoh and Assensoh, "Inner-City Contexts"; Spence and McClerking, "Context, Black Empowerment"; Gotham and Brumley, "Using Space"; Hayward, *How Americans Make Race*; McCurn, "Surviving the Grind"; Michener, *Fragmented Democracy*; Sampson, *Great American City*; Michener, "Neighborhood Disorder and Local Participation"; Cohen and Dawson, "Neighborhood Poverty"; Burch, *Trading Democracy for Justice*; Bolland and Moehle McCallum, "Neighboring and Community Mobilization"; Morenoff, Sampson, and Raudenbush, "Neighborhood Inequality"; Kang and Kwak, "Multilevel Approach to Civic Participation"; Peterson, Krivo, and Hagan, *Divergent Social Worlds*; Krivo, Peterson, and Kuhl, "Segregation, Racial Structure"; Trounstine, *Segregation by Design*; Rios, *Punished*.

84. Andrew Mercer et al., "Why 2016 Election Polls Missed the Mark," *Fact Tank: News in the Numbers*, November 9, 2016, http://www.pewresearch.org/fact-tank/2016/11/09/why-2016-election-polls-missed-their-mark/.

85. Cohen, *Democracy Remixed*.

86. Dawson, *Black Visions*.

87. Hanchard, *Party/Politics*.

88. James and Guy-Sheftall, *Seeking the Beloved Community*; Iton, *In Search of the Black Fantastic*.

BIBLIOGRAPHY

Acheson, Ray. *Abolishing State Violence: A World beyond Bombs, Borders, and Cages*. Chicago: Haymarket Books, 2022. https://www.haymarketbooks.org/books/1883-abolishing-state-violence.

Alexander-Floyd, Nikol G. "Radical Black Feminism and the Fight for Social and Epistemic Justice." In *Broadening the Contours in the Study of Black Politics: Political Development and Black Women*, edited by Michael Mitchell and David Covin, 63–73. New Brunswick, NJ: Routledge, 2016. https://www.taylorfrancis.com/chapters/edit/10.4324/9781315081939-5/radical-black-feminism-fight-social-epistemic-justice-nikol-alexander-floyd.

———. "Why Political Scientists Don't Study Black Women, but Historians and Sociologists Do: On Intersectionality and the Remapping of the Study of Black Political Women." In *Black Women in Politics: Identity, Power, and Justice in the New Millennium*, edited by Michael Mitchell and David Covin, 3–17. London: Routledge, 2017. https://doi.org/10.4324/9781351313681-1.

Alex-Assensoh, Yvette. "Race, Concentrated Poverty, Social Isolation, and Political Behavior." *Urban Affairs Review* 33, no. 2 (1997): 209–27.

Alex-Assensoh, Yvette, and A. B. Assensoh. "Inner-City Contexts, Church Attendance, and African-American Political Participation." *Journal of Politics* 63, no. 3 (2001): 886–901.

Backus, Fred. "More Americans Say They Are 'Cutting the Cord.'" *CBS News*, April 23, 2021. https://www.cbsnews.com/news/cord-cutting-americans-rising/.

Bakshi, Amar, Tracey Meares, and Vesla Weaver. "Portals to Politics: Perspectives on Policing from the Grassroots." Shared Studios: Research, 2016. https://www.sharedstudios.com/research.

Baron, Harold. *What Is Gautreaux? The Name of a Gallant Woman.* Chicago, IL: Business and Professional People for the Public Interest, 1991. https://www.bpichicago.org/wp-content/uploads/2013/12/what-is-gautreaux.pdf.

Bateson, Regina. "Crime Victimization and Political Participation." *American Political Science Review* 106, no. 3 (2012): 570–87. https://doi.org/10.1017/S0003055412000299.

Bennett, W. Lance. "The Personalization of Politics: Political Identity, Social Media, and Changing Patterns of Participation." *Annals of the American Academy of Political and Social Science* 644, no. 1 (2012): 20–39. https://doi.org/10.1177/0002716212451428.

Bennett, Larry, Janet L. Smith, and Patricia A. Wright. *Where Are Poor People to Live? Transforming Public Housing Communities.* Edited by Larry Bennett, Janet L. Smith, and Patricia A. Wright. Armonk, NY: M. E. Sharpe, 2006. https://www.routledge.com/Where-are-Poor-People-to-Live-Transforming-Public-Housing-Communities/Bennett-Smith-Wright/p/book/9780765610768.

Berger, Michele Tracy. *Workable Sisterhood: The Political Journey of Stigmatized Women with HIV/AIDS.* Princeton, NJ: Princeton University Press, 2006. https://doi.org/10.1057/palgrave.fr.9400401.

Black Public Sphere Collective, ed. *The Black Public Sphere: A Public Culture Book.* Chicago: University of Chicago Press, 1995.

Bobo, Lawrence, and Vincent L. Hutchings. "Perceptions of Racial Group Competition: Extending Blumer's Theory of Group Position to a Multiracial Social Context." *American Sociological Review* 61, no. 6 (1996): 951–72. https://doi.org/10.2307/2096302.

Bolland, John M., and Debra Moehle McCallum. "Neighboring and Community Mobilization in High-Poverty Inner-City Neighborhoods." *Urban Affairs Review* 38, no. 1 (2002): 42–69.

Brady, Henry E., Sidney Verba, and Kay Lehman Schlozman. "Beyond SES: A Resource Model of Political Participation." *American Political Science Review* 89, no. 2 (1995): 271–94. https://doi.org/10.2307/2082425.

Brinson, Clemolyn. "Altgeld Gardens Lawsuit Settlement." *We the People Media: Residents' Journal,* February 2004. https://wethepeoplemedia.org/altgeld-gardens-lawsuit-settlement/.

Brison, Susan J. *Aftermath: Violence and the Remaking of a Self.* Princeton, NJ: Princeton University Press, 2002. https://doi.org/10.5860/choice.40-0831.

Brown, Kevin J., and Frederick D. Weil. "Strangers in the Neighborhood: Violence and Neighborhood Boundaries." *Journal of Contemporary Ethnography* 49, no. 1 (2020): 86–117. https://doi.org/10.1177/0891241619857150.

Brown, Nadia E. "Political Participation of Women of Color: An Intersectional Analysis." *Journal of Women, Politics and Policy* 35, no. 4 (2014): 315–48. https://doi.org/10.1080/1554477X.2014.955406.

———. *Sisters in the Statehouse: Black Women and Legislative Decision Making.* Oxford: Oxford University Press, 2014. https://doi.org/10.1093/acprof:oso/9780199352432.001.0001.

Brown, Nadia E., and Lisa Young. "Ratchet Politics: Moving beyond Black Women's Bodies to Indict Institutions and Structures." *National Political Science Review* 17, no. 2 (2015): 45–56. https://www.proquest.com/scholarly-journals/ratchet-pol itics-moving-beyond-black-womens/docview/1747345067/se-2.

Bruch, Sarah K., and Joe Soss. "Schooling as a Formative Political Experience: Authority Relations and the Education of Citizens." *Perspectives on Politics* 16, no. 1 (2018): 36–57. https://doi.org/10.1017/S1537592717002195.

Bunyasi, Tehama Lopez, and Candis Watts Smith. "Do All Black Lives Matter Equally to Black People? Respectability Politics and the Limitations of Linked Fate." *Journal of Race, Ethnicity and Politics* 4, no. 1 (March 1, 2019): 180–215. https://doi .org/10.1017/rep.2018.33.

Burack, Cynthia. *Healing Identities: Black Feminist Thought and the Politics of Groups.* Ithaca, NY: Cornell University Press, 2004.

Burch, Traci. "Neighborhood Effects of Incarceration on Individual Perceptions of Discrimination and Political Efficacy." Paper presented at the Public Laws Colloquium at University of Chicago School of Law, Chicago, IL, 2010.

——. *Trading Democracy for Justice: Criminal Convictions and the Decline of Neighborhood Political Participation.* Chicago: University of Chicago Press, 2013.

Bush, Rod. Review of *Mobilizing Public Opinion: Black Insurgency and Racial Attitudes in the Civil Rights Era*, by Taeku Lee. *Contemporary Sociology* 32, no. 5 (September 2003): 618–20. https://doi.org/10.2307/1556504.

Butler, Alana. "Quiltmaking among African-American Women as a Pedagogy of Care, Empowerment, and Sisterhood." *Gender and Education* 31, no. 5 (2019): 590–603. https://doi.org/10.1080/09540253.2019.1594708.

Campbell, Andrea Louise. *How Policies Make Citizens: Senior Political Activism and the American Welfare State.* Princeton, NJ: Princeton University Press, 2005. https:// doi.org/10.1215/03616878-2006-007.

Campbell, Angus, Philip Converse, Warren Miller, and Donald Stokes. *The American Voter.* Chicago: University of Chicago Press, 1960. https://doi.org/10.2307/19 52653.

Campi, Ashleigh, and Jane Junn. "Racial Linked Fate and Gender in U.S. Politics." *Politics, Groups, and Identities* 7, no. 3 (July 3, 2019): 654–62. https://doi.org/10.1080 /21565503.2019.1638805.

Carruthers, Charlene A. *Unapologetic: A Black, Queer, and Feminist Mandate for Radical Movements.* Boston: Beacon, 2018. https://www.amazon.com/Unapolo getic-Feminist-Mandate-Radical-Movements-ebook/dp/B077WYW2D8/.

Carter, Lashonda, and Tiffany Willoughby-Herard. "What Kind of Mother Is She? From Margaret Garner to Rosa Lee Ingram to Mamie Till to the Murder of Korryn Gaines." *Theory and Event* 21, no. 1 (2018): 88–105. https://muse.jhu.edu/article /685971.

Chan, Rosalie. "The 40-Year Fight to Clean Up One of America's Most Polluted Projects." *Vice*, June 2017. https://www.vice.com/en_us/article/59pmvn/this-is-life-in -one-of-americas-most-polluted-housing-projects.

Charron, Katherine Mellen. *Freedom's Teacher: The Life of Septima Clark*. Chapel Hill: University of North Carolina Press, 2009. https://uncpress.org/book/97808078 72222/freedoms-teacher/.

Chase, Brett. "Public Housing Residents Kept in Dark about Toxic Sites, Report Says." *Chicago Sun Times*, July 1, 2020. https://chicago.suntimes.com/2020/7/1/21310566 /public-housing-cha-epa-shriver-hud.

Chaskin, Robert J., Mark L. Joseph, Sara Voelker, and Amy Dworsky. "Public Housing Transformation and Resident Relocation: Comparing Destinations and House-hold Characteristics in Chicago." *Cityscape* 14, no. 1 (2012): 183–214. https://www .huduser.gov/portal/periodicals/cityscpe/vol14num1/ch12.html.

Chen, Ching-In, Jai Dulani, and Leah Lakshmi Piepzna-Samarasinha, eds. *The Revolution Starts at Home: Confronting Intimate Partner Violence within Activist Communities*. Chico, CA: AK Press, 2016.

Chicago Housing Authority. "Altgeld Gardens and Phillip Murray Homes." *Altgeld Gardens and Phillip Murray Homes* (blog), May 29, 2023. https://www.thecha.org /residents/public-housing/find-public-housing/altgeld-gardens-and-phillip-mur ray-homes.

———. *The Plan for Transformation*. Chicago, IL: Chicago Housing Authority, 2010.

———. *Plan for Transformation, Year 3, Moving to Work (MTW): Annual Plan FY2002*. Chicago: Chicago Housing Authority, 2002.

Chicago Talks. "Occupy the Hood Strikes Back at Worst Food Desert in Chicago." 2011. http://www.chicagotalks.org/?p=17941.

Coalition to Protect Public Housing. "Written Submission of the Coalition to Protect Public Housing in Chicago, Illinois USA to the Human Rights Committee at Its 85th Session (2006)." Submitted to the 85th Session of the Human Rights Committee, Chicago, IL, 2006. https://www2.ohchr.org/english/bodies/hrc/docs/ngos /coalition.doc.

Coffey, Emily, Kate Walz, Debbie Chizewer, Emily A. Benfer, Mark N. Templeton, and Robert Weinstock. "Poisonous Homes: The Fight for Environmental Justice in Federally Assisted Housing." Shriver Center on Poverty Law, 2020. https://www .povertylaw.org/report/poisonoushomes/.

Cohen, Cathy J. *The Boundaries of Blackness: AIDS and the Breakdown of Black Politics*. Chicago: University of Chicago Press, 1999. https://doi.org/10.1086/210428.

———. *Democracy Remixed: Black Youth and the Future of American Politics*. Oxford, England: Oxford University Press, 2010.

———. "Deviance as Resistance: A New Research Agenda for the Study of Black Politics." *Du Bois Review* 1, no. 1 (2004): 27–45. https://doi.org/10.1017/S1742058X040 40044.

———. "Punks, Bulldaggers and Welfare Queens: The Radical Potential of Queer Politics?" In *Black Queer Studies: A Critical Anthology*, edited by E. Patrick Johnson and Mae G. Henderson, 21–51. Durham, NC: Duke University Press, 2005. https://www.degruyter.com/document/doi/10.1515/9780822387220-004/html? lang=en.

Cohen, Cathy J., and Michael C. Dawson. "Neighborhood Poverty and African American Politics." *American Political Science Review* 87, no. 2 (1993): 286–302. https://doi.org/10.2307/2939041.

Collins, Patricia Hill. *Black Feminist Thought: Knowledge, Consciousness, and the Politics of Empowerment*. Perspectives on Gender. New Brunswick, NJ: Routledge, 2000.

———. *From Black Power to Hip Hop: Racism, Nationalism and Feminism*. Philadelphia: Temple University Press, 2006.

———. *Intersectionality as Critical Social Theory*. Durham, NC: Duke University Press, 2019. https://www.dukeupress.edu/intersectionality-as-critical-social-theory.

———. "On Violence, Intersectionality and Transversal Politics." *Ethnic and Racial Studies* 40, no. 9 (2017): 1460–73.

———. "The Tie That Binds: Race, Gender, and US Violence." *Ethnic and Racial Studies* 21, no. 5 (1998): 917–38.

———. "Truth-Telling and Intellectual Activism." *Contexts* 12, no. 1 (February 1, 2013): 36–41. https://doi.org/10.1177/1536504213476244.

"The Combahee River Collective Statement." Combahee River Collective, April 1977. https://www.loc.gov/item/lcwaN0028151/.

Comey, Jennifer, Susan J. Popkin, and Katlin Franks. "MTO: A Successful Housing Intervention." *Cityscape* 14, no. 2 (2012): 87–107.

Cramer, Katherine J., and Benjamin Toff. "The Fact of Experience: Rethinking Political Knowledge and Civic Competence." *Perspectives on Politics* 15, no. 3 (2017): 754–70. https://doi.org/10.1017/S1537592717000949.

Crenshaw, Kimberle. "Mapping the Margins: Intersectionality, Identity Politics, and Violence against Women of Color." *Stanford Law Review* 43, no. 6 (July 1991): 1241. https://doi.org/10.2307/1229039.

Cudd, Ann E. *Analyzing Oppression*. Oxford: Oxford University Press, 2006. https://doi.org/10.1093/0195187431.001.0001.

Cutter, Susan L., Bryan J. Boruff, and W. Lynn Shirley. "Social Vulnerability to Environmental Hazards." *Social Science Quarterly* 84, no. 2 (June 2003): 242–61. https://doi.org/10.1111/1540-6237.8402002.

Davenport, Tiffany C. "Public Accountability and Political Participation: Effects of a Face-to-Face Feedback Intervention on Voter Turnout of Public Housing Residents." *Political Behavior* 32, no. 3 (2010): 337–68. https://doi.org/10.1007/s11109-010-9109-x.

Davies, Carole Boyce. *Left of Karl Marx: The Political Life of Black Communist Claudia Jones*. Illustrated ed. Durham, NC: Duke University Press Books, 2008.

Davis, Angela Y. *Women, Race and Class*. New York: Vintage Books, 1983.

Dawson, Michael C. *Behind the Mule: Race and Class in African American Politics*. Princeton, NJ: Princeton University Press, 1994. https://doi.org/10.2307/j.ctvzx x9d4.

———. *Black Visions: The Roots of Contemporary African-American Political Ideologies*. Chicago: University of Chicago Press, 2003. https://doi.org/10.2307/3089610.

———. "Hidden in Plain Sight: A Note on Legitimation Crises and the Racial Order." *Critical Historical Studies* 3, no. 1 (2016): 143–61. https://doi.org/10.1086/685540.

Desmond, Matthew, Andrew V. Papachristos, and David S. Kirk. "Police Violence and Citizen Crime Reporting in the Black Community." *American Sociological Review* 81, no. 5 (2016): 857–76. https://doi.org/10.1177/0003122416663494.

Desmond, Matthew, and Adam Travis. "Political Consequences of Survival Strategies among the Urban Poor." *American Sociological Review* 83, no. 5 (2018): 869–96. https://doi.org/10.1177/0003122418792836.

Dillard, Cynthia B. *Learning to (Re)Member the Things We've Learned to Forget: Endarkened Feminisms, Spirituality, and the Sacred Nature of Research and Teaching.* New York: Peter Lang, 2012.

Dion, Leon. "Political Ideology as a Tool of Functional Analysis in Socio-political Dynamics." *Canadian Journal of Economics and Political Science* 25, no. 1 (1959): 47–59.

Dreier, Peter, John Mollenkopf, and Todd Swanstrom. *Place Matters: Metropolitics for the 21st Century.* Lawrence: University of Kansas Press, 2013.

Dumke, Mick, Tim Novak, Chris Fusco, and Brett Chase. "Daley's CHA Plan Jolted Region." Better Government Association, 2016. https://www.bettergov.org/news /daleys-cha-plan-jolted-region.

Eliasoph, Nina. *Avoiding Politics: How Americans Produce Apathy in Everyday Life.* Cambridge Cultural Social Studies. Cambridge: Cambridge University Press, 1998. https://doi.org/10.1017/cbo9780511583391.

———. "The Evaporation of Politics in the Public Sphere." *Kettering Review* 28, no. 1 (2010): 37–48.

Evans-Winters, Venus E. *Black Feminism in Qualitative Inquiry: A Mosaic for Writing Our Daughter's Body.* New York: Routledge, 2019.

Feimster, Crystal. *Southern Horrors: Women and the Politics of Rape and Lynching.* Cambridge, MA: Harvard University Press, 2011. https://www.hup.harvard.edu /catalog.php?isbn=9780674061859.

Feldman, Roberta M., and Susan Stall. *The Dignity of Resistance: Women Residents' Activism in Chicago Public Housing.* Cambridge: Cambridge University Press, 2004. https://doi.org/10.1017/CBO9780511734977.

Ferguson, Kennan. "Why Does Political Science Hate American Indians?" *Perspectives on Politics* 14, no. 4 (December 2016): 1029–38. https://doi.org/10.1017/S153 7592716002905.

Fording, Richard C., Joe Soss, and Sanford F. Schram. "Race and the Local Politics of Punishment in the New World of Welfare." *American Journal of Sociology* 116, no. 5 (2011): 1610–57. https://doi.org/10.1086/657525.

Foreman, P. Gabrielle. *Activist Sentiments: Reading Black Women in the Nineteenth Century.* Chicago: University of Illinois Press, 2009.

Francis, Megan Ming. *Civil Rights and the Making of the Modern American State.* Cambridge: Cambridge University Press, 2014. https://doi.org/10.1017/cbo97811 39583749.

———. "The Strange Fruit of American Political Development." *Politics, Groups, and Identities* 6, no. 1 (2018): 128–37. https://doi.org/10.1080/21565503.2017.1420551.

Frasure-Yokley, Lorrie, Natalie Masuoka, and Matt A. Barreto. "Introduction to Dialogues: Linked Fate and the Politics of Groups and Identities." *Politics, Groups, and Identities* 7, no. 3 (July 3, 2019): 610–14. https://doi.org/10.1080/21565503.2019.1638802.

Frazer, Elizabeth. "Marry Wollstonecraft on Politics and Friendship." *Political Studies* 56 (2008): 237–56.

Friedrich, Mike. "Income, Poverty and Health Insurance Coverage in the United States: 2020." U.S. Census Bureau, press release no. CB21-151, September 14, 2021. https://www.census.gov/newsroom/press-releases/2021/income-poverty-health-insurance-coverage.html.

Fuerst, J. S., and D. Bradford Hunt. *When Public Housing Was Paradise: Building Community in Chicago.* Chicago: University of Illinois Press, 2004. https://doi.org/10.5860/choice.41-5604.

Gainous, Jason, and Kevin M. Wagner. *Tweeting to Power: The Social Media Revolution in American Politics.* Oxford Studies in Digital Politics. Oxford: Oxford University Press, 2014. https://doi.org/10.1093/acprof:oso/9780199965076.001.0001.

Gallagher, Julie A. *Black Women and Politics in New York City.* Chicago: University of Illinois Press, 2012.

Garcia, R. Marie, Ralph B. Taylor, and Brian A. Lawton. "Impacts of Violent Crime and Neighborhood Structure on Trusting Your Neighbors." *Justice Quarterly* 24, no. 4 (2007): 679–704. https://doi.org/10.1080/07418820701717169.

Gay, Claudine. "Moving to Opportunity: The Political Effects of a Housing Mobility Experiment." *Urban Affairs Review* 48, no. 2 (2012): 147–79. https://doi.org/10.1177/1078087411426399.

———. "Putting Race in Context: Identifying the Environmental Determinants of Black Racial Attitudes." *American Political Science Review* 98, no. 4 (2004): 547–62. https://doi.org/10.1017/S0003055404041346.

Gay, Claudine, and Katherine Tate. "Doubly Bound: The Impact of Gender and Race on the Politics of Black Women." *Political Psychology* 19, no. 1 (1998): 169–84. https://doi.org/10.1111/0162-895x.00098.

Gershon, Sarah Allen, Celeste Montoya, Christina Bejarano, and Nadia Brown. "Intersectional Linked Fate and Political Representation." *Politics, Groups, and Identities* 7, no. 3 (July 3, 2019): 642–53. https://doi.org/10.1080/21565503.2019.1639520.

Gil de Zúñiga, Homero. "Social Media Use for News and Individuals' Social Capital, Civic Engagement and Political Participation." *Journal of Computer-Mediated Communication* 17, no. 3 (2012): 319–36. https://doi.org/10.1111/j.1083-6101.2012.01574.x.

Gil de Zúñiga, Homero, Logan Molyneux, and Pei Zheng. "Social Media, Political Expression, and Political Participation: Panel Analysis of Lagged and Concurrent Relationships." *Journal of Communication* 64, no. 4 (2014): 612–34. https://doi.org/10.1111/jcom.12103.

Gilmore, Ruth Wilson. "Fatal Couplings of Power and Difference: Notes on Racism and Geography." *Professional Geographer* 54, no. 1 (2002): 15–24. https://doi.org/10.1111/0033-0124.00310.

Goetz, Edward G. *New Deal Ruins: Race, Economic Justice, and Public Housing Policy.* Ithaca, NY: Cornell University Press, 2013. https://doi.org/10.1177/009430611 5588487x.

Gold, Roberta. *When Tenants Claimed the City: The Struggle for Citizenship in New York City Housing.* Chicago: University of Illinois Press, 2014. https://doi.org/10 .5406/illinois/9780252038181.001.0001.

Gotham, Kevin Fox, and Krista Brumley. "Using Space: Agency and Identity in a Public-Housing Development." *City and Community* 1, no. 3 (2002): 267–89. https:// doi.org/10.1111/1540-6040.00023.

Greer, Christina M. *Black Ethnics: Race, Immigration, and the Pursuit of the American Dream.* Illustrated ed. Oxford: Oxford University Press, 2013.

Grotto, Jason, Laurie Cohen, and Sara Olkon. "Public Housing's Island." *Chicago Tribune*, October 10, 2008. https://www.chicagotribune.com/news/chi-altgeldoc t10-story.html.

Gurusami, Susila. "Motherwork under the State: The Maternal Labor of Formerly Incarcerated Black Women." *Social Problems* 66, no. 1 (2019): 128–43. https://doi .org/10.1093/socpro/spx045.

———. "Working for Redemption: Formerly Incarcerated Black Women and Punishment in the Labor Market." *Gender and Society* 31, no. 4 (2017): 433–56. https:// doi.org/10.1177/0891243217716114.

Guy-Sheftall, Beverly, ed. *Words of Fire: An Anthology of African-American Feminist Thought.* New York: New Press, 1995. https://thenewpress.com/books/words-of-fire.

Hackworth, Jason. *The Neoliberal City: Governance, Ideology, and Development in American Urbanism.* Ithaca, NY: Cornell University Press, 2014. https://doi.org /10.7591/9780801461590.

Haider, Areeba, Jocelyn Frye, and Rose Khattar. "Census Data Show Historic Investments in Social Safety Net Alleviated Poverty in 2020." Center for American Progress, September 14, 2021. https://www.americanprogress.org/article/census-data -show-historic-investments-social-safety-net-alleviated-poverty-2020/.

Hanchard, Michael. "Acts of Misrecognition: Transnational Black Politics, Anti-imperialism and the Ethnocentrisms of Pierre Bourdieu and Loïc Wacquant." *Theory, Culture and Society* 20, no. 4 (2003): 5–29. https://doi.org/10.1177/026327640 30204002.

———. "Contours of Black Political Thought: An Introduction and Perspective." *Political Theory* 38, no. 4 (2010): 510–36. https://doi.org/10.1177/0090591710366379.

———. *Party/Politics: Horizons in Black Political Thought.* Oxford: Oxford University Press, 2006. https://doi.org/10.1093/acprof:oso/9780195176247.001.0001.

Hancock, Ange Marie. *The Politics of Disgust: The Public Identity of the Welfare Queen.* New York: New York University Press, 2004. https://doi.org/10.1177/009430610 603500108.

Hansen, Helena, Philippe Bourgois, and Ernest Drucker. "Pathologizing Poverty: New Forms of Diagnosis, Disability, and Structural Stigma under Welfare Reform." *Social Science and Medicine* 103 (2014): 76–83. https://doi.org/10.1016/j .socscimed.2013.06.033.

Hansen, John Mark. "Mobilization, Participation, and Political Change." *Party Politics* 22, no. 2 (March 28, 2016): 149–57. https://doi.org/10.1177/1354068815605677.

Harcourt, Bernard. *Illusion of Order: The False Promise of Broken Windows Policing.* Cambridge, MA: Harvard University Press, 2002. https://doi.org/10.5860/choice .39-4270.

Harris, Duchess. *Black Feminist Politics from Kennedy to Obama.* London: Palgrave Macmillan, 2009.

Harris, Fredrick C. "The Rise of Respectability Politics." *Dissent* 61, no. 1 (2014): 33–37. https://doi.org/10.1353/dss.2014.0010.

Harris, Paisley Jane. "Gatekeeping and Remaking: The Politics of Respectability in African American Women's History and Black Feminism." *Journal of Women's History* 15, no. 1 (2003): 212–20. https://doi.org/10.1353/jowh.2003.0025.

Harris-Lacewell, Melissa Victoria. *Barbershops, Bibles, and BET.* Princeton, NJ: Princeton University Press, 2004. https://doi.org/10.1515/9781400836604.

Harris-Perry, Melissa V. *Sister Citizen: Shame, Stereotypes, and Black Women in America.* New Haven, CT: Yale University Press, 2011. https://doi.org/10.1057/fr.2012.31.

Hayward, Clarissa Rile. *How Americans Make Race: Stories, Institutions, Spaces.* Cambridge: Cambridge University Press, 2012. https://doi.org/10.1017/CBO9781107 358232.

Healy, Shawn. "Momentum Grows for Stronger Civic Education across States." *Human Rights Magazine,* January 4, 2022. https://www.americanbar.org/groups/crsj /publications/human_rights_magazine_home/the-state-of-civic-education-in -america/momentum-grows-for-stronger-civic-education-across-states/.

Hearsey, Tricia. "Sabbath Time!" *Nap Ministry* (blog), March 1, 2021. https://thenap ministry.wordpress.com/2021/03/01/sabbath-time/.

Holifield, Ryan. "Defining Environmental Justice and Environmental Racism." *Urban Geography* 22, no. 1 (February 1, 2001): 78–90. https://doi.org/10.2747/0272 -3638.22.1.78.

hooks, bell. *Ain't I a Woman: Black Women and Feminism.* Boston: South End, 1981.

———. *Belonging: A Culture of Place.* London: Routledge, 2008. http://www.amazon .com/Belonging-Culture-Place-bell-hooks/dp/041596816X.

———. *Feminist Theory: From Margin to Center.* Boston: South End, 2000. https:// www.amazon.com/Feminist-Theory-Margin-bell-hooks/dp/0896086135.

———. *Outlaw Culture: Resisting Representations.* New York: Routledge, 1994.

———. *Sisters of the Yam: Black Women and Self-Recovery.* New York: Routledge, 2014. https://www.amazon.com/Sisters-Yam-Black-Women-Self-Recovery/dp/1138821 683/.

———. *Teaching Community: A Pedagogy of Hope.* New York: Routledge, 2003.

———. *Teaching to Transgress: Education as the Practice of Freedom.* London: Routledge, 1994.

———. *Where We Stand: Class Matters.* New York: Routledge, 2000.

Hopkins, Daniel J., and Gary King. "Improving Anchoring Vignettes: Designing Surveys to Correct Interpersonal Incomparability." *Public Opinion Quarterly* 74, no. 2 (2010): 201–22.

Huckfeldt, Robert. *Politics in Context: Assimilation and Conflict in Urban Neighborhoods.* New York: Agathon, 1986.

———. "Variable Responses to Neighborhood Social Contexts: Assimilation, Conflict, and Tipping Points." *Political Behavior* 2, no. 3 (1980): 231–57. https://doi.org/10.1007/BF00990481.

Hudson, Wendell. "Altgeld Gardens: Home Away from Nearly Everything." *Chicago Defender*, September 9, 2009. https://chicagodefender.com/altgeld-gardens-home-away-from-nearly-everything/.

Hull, Gloria T., Patricia Bell Scott, and Barbara Smith, eds. *But Some of Us Are Brave: All the Women Are White, All the Blacks Are Men; Black Women's Studies.* New York: Feminist Press at the City University of New York, 1982. https://www.feministpress.org/books-a-m/but-some.

Hunt, D. Bradford. *Blueprint for Disaster: The Unraveling of Chicago Public Housing.* Chicago: University of Chicago Press, 2010. https://doi.org/10.1177/0094306110373238y.

Hurston, Zora Neale. *Dust Tracks on a Road: An Autobiography.* New York: Amistad, 2006. https://www.zoranealehurston.com/books/dust-tracks-on-a-road/.

INCITE! Women of Color against Violence. *Color of Violence: The Incite! Anthology.* Durham, NC: Duke University Press, 2016. https://doi.org/10.5860/choice.44-5336.

"Isabel Wilkerson: How Did the Great Migration Change the Course of Human History?" Radio interview transcript. *TED Radio Hour.* NPR, April 30, 2021. https://www.npr.org/2021/04/30/992040563/isabel-wilkerson-how-did-the-great-migration-change-the-course-of-human-history.

Isoke, Zenzele. "Black Ethnography, Black (Female) Aesthetics: Thinking/Writing/Saying/Sounding Black Political Life." *Theory and Event* 21, no. 1 (2019): 148–68.

———. "The Politics of Homemaking: Black Feminist Transformations of a Cityscape." *Transforming Anthropology* 19, no. 2 (2011): 117–30. https://doi.org/10.1111/j.1548-7466.2011.01136.x.117.

———. Review of *The Suffering Will Not Be Televised: African American Women and Sentimental Political Storytelling*, by Rebecca Wanzo, and *Behind the Mask of the Strong Black Woman: Voice and the Embodiment of a Costly Performance*, by Tamara Beauboeuf-Lafontant. *Feminist Formations* 24, no. 2 (2012): 217–21. https://doi.org/10.1353/ff.2012.0016.

———. *Urban Black Women and the Politics of Resistance.* New York: Palgrave Macmillan, 2013.

Iton, Richard. *In Search of the Black Fantastic: Politics and Popular Culture in the Post–Civil Rights Era.* Oxford: Oxford University Press, 2010.

Jackson, Sherman A. *Islam and the Blackamerican: Looking toward the Third Resurrection.* New York: Oxford University Press, 2005. https://doi.org/10.1093/ACPROF:OSO/9780195180817.001.0001.

James, Joy. "Framing the Panther: Assata Shakur and Black Female Agency." In *Want to Start a Revolution? Radical Women in the Black Freedom Struggle*, edited by Jeanne Theoharis. New York: NYU Press 2009.

———. *Shadowboxing: Representations of Black Feminist Politics*. London: Palgrave Macmillan, 2016. https://doi.org/10.1007/978-1-137-06751-7.

James, Joy, and Beverly Guy-Sheftall. *Seeking the Beloved Community: A Feminist Race Reader*. 2nd ed. Albany: SUNY Press, 2013.

Jeffrey, Ashley, and Scott Sargrad. "Strengthening Democracy with a Modern Civics Education." Center for American Progress, December 14, 2019. https://www.amer icanprogress.org/article/strengthening-democracy-modern-civics-education/.

Johnson, Eric. "Altgeld Gardens Moved out of Black Ward under New Chicago Map." *Chicago Crusader*, 2022. https://chicagocrusader.com/altgeld-gardens-moved-out -of-black-ward-under-new-chicago-map/.

Jones, Claudia. "An End to the Neglect of the Problems of the Negro Woman!" In *Words of Fire: An Anthology of African-American Feminist Thought*, edited by Beverly Guy-Sheftall, 107–23. New York: New Press, 1995. https://thenewpress.com /books/words-of-fire.

Jones, Nicholas, Rachel Marks, Roberto Ramirez, and Merarys Rios-Vargas. "Improved Race and Ethnicity Measures Reveal U.S. Population Is Much More Multiracial: 2020 Census Illuminates Racial and Ethnic Composition of the Country." America Counts: Stories. U.S. Census Bureau, August 12, 2021. https://www .census.gov/library/stories/2021/08/improved-race-ethnicity-measures-reveal -united-states-population-much-more-multiracial.html.

Jordan-Zachery, Julia S. "Beyond the Side Eye: Black Women's Ancestral Anger as a Liberatory Practice." *Journal of Black Sexuality and Relationships* 4, no. 1 (2017): 61–81. https://doi.org/10.1353/bsr.2017.0021.

———. "'I Ain't Your Darn Help': Black Women as the Help in Intersectionality Research in Political Science." In *Black Women in Politics: Identity, Power, and Justice in the New Millennium*, edited by Michael Mitchell and David Covin, 19–30. London: Routledge, 2014. https://doi.org/10.4324/9781351313681-2.

———. "Resistance and Redemption Narratives: Black Girl Magic and Other Forms of Black Girls and Women's Political Self-Articulations." *National Political Science Review* 19, no. 2 (2018): 2–10. https://www.proquest.com/docview/2502299247.

Jordan-Zachery, Julia S., and Nikol G. Alexander-Floyd, eds. *Black Women in Politics: Demanding Citizenship, Challenging Power, and Seeking Justice*. Albany: State University of New York Press, 2018.

Junn, Jane. "Participation in Liberal Democracy: The Political Assimilation of Immigrants and Ethnic Minorities in the United States." *American Behavioral Scientist* 42, no. 9 (1999): 1417–38. https://doi.org/10.1177/00027649921954976.

Junn, Jane, Nadia E. Brown, Christina Wolbrecht, Karen Beckwith, and Lisa Baldez. "What Revolution? Incorporating Intersectionality in Women and Politics." In *Political Women and American Democracy*, 64–78. Cambridge: Cambridge University Press, 2008. https://doi.org/10.1017/CBO9780511790621.007.

Kaba, Mariame. *Against Punishment: A Resource by Project Nia and Interrupting Criminalization*. Chicago: Project Nia, 2020. https://issuu.com/projectnia/docs /against_punishment_curriculum_final.

Kang, Naewon, and Nojin Kwak. "A Multilevel Approach to Civic Participation: Individual Length of Residence, Neighborhood Residential Stability, and Their Interactive Effects with Media Use." *Communication Research* 30, no. 1 (2003): 80–106. https://doi.org/10.1177/0093650202239028.

Kasakove, Sophie. "A Major Chicago Public-Housing Lawsuit Is Wrapping Up. The Segregation It Fought Against Lives On." *Pacific Standard*, March 2019. https://psmag.com/social-justice/a-major-chicago-public-housing-lawsuit-is-wrapping-up-the-segregation-it-fought-against-lives-on.

Katznelson, Ira. *City Trenches: Urban Politics and the Patterning of Class in the United States*. New York: Pantheon Books, 1981. https://doi.org/10.1017/S0003055400188628.

Kelley, Robin D. G. *Race Rebels: Culture, Politics, and the Black Working Class*. New York: Free Press, 1996. https://doi.org/10.2307/2211261.

———. *Yo' Mama's Disfunktional! Fighting the Culture Wars in Urban America*. Boston: Beacon, 1997.

Kim, Claire Jean. *Bitter Fruit: The Politics of Black-Korean Conflict in New York City*. New Haven, CT: Yale University Press, 2003. https://doi.org/10.2307/2700765.

King, Deborah K. "Multiple Jeopardy, Multiple Consciousness: The Context of a Black Feminist Ideology." *Signs* 14, no. 1 (Autumn 1988): 42–72. https://doi.org/10.4324/9780203705841-21.

King, Gary, Christopher J. L. Murray, Joshua A. Salomon, and Ajay Tandon. "Enhancing the Validity and Cross-cultural Comparability of Measurement in Survey Research." *American Political Science Review* 98, no. 1 (2004): 191–207. https://doi.org/10.1017/S000305540400108X.

King, Gary, and Jonathan Wand. "Comparing Incomparable Survey Responses: Evaluating and Selecting Anchoring Vignettes." *Political Analysis* 15, no. 1 (2007): 46–66. https://doi.org/10.1093/pan/mpl011.

Kirk, David S., and Sara Wakefield. "Collateral Consequences of Punishment: A Critical Review and Path Forward." *Annual Review of Criminology* 1 (2018): 171–94. https://doi.org/10.1146/annurev-criminol-032317-092045.

Krivo, Lauren J., Ruth D. Peterson, and Danielle C. Kuhl. "Segregation, Racial Structure, and Neighborhood Violent Crime." *American Journal of Sociology* 114, no. 6 (2009): 1765–1802. https://doi.org/10.1086/597285.

Le Mignot, Suzanne. "4 Dead, 2 Wounded in Altgeld Gardens Store Shooting." *CBS Chicago*, 2011. https://www.cbsnews.com/chicago/news/4-dead-2-wounded-in-altgeld-gardens-store-shooting/.

Lerman, Amy E., and Vesla M. Weaver. *Arresting Citizenship: The Democratic Consequences of American Crime Control*. Chicago Studies in American Politics. Chicago: University of Chicago Press, 2014. https://doi.org/10.7208/chicago/9780226137971.001.0001.

Levenstein, Lisa. *A Movement without Marches: African American Women and the Politics of Poverty in Postwar Philadelphia*. Chapel Hill: University of North Carolina Press, 2009. https://doi.org/10.5149/9780807889985_levenstein.

Lipsky, Michael. *Street-Level Bureaucracy: Dilemmas of the Individual in Public Services*. New York: Russell Sage Foundation, 2010. https://doi.org/10.2307/2392554.

Lorde, Audre. "Keynote Address: The Uses of Anger." National Women's Studies Association Convention, 1981.

Love, Bettina. *We Want to Do More Than Survive: Abolitionist Teaching and the Pursuit of Educational Freedom*. Illustrated ed. Boston: Beacon, 2019.

Loyd, Jenna M., and Anne Bonds. "Where Do Black Lives Matter? Race, Stigma, and Place in Milwaukee, Wisconsin." *Sociological Review* 66, no. 4 (2018): 898–918. https://doi.org/10.1177/0038026118778175.

Lyons, Schley R. "The Political Socialization of Ghetto Children: Efficacy and Cynicism." *Journal of Politics* 32, no. 2 (1970): 288–304.

Mansfield, Howard. *Dwelling in Possibility: Searching for the Soul of Shelter*. Peterborough, NH: Bauhan, 2013. https://bauhanpublishing.com/shop/dwelling-possibility-2/.

Maroni, Emily. "Americans' Civics Knowledge Drops on First Amendment and Branches of Government." Higher Education. *Annenberg Public Policy Center of the University of Pennsylvania* (blog), September 13, 2022. https://www.annenbergpublicpolicycenter.org/americans-civics-knowledge-drops-on-first-amendment-and-branches-of-government/.

Massey, Douglas S., and Shawn M. Kanaiapuni. "Public Housing and the Concentration of Poverty." *Social Science Quarterly* 74, no. 1 (1993): 109–22. http://www.jstor.org/stable/42863165.

Masuoka, Natalie, and Jane Junn. *The Politics of Belonging: Race, Public Opinion, and Immigration*. Chicago Studies in American Politics. Chicago: University of Chicago Press, 2013. https://doi.org/10.7208/chicago/9780226057330.001.0001.

McAdam, Doug. *Political Process and the Development of Black Insurgency, 1930–1970*. Chicago: University of Chicago Press, 1999.

McAvoy, Spencer. "Lost in the Shuffle: The Future of Traditional Public Housing under the CHA's Plan for Transformation." *Southside Weekly* (Chicago), January 8, 2014. https://southsideweekly.com/lost-in-the-shuffle/.

McCurn, Alexis S. "Surviving the Grind: How Young Black Women Negotiate Physical and Emotional Labor in Urban Space." *Sociological Spectrum* 40, no. 4 (2020): 227–46. https://doi.org/10.1080/02732173.2020.1760155.

McGregor, Shannon C., Rachel R. Mourão, and Logan Molyneux. "Twitter as a Tool for and Object of Political and Electoral Activity: Considering Electoral Context and Variance among Actors." *Journal of Information Technology and Politics* 14, no. 2 (2017): 154–67. https://doi.org/10.1080/19331681.2017.1308289.

McGuire, Danielle L. *At the Dark End of the Street: Black Women, Rape, and Resistance—a New History of the Civil Rights Movement from Rosa Parks to the Rise of Black Power*. New York: Vintage, 2011. https://www.penguinrandomhouse.com/books/111678/at-the-dark-end-of-the-street-by-danielle-l-mcguire/.

McKittrick, Katherine. *Demonic Grounds: Black Women and the Cartographies of Struggle*. Minneapolis: University of Minnesota Press, 2006.

McRoberts, Omar M. "Beyond Mysterium Tremendum: Thoughts toward an Aesthetic Study of Religious Experience." *Annals of the American Academy of Political and Social Science* 595 (September 1, 2004): 190–203. https://doi.org/10.1177/000 2716204267111.

Mettler, Suzanne. *Soldiers to Citizens: The G.I. Bill and the Making of the Greatest Generation.* Oxford: Oxford University Press, 2005.

Mettler, Suzanne, and Joe Soss. "The Consequences of Public Policy for Democratic Citizenship: Bridging Policy Studies and Mass Politics." *Perspectives on Politics* 2, no. 1 (2004): 55–73. https://doi.org/10.1017/S1537592704000623.

Micheletti, Michele, Andreas Follesdal, and Dietlind Stolle, eds. *Politics, Products, and Markets: Exploring Political Consumerism Past and Present.* New Brunswick, NJ: Transaction, 2009. https://doi.org/10.1111/j.1944-8287.2008.tb00400.x.

Michener, Jamila. *Fragmented Democracy: Medicaid, Federalism, and Unequal Politics.* New York: Cambridge University Press, 2018. https://doi.org/10.1017/97811 08224987.

———. "Medicaid and the Policy Feedback Foundations for Universal Healthcare." *Annals of the American Academy of Political and Social Science* 685, no. 1 (2019): 116–34. https://doi.org/10.1177/0002716219867905.

———. "Neighborhood Disorder and Local Participation: Examining the Political Relevance of 'Broken Windows.'" *Political Behavior* 35, no. 4 (2018): 777–806. https:// link.springer.com/article/10.1007/s11109-012-9217-x.

———. "People, Places, Power: Medicaid Concentration and Local Political Participation." *Journal of Health Politics, Policy and Law* 42, no. 5, (2017): 865–900. https:// doi.org/10.1215/03616878-3940468.

———. "Policy Feedback in a Racialized Polity." *Policy Studies Journal* 47 (2019): 423–50. https://doi.org/10.1111/psj.12328.

———. "Power from the Margins: Grassroots Mobilization and Urban Expansions of Civil Legal Rights." *Urban Affairs Review* 56, no. 5 (2020): 1390–1422. https:// doi.org/10.1177/1078087419855677.

Michener, Jamila, and Margaret Teresa Brower. "What's Policy Got to Do with It? Race, Gender and Economic Inequality in the United States." *Daedalus* 149, no. 1 (2020): 100–118. https://doi.org/10.1162/daed_a_01776.

Miller, Jody. *Getting Played: African American Girls, Urban Inequality, and Gendered Violence.* New York: New York University Press, 2010.

Mitchell, Koritha. *From Slave Cabins to the White House: Homemade Citizenship in African American Culture.* Chicago: University of Illinois Press, 2020.

———. *Living with Lynching: African American Lynching Plays, Performance, and Citizenship, 1890–1930.* Champaign: University of Illinois Press, 2011. https://www .press.uillinois.edu/books/?id=p078804.

Mitchell, Michael, David Covin, Nikol Alexander-Floyd, and Julia S. Jordan-Zachery, eds. *Black Women in Politics: Identity, Power, and Justice in the New Millenium.* London: Routledge, n.d.

Mitchell-Walthour, Gladys L. *The Politics of Survival: Black Women Social Welfare Beneficiaries in Brazil and the United States.* New York: Columbia University Press,

2023. https://cup.columbia.edu/book/the-politics-of-survival/9780231207
676.

Moffett-Bateau, Alex J. "'I Can't Vote If I Don't Leave My Apartment': The Problem of Neighborhood Violence and Its Impact on the Political Behavior of Black American Women Living below the Poverty Line." *Urban Affairs Review* 60, no. 1 (2023). https://doi.org/10.1177/10780874231162930.

Moffett-Bateau, Alex, and Jenn M. Jackson. "Moving beyond Niceness: Reading bell hooks into the Radical Potential for the Discipline." *Journal of Women, Politics and Policy* 43, no. 3 (2022): 409–16. https://doi.org/10.1080/1554477X.2022.2075 681.

Moffett-Bateau, Alexandra. "Feminist Erasures: The Development of a Black Feminist Methodological Theory." In *Feminist Erasures: Challenging Backlash Culture*, edited by Silva Kumarini and Kaitlynn Mendes, 1:54–71. London: Palgrave Macmillan, 2015. https://doi.org/10.1057/9781137454928_4.

———. "Strategies of Resistance in the Everyday: The Political Approaches of Black Women Living in a Public Housing Development in Chicago." *Journal of Women, Politics and Policy* 44, no. 4 (2023).

Moore, Natalie. "Chicago Housing Authority Residents Want Housing Agency to Supply More Jobs." WBEZ Chicago, July 15, 2011. https://www.wbez.org/stories/cha-residents-want-housing-agency-to-supply-more-jobs/4f50b93b-06eb-4e0e-8d61-3c748bab7f50.

———. "Residents Question Chicago Housing Authority Plans for Altgeld Gardens." WBEZ Chicago, May 4, 2010. https://www.wbez.org/stories/residents-question-chaas-plans-for-altgeld/3e83dfe7-9db1-439f-a8d4-943f5b5de3be.

Moraga, Cherríe L., and Gloria E. Anzaldúa, eds. *This Bridge Called My Back: Writings by Radical Women of Color.* 4th ed. Albany: SUNY Press, 2015. https://suny press.edu/Books/T/This-Bridge-Called-My-Back-Fourth-Edition.

Morenoff, Jeffrey D., Robert J. Sampson, and Stephen W. Raudenbush. "Neighborhood Inequality, Collective Efficacy, and the Spatial Dynamics of Urban Violence." *Criminology* 39, no. 3 (2001): 517–58. https://doi.org/10.1111/j.1745-9125.2001.tb 00932.x.

Mouffe, Chantal. "Democratic Citizenship and the Political Community." In *The Return of the Political*, edited by Chantal Mouffe, 60–73. New York: Verso, 1991. https://www.versobooks.com/products/1437-the-return-of-the-political.

———. *On the Political: Thinking in Action.* London: Routledge, 2005. https://www.routledge.com/On-the-Political/Mouffe/p/book/9780415305211.

——— eds. *The Return of the Political.* New York: Verso, 1991. https://www.verso books.com/products/1437-the-return-of-the-political.

Naples, Nancy A. *Grassroots Warriors: Activist Mothering, Community Work, and the War on Poverty.* London: Routledge, 1998. https://doi.org/10.4324/9781315811598.

National Partnership for Women and Families. *Black Women and the Wage Gap.* Fact Sheet. Washington, DC: National Partnership for Women and Families, 2022.

New York Times Editorial. "Opinion: Ex-offenders and the Vote." *New York Times*, March 21, 2010. https://www.nytimes.com/2010/03/22/opinion/22mon3.html.

Nunnally, Shayla C. *Trust in Black America: Race, Discrimination, and Politics*. New York: New York University Press, 2012. https://doi.org/10.5860/choice.50-0557.

Office of Standards and Instruction. "Civic Readiness Initiative." New York State Education Department. Accessed June 29, 2023. https://www.nysed.gov/curriculum-instruction/civic-readiness-initiative.

Osterweil, Vicky. *In Defense of Looting: A Riotous History of Uncivil Action*. New York: Bold Type Books, 2020.

Oyserman, D., and S. Fryberg. "The Possible Selves of Diverse Adolescents." In *Possible Selves: Theory, Research, and Application*, edited by Curtis Dunkel and Jennifer Kerpelman, 1–26. Hauppauge: Nova Science Publishers, 2006. https://psycnet.apa.org/record/2006-04587-000.

Oyserman, Daphna, Deborah Bybee, Kathy Terry, and Tamera Hart-Johnson. "Possible Selves as Roadmaps." *Journal of Research in Personality* 38, no. 2 (2004): 130–49. https://doi.org/10.1016/S0092-6566(03)00057-6.

Oyserman, Daphna, Larry Gant, and Joel Ager. "A Socially Contextualized Model of African American Identity: Possible Selves and School Persistence." *Journal of Personality and Social Psychology* 69, no. 5 (1995): 1216–32. https://doi.org/10.1037/0022-3514.69.6.1216.

Pateman, Carole. "Feminist Critiques of the Public/Private Dichotomy." In *The Disorder of Women: Democracy, Feminism and Political Theory*, 118–40. Cambridge: Polity, 1989.

Pattillo, Mary. *Black on the Block: The Politics of Race and Class in the City*. Chicago: University of Chicago Press, 2013. https://doi.org/10.7208/chicago/9780226649337.001.0001.

Perry, Keisha-Khan. *Black Women against the Land Grab: The Fight for Racial Justice in Brazil*. Minneapolis: University of Minnesota Press, 2013.

Peterson, Ruth D., Lauren J. Krivo, and John Hagan. *Divergent Social Worlds: Neighborhood Crime and the Racial-Spatial Divide*. New York: Russell Sage Foundation, 2010. https://doi.org/10.1177/0094306111419111gg.

Pfeiffer, Deirdre. "Displacement through Discourse: Implementing and Contesting Public Housing Redevelopment in Cabrini Green." *Urban Anthropology and Studies of Cultural Systems and World Economic Development* 35, no. 1 (2006): 39–74.

Polikoff, Alexander. *Waiting for Gautreaux: A Story of Segregation, Housing, and the Black Ghetto*. Evanston, IL: Northwestern University Press, 2006.

Popkin, Susan J. *No Simple Solutions: Transforming Public Housing in Chicago*. Lanham, MD: Rowman and Littlefield, 2016. https://doi.org/10.1177/0094306118792220hh.

Popkin, Susan J., Diane K. Levy, Laura E. Harris, Jennifer Comey, Mary K. Cunningham, and Larry F. Buron. "The HOPE VI Program: What about the Residents?" *Housing Policy Debate* 15, no. 2 (2010): 385–414. https://doi.org/10.1080/10511482.2004.9521506.

Popkin, Susan J., Michael J. Rich, Leah Hendey, Chris Hayes, Joe Parilla, and George Galster. "Public Housing Transformation and Crime: Making the Case for Responsible Relocation." *Cityscape* 14, no. 3 (2012): 137–60.

Prestage, Jewell. "In Quest of African American Political Woman." *Annals of the American Academy of Political and Social Science* 515 (1991): 88–103.

Prowse, Gwen, Vesla M. Weaver, and Tracey L. Meares. "The State from Below: Distorted Responsiveness in Policed Communities." *Urban Affairs Review* 56, no. 5 (2019): 1423–71. https://doi.org/10.1177/1078087419844831.

Ralph, Laurence. *Renegade Dreams: Living through Injury in Gangland Chicago.* Chicago: University of Chicago Press, 2014. https://doi.org/10.1177/0094306116641407jj.

Ransby, Barbara. *Ella Baker and the Black Freedom Movement: A Radical Democratic Vision.* Gender and American Culture. Chapel Hill: University of North Carolina Press, 2005. https://www.amazon.com/Ella-Baker-Black-Freedom-Movement-dp-0807856169/.

———. *Making All Black Lives Matter: Reimagining Freedom in the Twenty-First Century.* Berkeley: University of California Press, 2018. https://www.amazon.com/Making-All-Black-Lives-Matter-ebook/dp/B07DH5NCD5.

Reingold, David A. "Public Housing, Home Ownership, and Community Participation in Chicago's Inner City." *Housing Studies* 10, no. 4 (1995): 445–69. https://doi.org/10.1080/02673039508720832.

Richie, Beth E. *Arrested Justice: Black Women, Violence, and America's Prison Nation.* New York: New York University Press, 2012. https://doi.org/10.1177/009430611456220luu.

Rios, Victor M. *Punished: Policing the Lives of Black and Latino Boys.* New York: New York University Press, 2011. https://doi.org/10.1177/0094306112449614y.

Ritchie, Andrea J. *Invisible No More: Police Violence against Black Women and Women of Color.* Boston: Beacon, 2017.

———. *Shrouded in Silence, Police Sexual Violence: What We Know and What We Can Do about It.* New York: Interrupting Criminalization, 2021. https://www.interruptingcriminalization.com/publications.

Roberts, Dorothy E. *Killing the Black Body: Race, Reproduction, and the Meaning of Liberty.* New York: Random House/Pantheon, 1997. https://scholarship.law.upenn.edu/faculty_scholarship/2776/.

———. *Shattered Bonds: The Color of Child Welfare.* New York: Basic Books, 2002.

Robnett, Belinda. *How Long? How Long? African-American Women in the Struggle for Civil Rights.* New York: Oxford University Press, 1997. https://global.oup.com/academic/product/how-long-how-long-9780195114911.

Roth, Benita. "The Making of the Vanguard Center: Black Feminist Emergence in the 1960s and 1970s." In *Still Lifting, Still Climbing: Contemporary African American Women's Activism*, edited by Kimberly Springer, 70–90. New York: New York University Press, 1999.

———. *Separate Roads to Feminism: Black, Chicana, and White Feminist Movements in America's Second Wave.* Cambridge: Cambridge University Press, 2003. https://doi.org/10.1017/CBO9780511815201.

Sampson, Robert J. *Great American City: Chicago and the Enduring Neighborhood Effect.* Chicago: University of Chicago Press, 2013. https://doi.org/10.1080/10511253.2012.759767.

Sampson, Robert J., Stephen W. Raudenbush, and Felton Earls. "Neighborhoods and Violent Crime: A Multilevel Study of Collective Efficacy." *Science* 277 (1997): 918–24.

Sampson, Robert J., William Julius Wilson, and Hanna Katz. "Reassessing toward a Theory of Race, Crime, and Urban Inequality." *Du Bois Review* 15, no. 1 (2018): 13–34. https://doi.org/10.1017/S1742058X18000140.

Schmidt, Ronald. *Interpreting Racial Politics in the United States.* Vol. 1. London: Routledge, 2020. https://www.routledge.com/Interpreting-Racial-Politics-in-the-United-States/Schmidt-Sr/p/book/9781138204324.

Schneider, Cathy Lisa. *Police Power and Race Riots: Urban Unrest in Paris and New York.* Philadelphia: University of Pennsylvania Press, 2014.

Scholz, Sally J. "Empowering Resistance: Comments on Cudd's *Analyzing Oppression.*" *Symposia on Gender, Race and Philosophy* 5, no. 1 (2009).

Scott, James C. *Domination and the Arts of Resistance: Hidden Transcripts.* New Haven, CT: Yale University Press, 1992. https://yalebooks.yale.edu/book/9780300056693/domination-and-the-arts-of-resistance/.

Shingles, Richard D. "Black Consciousness and Political Participation: The Missing Link." *American Political Science Review* 75, no. 1 (1981): 76–91. https://doi.org/10.2307/1962160.

Simien, Evelyn M. *Black Feminist Voices in Politics.* Albany: State University of New York Press, 2006.

———. "Gender Differences in Attitudes toward Black Feminism among African Americans." *Political Science Quarterly* 119, no. 2 (2004): 315–38. https://doi.org/10.2307/20202348.

———. "Race, Gender, and Linked Fate." *Journal of Black Studies* 35, no. 5 (May 2005): 529–50. https://doi.org/10.1177/0021934704265899.

Sinclair, Betsy. *The Social Citizen: Peer Networks and Political Behavior.* Chicago: University of Chicago Press, 2012. https://doi.org/10.7208/CHICAGO/9780226922836.001.0001.

Sisson, Patrick, Sara Freund, and Jay Koziarz. "How Mayor Rahm Emanuel Changed the Look of Chicago." *Curbed: Chicago,* May 17, 2019. https://chicago.curbed.com/2019/5/17/18623391/chicago-mayor-rahm-emanuel-legacy-development.

Skocpol, Theda. *Protecting Soldiers and Mothers.* Cambridge, MA: Harvard University Press, 2009. https://doi.org/10.2307/j.ctvjz81v6.

Soss, Joe. "Classes, Races, and Marginalized Places: Notes on the Study of Democracy's Demise." *Annals of the American Academy of Political and Social Science* 651, no. 1 (2014): 250–54. https://doi.org/10.1177/0002716213502932.

———. "Lessons of Welfare: Policy Design, Political Learning, and Political Action." *American Political Science Review* 93, no. 2 (1999): 363–80. https://doi.org/10.2307/2585401.

———. *Unwanted Claims: The Politics of Participation in the U.S. Welfare System.* Ann Arbor: University of Michigan Press, 2000. https://doi.org/10.3998/mpub.16475.

Soss, Joe, and Vesla Weaver. "Police Are Our Government: Politics, Political Science, and the Policing of Race–Class Subjugated Communities." *Annual Review of Po-*

litical Science 20, no. 1 (2017): 565–91. https://doi.org/10.1146/annurev-polisci-06 0415-093825.

Souza Briggs, Xavier de, Susan J. Popkin, and John Goering. *Moving to Opportunity: The Story of an American Experiment to Fight Ghetto Poverty.* Oxford: Oxford University Press, 2010. https://global.oup.com/academic/product/moving-to-op portunity-9780195392845.

Spence, Lester. "Ella Baker and the Challenge of Black Rule." *Contemporary Political Theory* 19, no. 4 (December 1, 2020): 551–72. https://doi.org/10.1057/s41296-020 -00448-8.

———. *Knocking the Hustle: Against the Neoliberal Turn in Black Politics.* Brooklyn: punctum books, 2015.

Spence, Lester, and Harwood McClerking. "Context, Black Empowerment, and African American Political Participation." *American Politics Research* 38, no. 5 (2010): 909–30.

Squires, Catherine R. "Rethinking the Black Public Sphere: An Alternative Vocabulary for Multiple Public Spheres." *Communication Theory* 12, no. 4 (November 1, 2002): 446–68. https://doi.org/10.1111/J.1468-2885.2002.TB00278.X.

Stake, Robert E. *The Art of Case Study Research.* Thousand Oaks, CA: SAGE, 1996. https://doi.org/10.2307/329758.

Staples, Brent. "The Death of the Black Utopia." *New York Times*, November 28, 2019. https://www.nytimes.com/2019/11/28/opinion/seneca-central-park-nyc.html.

Stolle, Dietlind, Marc Hooghe, and Michele Micheletti. "Politics in the Supermarket: Political Consumerism as a Form of Political Participation." *International Political Science Review* 26, no. 3 (2005): 245–69. https://doi.org/10.1177/019251210 5053784.

Stucky, Thomas D. "Local Politics and Violent Crime in U.S. Cities." *Criminology* 41, no. 4 (2003): 1101–36. https://doi.org/10.1111/j.1745-9125.2003.tb01015.x.

Su, Celina. *Streetwise for Book Smarts: Grassroots Organizing and Education Reform in the Bronx.* Ithaca, NY: Cornell University Press, 2009.

Tanous, Osama, and Rabea Eghbariah. "Organized Violence and Organized Abandonment beyond the Human: The Case of Brucellosis among Palestinians in Israel." *MSystems* 7, no. 3 (2022): 1–9. https://pubmed.ncbi.nlm.nih.gov/35467394/.

Tate, Katherine. "Black Political Participation in the 1984 and 1988 Presidential Elections." *American Political Science Review* 85, no. 4 (1991): 1159–76. https://doi.org /10.2307/1963940.

Theoharris, Jeanne. *The Rebellious Life of Mrs. Rosa Parks.* Boston: Beacon, 2014. http:// www.beacon.org/The-Rebellious-Life-of-Mrs-Rosa-Parks-P1157.aspx.

Thurston, Chloe N. "Black Lives Matter, American Political Development, and the Politics of Visibility." *Politics, Groups, and Identities* 6, no. 1 (2018): 162–70. https:// doi.org/10.1080/21565503.2017.1420547.

Trounstine, Jessica. *Segregation by Design: Local Politics and Inequality in American Cities.* Cambridge: Cambridge University Press, 2018. https://doi.org/10.1017/97 81108555722.

Vasilogambros, Matt. "After Capitol Riot, Some States Turn to Civics Education." *Stateline*, May 19, 2021. https://pew.org/2SVnhbr.

Venkatesh, Sudhir Alladi. *American Project: The Rise and Fall of a Modern Ghetto.* Cambridge, MA: Harvard University Press, 2002. https://doi.org/10.2307/3089389.

Verba, Sidney, Kay Lehman Schlozman, and Henry E. Brady. *Voice and Equality: Civic Voluntarism in American Politics.* Cambridge, MA: Harvard University Press, 1996. https://doi.org/10.2307/2152095.

Warren, Mark E. "Voting with Your Feet: Exit-Based Empowerment in Democratic Theory." *American Political Science Review* 105, no. 4 (2011): 683–701. https://doi.org/10.1017/S0003055411000323.

Washington, Nabeela. "Narrowing the Digital Divide on Chicago's South and West Sides." *South Side Weekly* (Chicago), 2022. https://southsideweekly.com/narrowing-the-digital-divide-on-chicagos-south-and-west-sides/.

Watkins-Hayes, Celeste. *The New Welfare Bureaucrats.* Chicago: University of Chicago Press, 2009. https://doi.org/10.7208/chicago/9780226874937.001.0001.

———. *Remaking a Life: How Women Living with HIV/AIDS Confront Inequality.* Berkeley: University of California Press, 2019. https://doi.org/10.2307/j.ctvp2n290.

Weaver, Vesla, Gwen Prowse, and Spencer Piston. "Too Much Knowledge, Too Little Power: An Assessment of Political Knowledge in Highly Policed Communities." *Journal of Politics* 81, no. 3 (2019): 1153–66. https://doi.org/10.1086/703538.

Western, Bruce. *Punishment and Inequality in America.* New York: Russell Sage Foundation, 2007.

White, Brandi M., and Eric S. Hall. "Perceptions of Environmental Health Risks among Residents in the 'Toxic Doughnut': Opportunities for Risk Screening and Community Mobilization." *BMC Public Health* 15, no. 1 (December 10, 2015): 1230. https://doi.org/10.1186/s12889-015-2563-y.

Williams, Debra. "Altgeld Gardens: Isolated Schools, Community Get Repairs, No Transformation." *Chicago Reporter*, October 5, 2005. http://www.chicagoreporter.com/altgeld-gardens-isolated-schools-community-get-repairs-no-transformation/.

Williams, Kidada E. *They Left Great Marks on Me: African American Testimonies of Racial Violence from Emancipation to World War I.* New Haven, CT: New York University Press, 2012. https://doi.org/10.1093/jahist/jas406.

Williams, Rhonda Y. *The Politics of Public Housing: Black Women's Struggle against Urban Inequality.* Chicago: University of Chicago Press, 2005. https://doi.org/10.2307/27648973.

Williamson, Terrion L. *Scandalize My Name: Black Feminist Practice and the Making of Black Social Life.* New York: Fordham University Press, 2016.

Williamson, Vanessa, Kris Stella Trump, and Katherine Levine Einstein. "Black Lives Matter: Evidence That Police-Caused Deaths Predict Protest Activity." *Perspectives on Politics* 16, no. 2 (2018): 400–415. https://doi.org/10.1017/S1537592717004273.

Wilson Gilmore, Ruth. *Golden Gulag: Prisons, Surplus, Crisis, and Opposition in Globalizing California*. Berkeley: University of California Press, 2007.

———. "Organized Abandonment and Organized Violence: Devolution and the Police." Invited talk at the UC Presidential Chair in Feminist Critical Race and Ethnic Studies Presents, Santa Cruz, CA, 2015. https://thi.ucsc.edu/event/ruth-wilson-gilmore-2/.

Wolfinger, Raymond, and Steven J. Rosenstone. *Who Votes?* New Haven, CT: Yale University Press, 1981. https://doi.org/10.2307/2130227.

Wong, Cara J. *Boundaries of Obligation in American Politics: Geographic, National, and Racial Communities*. Cambridge Studies in Public Opinion and Political Psychology. New York: Cambridge University Press, 2012. https://doi.org/10.1017/cbo9780511802874.004.

Wong, Diane. "Shop Talk and Everyday Sites of Resistance to Gentrification in Manhattan's Chinatown." *WSQ: Women's Studies Quarterly* 47, nos. 1 and 2 (2019): 133–48. https://doi.org/10.1353/wsq.2019.0032.

Wright Mills, C. *The Sociological Imagination*. 40th anniversary ed. Oxford: Oxford University Press, 2000. https://www.amazon.com/Sociological-Imagination-C-Wright-Mills/dp/0195133730.

Yin, Robert K. *Case Study Research Design and Methods*. 4th ed. Applied Social Research Methods. Thousand Oaks, CA: SAGE, 2017.

Young, Iris Marion. *Justice and the Politics of Difference*. Princeton, NJ: Princeton University Press, 1990.

Index

Page numbers followed by the letter f refer to figures.

Alex J. Moffett-Bateau is Assistant Professor of Political Science at John Jay College of Criminal Justice at the City University of New York.